MIRACLES IN
GRECO-ROMAN ANTIQUITY

Miracles in Greco-Roman Antiquity is a sourcebook which presents a concise selection of key miracle stories from the Greco-Roman world, together with contextualizing texts from ancient authors as well as footnotes and commentary by the author herself.

The sourcebook is organized into four parts that deal with the main miracle story types and magic: Gods and Heroes who Heal and Raise the Dead, Exorcists and Exorcisms, Gods and Heroes who Control Nature, and Magic and Miracle. Two appendixes add richness to the contextualization of the collection: Diseases and Doctors features ancient authors' medical diagnoses, prognoses and treatments for the most common diseases cured in healing miracles; Jesus, Torah and Miracles selects pertinent texts from the Old Testament and Mishnah necessary for the understanding of certain Jesus miracles.

This collection of texts not only provides evidence of the types of miracle stories most popular in the Greco-Roman world, but even more importantly assists in their interpretation. The contextualizing texts enable the student to reconstruct a set of meanings available to the ordinary Greco-Roman, and to study and compare the forms of miracle narrative across the whole spectrum of antique culture.

Wendy Cotter C.S.J. is Associate Professor of Scripture at Loyola University, Chicago.

MIRACLES IN GRECO-ROMAN ANTIQUITY

A sourcebook

Wendy Cotter, C.S.J.

First published 1999
by Routledge
11 New Fetter Lane, London EC4P 4EE

Simultaneously published in the USA and Canada
by Routledge
29 West 35th Street, New York, NY 10001

Routledge is an imprint of the Taylor & Francis Group

Typeset in Garamond by The Florence Group, Stoodleigh, Devon

Printed and bound in Great Britain by Mackays of Chatham plc, Chatham, Kent

British Library Cataloguing in Publication Data
A catalogue record for this book is available
from the British Library

Library of Congress Cataloging in Publication Data
Cotter, Wendy, 1946–
Miracles in Greco-Roman Antiquity : a sourcebook / Wendy Cotter.
p. cm.
Includes bibliographical references and index.
ISBN 0–415–11863–8. -- ISBN 0–415–11864–6 (pbk.)
1. Miracles. 2. Greece--Religion. 3. Rome--Religion. I. Title.
BL785.C35   1999
292.2'117—dc21   98–19320
CIP

ISBN 0–415–11863–8 (hbk)
ISBN 0–415–11864–6 (pbk)

FOR MY MOTHER,
ISABEL COTTER
WITH MY GRATITUDE AND LOVE

CONTENTS

CONTENTS

PREFACE

This book is the result of David Aune's invitation one afternoon several years ago in the Theology Department library as I had just finished expounding to him my concern over the lack of proper cultural contextualization in miracle story analysis. My own involvement with the interpretation of miracle stories had begun with the research for my doctoral dissertation, "The Markan Sea Miracles: Their history, formation, and function in the literary context of Greco-Roman Antiquity" (Ph.D. dissertation: University of St Michael's College, Toronto, 1991). It was during those years that I discovered what few tools were readily available for situating miracle story claims and heroes in the reality of the first-century Mediterranean world. That afternoon, David informed me that he had just agreed to be editor of Routledge's new series, *Christianity in Context*, in which forms in Christian texts would be provided their proper cultural settings through illuminating extracts from Greco-Roman texts. David's invitation to me to prepare the sourcebook for miracle story contextualization was an honour as it was a practical answer to my concern, and I would like to express my sincerest thanks to him. I hope that this volume of selected texts will be found helpful by many scholars and students who have searched for a book of pertinent sources to assist them in their interpretation of Greco-Roman miracle stories.

I would like to acknowledge in a special way the generosity of Loyola University of Chicago in awarding me a summer research grant to begin the necessary research for the book, and then adding to this a paid semester sabbatical to bring it to completion.

Profound thanks go to my own religious community, the Sisters of St Joseph of London, Ontario, Canada, for their kind funding of a summer field study in Rome as part of the research for this volume.

I am so grateful for their constant support, their warm friendship and their fond appreciation of my scholarly endeavours.

My thanks also go to those who have been of enormous assistance in the publication of this sourcebook. First I would like to mention Richard Stoneman, Senior Editor at Routledge, for his encouragement, patience and helpful advice. I am greatly indebted to Ms Coco Stevenson, Editorial Assistant to Richard Stoneman, about whom the saying was written: "Swift kindnesses are best." I thank her for her graciousness in answering my countless queries relative to the organization and presentation of the volume. A special thanks to Ms Pauline Marsh, the copy-editor, for her meticulous attention to the smallest details of the manuscript and for her erudition in raising questions of clarification.

Finally, I would like to thank my family, friends and my colleagues here in the Theology Department of Loyola University whose kind and steady interest in this project has supported me throughout its lengthy preparation.

Dr Wendy Cotter C.S.J.,
Loyola University,
Chicago.
July, 1998.

INTRODUCTION

Miracle stories as we call them, were plentiful and popular in the Greco-Roman world, and we find them told by persons from simple as well as elite backgrounds in the extant sources. Unlike the witty apophthegms or *chreiai*, however, miracle stories had little status as a "form." They were not the subject of examination, memorization and imitation in the classroom as were the famous wisdom stories of the greats.[1] Theon's teacher manual defined the form of the *chreia* as

> a concise statement or action which is attributed with aptness to some specified character or something analogous to a character,[2]

but there is no one from Greco-Roman antiquity who even comments on the form expected of a miracle story.

We hasten to distinguish the miracle stories from those lists of nature's freakish wonders that were indeed noted, published and discussed by the *literati*. Nature's genetic anomalies, often called *terrata*, or nature's strange inexplicable phenomena, sometimes

---

1 "Dio Chrysostom remarks that everyone could recite *chreiai* about Diogenes and thousands of *chreiai* can be found in the writings of, say, Plutarch, Quintillian, Aulus Gellius, Lucian, Diogenes Laertius, Aelian, Philostratus, and Stobaeus." See the treatment of the popularity of the *chreiai* by Ronald F. Hock and Edward N. O'Neil, *The Chreia in Ancient Rhetoric, Volume 1: The Progymnasmata* (Society of Biblical Literature Texts and Translations 27; Atlanta: Scholars Press, 1986), 7.

2 Theon, *Progymnasmata* 1; Hock and O'Neil, "Aelius Theon of Alexandria: On the Chreia," in *The Chreia in Ancient Rhetoric*, 82–83.

1

called *paradoxographia*,[3] might well be termed *mirabili* (miracles) by anyone in the Greco-Roman world, but they are not stories and not the miracles to which we refer. Rather, we mean those narratives in which a wonderful rescue or salvation of someone takes place by the overturning of "the canons of the ordinary"[4] through the intervention of a deity or hero.

Attention to such stories in any scholarly way really only began with the form-critical movement in New Testament studies at the beginning of the twentieth century in the work of Martin Dibelius and Rudolf Bultmann. In Dibelius' examination of these little stories about Jesus' wonders, he concluded that they belonged to the general category of "tales"[5] so popular in the Greco-Roman world. It was Rudolf Bultmann who identified these accounts as "miracle stories" *per se*, noted their common three-part sequence (a. the problem; b. the hero's miraculous act; c. the demonstration or acclamation of the miracle's effect) and derived the four classes: 1. healings, 2. exorcisms, 3. raisings from the dead and 4. nature miracles.[6] The question remained how such subdivisions could be used to reconstruct first-century authorial intent when their "form" and kinds were completely unattested formally anywhere in Greco-Roman evidence.

For his part, however, Bultmann agreed with Dibelius that miracle stories and the pithy apophthegms could be counted upon to be devoid of any interest in "portraiture." Each form was focused on one point, and in the case of the miracle stories, this would be the miraculous act itself.

> The style of a miracle story is related to that of the apophthegm (pp. 63f.) to this extent – the "absence of

---

3 See the scholarly discussion of these by Pseudo-Aristotle, *Mirabiles Auscultationes*. In A. Giannini (ed. and trans.) *Paradoxographorum Graecorum Reliquiae* (*Classici Greci e Latini, Sezioni Testi e Commenti* 3; Milan: Instituto Editoriale Italiano, 1965). On genetic malformations see Aristotle, *De Generatione Animalium* 770a 16ff.; 772b 13–14. I am indebted to Harold Remus, *Pagan–Christian Conflict Over Miracle in the Second Century* (Patristic Monograph Series 10; Cambridge, MA: The Philadelphia Patristic Foundation, 1983), 27–72.

4 Harold Remus' term to express the system that holds within the cosmic order. See his *Pagan–Christian Conflict Over Miracle in the Second Century*, 7–26.

5 Martin Dibelius, *From Tradition to Gospel* (trans. Bertram Lee Wolf; 2nd ed.; New York: Charles Scribner's Sons, 1935), 70.

6 Rudolf Bultmann, *The History of the Synoptic Tradition* (trans. John Marsh from 1931 German ed.; Oxford: Basil Blackwell, 1972 revised ed.).

portraiture" (Dibelius loc. cit.) and all that it involves is characteristic of both. Here as there nothing but the point matters – there a saying of Jesus, here a miracle.[7]

Now, Dibelius and Bultmann had already admitted that miracle stories were "narratives" or "tales," and quite distinct from apophthegms, which belonged to "sayings." They needed to recognize that any narrative automatically holds a *possibility* for portraiture, and in the case of the miracle stories, even more so, since no objective criterion was known for them in the ancient world, except that they tell about a miraculous happening. Any ancient author was free to tell the story his/her own way, turning it to whatever purpose might seem most attractive or advantageous. We have to see that these supposed "similarities" between apophthegms and miracle stories with respect to their purpose and focus are entirely artificial. The "miracle-story" writer was creating a story, and s/he was free of such restraints.

Every narrative holds within itself clues to its own interpretation. The delicate and painstaking task of reconstructing authorial intent for a story requires a recognition of the author's every appeal to ideas and images s/he has presupposed as obvious to the intended audience. And this principle is just as true for the narratives we designate as "miracle stories." To unlock the meaning of the story, we need to contextualize a story within its world. How we become familiar with that reality requires a great deal of study, but one way we can begin is to set the stories among others of their type, together with contextualizing discussions by people of that age. In this way, we can better estimate the weight and significance of a miracle and the god or hero who is given responsibility for it.

Since the initial work of Bultmann, the interpretation of miracle stories has continued to be explored by a number of important scholars. Among these we would want to pay special attention to the meticulous analysis of Gerd Theissen's *The Miracle Stories of the Early Christian Tradition*,[8] and the erudite discussions in Howard Kee's two volumes, *Miracle in the Early Christian World: A Study in Socio-historical Method*[9] and *Medicine, Miracle and Magic in New*

---

7 Ibid., 220.

8 Gerd Theissen, *The Miracle Stories of the Early Christian Tradition* (trans. Francis McDonagh; Philadelphia: Fortress Press, 1983).

9 Howard Clark Kee, *Miracle in the Early Christian World: A Study in Socio-historical Method* (New Haven and London: Yale University Press, 1983).

Testament Times.[10] But in all these examinations, there has been no English-language sourcebook to supply selected texts from the Greco-Roman world in order to contextualize these important exegetical endeavors and to further facilitate study and discussion of the significance of miracle narratives. This volume is intended to meet that need. It provides a basic set of texts, a selection of representative stories and discussions that illustrate the most common ideas available to a Greco-Roman audience. Organized around the most general types of miracle stories and including pertinent comments from ancient sources related to each miracle story "type," this sourcebook aims to help in the accurate estimation of the meaning of the miracle and the claims being made for both the act of power and its significance for identity of the god or hero who intervenes.

THE ORGANIZATION OF THE VOLUME

Although Rudolf Bultmann's four miracle-story types were created from his analysis of the Jesus miracles in the Christian gospels, they prove to be accommodating to the classification of any miracle story, no matter what its provenance. For this reason, the greater part of the sourcebook has been organized according to these miracle-story types.

The book is divided into four parts and two ancillary appendices. Part 1 features the stories and texts about those deities and heroes most commonly attributed with healings. Since the few raising of the dead stories are attached to the same gods and heroes who heal, I have maintained that connection by including them with the healings associated with those gods and heroes.

Part 2 addresses the exorcisms of antiquity. As a necessary preliminary to these miracle stories, a series of texts review various ideas about the nature and identity of daimons/demons in the Greco-Roman world. A second issue demanding attention is the cosmology served by the story of a daimon's/demon's expulsion. This is particularly significant for the Jesus exorcisms, since many scholars assume that his miracles serve an apocalyptic expectation, Satan's overthrow and the in-breaking of the Kingdom. But does the apocalyptic lens

---

10 Howard Clark Kee, *Medicine, Miracle and Magic in New Testament Times* (Cambridge: Cambridge University Press, 1986).

show itself to have been intended by the writer of the story? What distinct features should be expected of the story to signal to the reader a deliberate appeal to such an unconventional worldview? Such questions demand the inclusion of comparative examples of Jewish material, first exorcism stories of a non-apocalyptic interpretation, and then distinctive Jewish treatments of demons found in apocalyptic texts extant by the first century CE (I have chosen 1 Enoch and Jubilees.)

Part 3 presents stories of gods and heroes who control nature, in four particular ways: 1. Controlling the wind and the sea; 2. Walking/traveling over the surface of the sea; 3. Changing water into wine and 4. Multiplying food for the hungry. Clearly, this four-part division is influenced by the four great nature miracles of the Jesus tradition. At the same time, however, these major miracles are a fair representation of the type of benevolent nature miracles to be expected of gods or heroes of antiquity.

Part 4 faces the very real world of blatant magic and its claims to efficacious miracles. Certainly, for the populace of antiquity, no firm lines divided magic from miracle or medicine. Nevertheless, there should be a special set of texts in which authors from the Greco-Roman world discuss magic, by name, as well as its promises of manipulations of the cosmic "canons of the ordinary" through the intervention of magicians so named. Pliny, Plutarch and Seneca provide the ancient texts on the nature of magic, while the heroes Empedocles and Apuleius are examples of heroes attributed with its powers. Part 4 concludes with a sample of magical spells from the Magical Papyri for healings and for exorcisms.

Two appendices bring the book to its conclusion. Appendix A, Diseases and Doctors, presents a selection of texts describing the diseases most commonly cured in the healing miracles, as well as the treatments these diseases normally would have received. Studying these readings, one can better evaluate the degree of importance of a miracle in the eyes of the Greco-Roman person, not only for the alleviation of the disease, but also for the rescue from its medical cure.

Appendix B is included for the special study of the Jesus miracles. It provides the texts from the Torah and the Mishnah that directly relate to specific miracles told of Jesus, and cover seven topics: a. leprosy; b. they that suffer a flux; c. touching a corpse; d. sabbath observance; e. Jewish dealings with Gentiles; f. the deaf-mute and Torah; and g. uttering a charm over a wound.

THE SELECTION OF SOURCE TEXTS

Date: a center point in the first century CE

Since I intend this sourcebook to be helpful also to those scholars particularly focused on the Jesus miracles, I have chosen the first century as a sort of median, a chronological center for the sources. Second- or even third-century sources, like Lucian and Dio Cassius, are included only if their ideas fairly represent ideas available to a first-century populace as well. For example, in the selection of texts for appendix A, I did not include the particular methods and treatments of Galen since they would have been unknown to the ordinary person of the first century.

Ideas available to the ordinary populace of the Greco-Roman world

My goal is to represent a range of the most common ideas about sickness and healings, daimons/demons and exorcisms, the role of nature and the powers of magic that belong to the first-century world. My idea of the "ordinary" refers to a populace of non-elites. We do need to note that the writers of miracle stories have had schooling sufficient to compose in Greek. It is in their allusions and details of narrative that their expectations of their audience are evinced. This holds true for the Jesus miracles as well, unless one argues that the miracles in Mark were kept in an oral state for over thirty years until he wrote them down for the first time. Texts from Pliny the Elder and Plutarch, two obvious elites, are presented not because we imagine that non-elites had access to their aristocratic world or writings, but because these authors often report customs, trends and cultural ideas that circulated throughout the empire, even if only to ridicule them.

The absence of later Christian texts

It will be noticed that this sourcebook will include excerpts from non-Christian sources from the third century CE, but not Christian texts from the same period. The reason for this seeming imbalance is that our purpose is to recapture evidence about the Greco-Roman view of miracles of various kinds. Even in the third century, we have pagans who are ignorant of Christian material and can blithely comment on miracle stories without the pointedness of an apologetic against Christian claims. Patristic commentaries, however, represent generations of Christian reflection, and Christological development internal to the religious group. The use of the miracle stories by the Fathers either supports later developments in theology or is used for apologetic purposes. This approach to the Christian miracle stories has already been meticulously analyzed in the erudite work of Harold Remus.[11] In this book, however, the sources are meant to help the reconstruction of the miracle story writer's own intention as found in his story from the early first century.

THE USES OF THE SOURCEBOOK

There are several uses of the sourcebook. But first, it is important to underline that I do not wish to suggest genetic influences on miracles of a similar type. I join Samuel Sandmel in deploring "parallelomania":

> that extravagance among scholars which first overdoes the supposed similarities in passages and then proceeds to describe source and derivation as if implying literary connection flowing in an inevitable or predetermined direction.[12]

Miracle stories and the texts that help contextualize their possible meanings are grouped by type in order to interpret their individual claims better, to hear the nuances of the miracle's significance and that of the god or hero who performs the wonder.

SUGGESTED WAYS TO USE THIS BOOK
FOR STUDY AND DISCUSSION

1. The sources and notes throughout the book allow it to be used as a basic text for a graduate course on miracles in the Greco-Roman world.

---

11 Remus, *Pagan–Christian Conflict Over Miracle in the Second Century*.
12 Samuel Sandmel, "Parallelomania," *JBL* (1962), 1–13, esp. p. 1.

2. Individual Jesus miracles can be investigated in the light of the contextualizing material found in the chapter pertinent to their type. As an illustrative exercise students can be invited to tabulate the interpretation of a Jesus miracle found in four or five recent commentaries and then compare these with their own conclusions drawn from the careful examination and discussion of the miracle with contextualizing sources.

3. One prominent theme throughout the book is the way in which miracles are claimed to be performed not only by philosophers and holy men but by military leaders, kings and emperors. The place of miracles in the political imagination of the Greco-Roman world deserves special attention. What did these supporters of political rulers presume was the connection between healing the sick and the command of the world?

4. With respect to the Jesus miracles, do we see political statements made about his power in the miracles? The sources in this volume provide us with ample material for our discussion.

5. Matthew and Luke often edit the Markan miracle stories in accordance with their own Christology. This sourcebook provides a textbook to further the discussion about their particular redactions which created in the Greco-Roman audience a new significance for the miracle, and especially for the portraiture of Jesus.

Part I

GODS AND HEROES
WHO HEAL

1

GODS WHO HEAL

INTRODUCTION

The significance of a hero's healing miracle is profoundly affected by any likeness it bears to actions of gods or heroes already known to the audience. Part 1 presents a selection of texts which represent those favorite gods and heroes who were attributed with the power to heal. Since it is particularly helpful if a narrator comments about the significance of the hero or god's miracle, I also include any interpretive remarks attached to the story's presentation. In this way we can better reconstruct the "lens" of the Greco-Roman world, better understand why certain tellings of miracle stories were especially popular so that they survived. The particular telling of the Jesus miracles that survived until the writing of the gospels must have held special significance. The texts in this part help to create a set of meanings and "echoes" that were available as reasons, at least in part, for the unforgettable character of those gospel accounts.

THE HEALING GODS: HERCULES, ASCLEPIUS AND ISIS

In principle, any deity or any divinely empowered hero of the Greco-Roman period could be claimed to have performed a healing miracle. But in fact, there are only a few deities who were regularly attributed with healings. In the Greek pantheon, Heracles/Hercules is famous for his enormous compassion for humanity. Once human, he was eventually raised to the status of a god. Yet, he never forgets the pains and troubles of the human condition. Among the foreign deities, it is the Egyptian goddess Isis who is worshiped for her beneficence toward humanity and can be approached for healings, especially in her role as loving mother to all her devotees, no matter what their social rank or status.

11

But the greatest of all the healing deities, Greek or foreign, is Asclepios (Asclepius or Aesculapius), the Greek physician who is raised to the status of a god. He is the one who guides the hands of all the physicians, the one to whom all the sick may turn hopefully. The shrine at Epidaurus, the many references to him in commemorative inscriptions and plaques, the amulets and statues all testify to his reputation as the healing god throughout the Greco-Roman world.

It is intriguing that the legends of all three deities, Hercules, Isis and Asclepius also feature a story of their raising someone from the dead. Thus, the particular type of miracle that Bultmann identified as "raising from the dead" belongs naturally in the section on healing. It seems that this type of miracle is a healing gone to its extreme.

Greek heroes now divine: Hercules and Asclepius

Hercules

Heals diseases

AELIUS ARISTIDES

1.1.1. Hercules, a Hero Now Divine, is Beyond Human Nature

Aelius Aristides, *Heracles* 40.11[1]

For when Heracles, purified in the manner told, left the human race, Apollo immediately proclaimed the establishment of temples to Heracles and that sacrifices be made to him as to a god, and at that he revealed it to Athens which was the oldest Greek city, and as it were, a guide for all men in the matter of piety toward the gods and in all other serious activities. Further it also had many other ties of friendship with Heracles, including the fact that he was the first foreigner to be initiated,[2] while he was among men. And the manifestation of the Athenians' zeal was so great and his position was adjudged as so very much superior that they even changed all the shrines built in honor of Theseus throughout the demes and made them shrines in honor of Heracles instead of Theseus in the belief that Theseus was the best of their citizens, but that Heracles was beyond human nature.

---

1 All quotations are taken from P. Aelius Aristides, *The Complete Works* (trans. Charles A. Behr; Leiden: Brill, 1981), 240–241.
2 The reference is to the Eleusinian Mysteries.

1.1.2. Even Now Hercules Heals All Diseases

Aelius Aristides, *Heracles* 40.12

But why should we speak of ancient history. For the activity of the god is still now manifest. On the one hand, as we hear he does marvelous deeds at Gadira[3] and is believed to be second to none of all the gods. And on the other hand, in Messene in Sicily he frees men from all diseases, and those who have escaped danger on the sea attribute the benefaction equally to Poseidon and Heracles. One could list many other places sacred to the god, and other manifestations of his power.

Raises the dead

APOLLODORUS (CIRCA FIRST CENTURY CE)

1.2. Hercules Fought with Hades and Brought Alcestis Back to Life

Apollodorus, *The Library*, 1.9.15[4]

Now Pelias had promised to give his daughter [Alcestis] to him who should yoke a lion and a boar to a car, and Apollo yoked and gave them to Admetus, who brought them to Pelias and so obtained Alcestis. But in offering a sacrifice at his marriage, he forgot to sacrifice to Artemis; therefore when he opened the marriage chamber he found it full of coiled snakes. Apollo bade him appease the goddess and obtained as a favour of the Fates that, when Admetus should be about to die, he might be released from death if someone should voluntarily choose to die for him. And when the day of his death came neither his father nor his mother would die for him, but Alcestis died in his stead. But the Maiden [Artemis] sent her up again, or as some say, Hercules fought with Hades and brought her up to him.

EURIPIDES (485–406 BCE)

The text from Euripides will be placed after Apollodorus, because the latter provides a fine review of the story's background. Euripides' play *Alcestis* reaches its climax with Hercules' restoration of the loving wife to her bereaved husband. In this last scene, Hercules meets Admetus, Alcestis' husband, as he returns from the funeral of his wife. He is especially grief-stricken because Alcestis has given her life in his place. With Hercules is a veiled woman, who stands

---

3 Cadiz. Diodorus 5.20.
4 Apollodorus, *The Library*, vol. 1 (trans. Sir James George Frazer; London: Heinemann, 1921), 1.9.15.

by silently as he and Admetus enter into the telling conversation that will reveal the miraculous event.

Hercules brings back from the dead Admetus' wife, Alcestis

1.3.1. Hercules Explains to Admetus that He Ambushed Hades at the Tomb

Euripides, *Alcestis* 1136–1142[5]

> *Admetus:* O scion nobly-born of Zeus most high,
> Blessings on thee! The Father who begat thee
> Keep thee! Thou only has restored my fortunes.
> How didst thou bring her from shades to light?
> *Hercules:* I closed in conflict with the Lord of Spirits.
> *Admetus:* Where, say'st thou, didst thou fight this fight with Death?
> *Hercules:* From ambush by the tomb mine hands ensnared him.

1.3.2. Alcestis Must Wait Till the Third Day to be Unconsecrated to the Powers Beneath the Earth

Euripides, *Alcestis* 1143–1150

> *Admetus:* Now wherefore speechless standeth thus my wife?
> *Hercules:* 'Tis not vouchsafed thee yet to hear her voice,
> Ere to the Powers beneath the earth she be
> Unconsecrated, and the third day come.
> But lead her in, and, just man as thou art,
> Henceforth, Admetus, reverence still the guest.
> Farewell. But I must go, and work the work
> Set by the king, the son of Sthenelaus.

1.3.3. Hercules Takes His Leave While Admetus Promises Sacrifices of Praise and Rejoicing

Euripides, *Alcestis* 1151–1158

> *Admetus*: Abide with us, a sharer of our hearth.
> *Hercules*: Hereafter this: now must I hasten on.
> *Admetus*: O prosper thou, and come again in peace!
> (Exit Hercules)

---

5 All quotations are taken from Euripides, *Alcestis*, *Euripides*, vol. 4 (trans. Arthur S. Way; London: Heinemann, 1912).

Through all my realm, I publish to my folk
That, for these blessings, dances they array,
And that atonement-fumes from altars rise.
For now to happier days than those o'erpast
Have we attained. I own me blest indeed.

1.3.4. The Chorus Praises this "Marvellous Thing," a Path Undiscerned in our Eyes

Euripides, *Alcestis* 1159–1163

Chorus: O the works of the Gods – in manifold forms they reveal
them:
Manifold things unhoped-for the Gods to accomplishment bring.
And the things that we looked for, the Gods deign not to fulfil
them;
And the paths undiscerned of our eyes, the Gods
unseal them.
So fell this marvellous thing.

Asclepius

1.4. Asclepius is worshipped everywhere

Of these [good daimones] they deem gods only those who,
having guided the chariot of their lives wisely and justly
and having been endowed afterward by men as divinities
with shrines and religious ceremonies
are commonly worshipped as Amphiaraus in Boeotia
Mopsus in Africa, Osiris in Egypt,
one in one part of the world and another in another part,
Asclepius everywhere.

(Apuleius)[6]

The most thorough treatment of this important deity is the two-volume work *Asclepius* by Emma J. Edelstein and Ludwig Edelstein.[7] This exhaustive collection of ancient texts (volume 1) and discussion of their significance (volume 2) is the treasure from which

6 Apuleius, *De Deo Socratis* 15.153. Trans. Emma J. Edelstein and Ludwig Edelstein, *Asclepius* (2 vols; Baltimore: The Johns Hopkins Press, 1945), vol. 1, p. 116.
7 See n. 6 above.

I have drawn a few especially pertinent references and translations for the contextualization of the Jesus miracles.

The physician Asclepius (Aesculapius for the Romans) first appears in Homer as a human being who would attend the Argonauts. But his legend would alter his status to that of a semi-divine being, the product of a union between Apollo and his human mother, Coronis.[8] Raised by a Thessalian centaur, Chiron, Asclepius learned from him the arts of healing. Asclepius' legend holds that it was his own compassionate raising of the dead that roused Zeus's anger to slay him with lightning. Asclepius was revered for his reliable philanthropy; Aelian describes him as "the god most loving towards humanity."[9]

In the hellenic period, his shrine at Epidaurus was already famous as a place for miraculous healings. The main feature of the rite involved a preliminary purification of the devotee and an "incubation," sleeping in the temple of the deity. During the night, the priest, embodying the presence of the god, moved through the temple, while the faithful slept, hoping for a dream in which the god would reveal the necessary measures to ensure prompt healing.

By the Imperial period, Asclepius was so elevated that his statue stood in the temple of Apollo, who in legend was his father.[10] The easy association between "healer" and "saviour" explains the appeal to him in any matter involving the extension of life.

Aside from one infrequently mentioned tradition that claimed that Asclepius was guilty of greed,[11] all the traditions around this deity set him apart for his unfailing compassion and kindness to humankind. Unlike the Olympians, Asclepius has no legend of jealous, vindictive anger or crafty machinations against his foes.

---

8   See Homer, *Hymns* 3.207–213 and 16.216.1–6; Hesiod, *Fragments* 122, 123; Apollonius of Rhodes, *Argonautica* 4.611–617; Diodorus, *Library of History* 5.74.6; Pausanias, *Description of Greece* 2.26.6; Hyginus, *Astronomica* 4.40; Servius, *Commentary on the Aeneid* 6.618.

9   Aelian, *De Natura Animalium* 8.12.

10 See the account of Pausanias, *Corinth, Description of Greece* 2.3–7.

11 Pindar, *Pythians* 3.55–58 is the main source of this tradition, referred to by Plato, *Republic* 3.408B–C; and subsequently by the Christian apologists against Asclepius, Clement of Alexandria (*Protrepticus* 2.30.1); Tertullian (*Apologeticus* 14.5–6 and *Ad Nationes* 2.14).

The majority of the testimonies to Asclepius here are taken from a stele dated about the second half of the fourth century BCE, or about 350 BCE. Others belong to the Greco-Roman period and will each be designated with the approximate date of inscription.

Asclepius heals the blind

Ambrosia, the woman blind in one eye

1.5. Ambrosia, Who Scoffed at Asclepius' Healings Through Dreams, is Asked to Dedicate a Silver Pig to Him in Memory of Her Ignorance

Inscriptiones Graecae 4.1.121–122: Stele 1.4

Ambrosia from Athens, blind of one eye. She came as a suppliant to the god. As she walked about in the Temple she laughed at some of the cures as incredible and impossible, that the lame and the blind should be healed by merely seeing a dream. In her sleep she had a vision. It seemed to her that the god stood by her and said that he would cure her, but that in payment he would ask her to dedicate to the Temple a silver pig as a memorial of her ignorance. After saying this, he cut the diseased eyeball and poured in some drug. When day came she walked out sound.

The man with no eye but only an eye socket

1.6. Ignoring People's Derision, the Man With Only an Eye Socket Trusted in Asclepius, and the God Restored his Eye

Inscriptiones Graecae 4.1.121–122: Stele 1.9

A man came as a suppliant to the god. He was so blind that of one of his eyes he had only the eyelids left – within them was nothing, but they were entirely empty. Some of those in the Temple laughed at his silliness to think that he could recover his sight when one of his eyes had not even a trace of the ball, but only the socket. As he slept a vision appeared to him. It seemed to him that the god prepared some drug, then, opening his eyelids, poured it into them. When day came he departed with the sight of both eyes restored.

Alcetas the blind man

1.7. Alcetas Dreams that Asclepius Opens his Eyes With his Fingers

Inscriptiones Graecae 4.1.121–122: Stele 1.18

Alcetas of Halieis. The blind man saw a dream. It seemed to him that the god came up to him and with his fingers opened his eyes, and that he first saw the trees in the sanctuary. At daybreak he walked out sound.

Hermon's blindness is healed

1.8. Hermon Has his Blindness Return Until he Returns to Thank Asclepius

Inscriptiones Graecae 4.1.121–122: Stele 2.22

Hermon of Thasus. His blindness was cured by Asclepius. But, since afterwards he did not bring the thank-offerings, the god made him blind again. When he came back and slept again in the Temple, he [sc. the god] made him well.

Valerius Aper, a blind soldier

1.9. Asclepius Prescribed an Eye Salve Which Restored Valerius' Sight

Inscriptiones Graecae 14.966 (second century CE)

To Valerius Aper, a blind soldier, the god revealed that he should go and take the blood of a white cock along with honey and compound an eye salve and for three days should apply it to his eyes. And he could see again and went and publicly offered thanks to the god.

Asclepius heals a woman of dropsy

Arata, the dropsical woman, is healed from a distance

1.10. While Arata's Mother Receives the Dream of Arata's Healing in Epidaurus, Arata Receives the Same One in Lacedaemon (Sparta)

Inscriptiones Graecae, 4.1.121–122: Stele 2.21

Arata, a woman of Lacedaemon, dropsical. For her, while she remained in Lacedaemon, her mother slept in the temple and sees a dream. It seemed to her that the god cut off her daughter's head and hung up her body in such a way that her throat was turned downwards. Out of it came a huge quantity of fluid matter. Then he took down the body and fitted the head back on to the neck. After she had seen this dream she went back to Lacedaemon, where she found her daughter in good health; she had seen the same dream.

Dumbness

Asclepius heals a mute boy

1.11. When the Servant of Asclepius Asked the Mute Boy's Father to Promise a Thank-offering, the Boy Himself Said, "I Promise!"

Inscriptiones Graecae 4.1.121–122: Stele 1.5

A voiceless boy. He came as a supplicant to the Temple for his voice. When he had performed the preliminary sacrifices and fulfilled the usual rites, thereupon the temple servant who brings in the fire for the god, looking at the boy's father, demanded he should promise to bring within a year the thank-offering for the cure if he obtained that for which he had come. But the boy suddenly said, "I promise." His father was startled at this and asked him to repeat it. The boy repeated the words and after that became well.

Epilepsy

Asclepius heals a man with epilepsy

1.12. Asclepius Cures Epilepsy by Substituting a Quartan Fever

Oribasius, Collectiones Medicae 45.30.10–14[12]

Also, epilepsy is a cramp; of this quartan fever, therefore, is a cure, so that if it supervenes afterwards epilepsy is broken up, while if it comes previously epilepsy does not befall that man any more. How it happened to Teucer, the Cyzicenean [circa 100 CE], is worth telling: when he was afflicted with epilepsy he came to Pergamum to Asclepius, asking for liberation from the disease. The god, appearing to him holds converse with him and asks if he wants to exchange his present disease against another one. And he said he surely did not want that but would rather get some immediate relief from the evil. But if at all, he wished that the future might not be worse than the present. When the god had said it would be easier and this would cure him more plainly than anything else, he [sc. Teucer] consents to the disease, and a quartan fever attacks him, and thereafter he is free from epilepsy.

---

12 "The passage is taken from Rufus, a physician of the 1st century CE" E. Edelstein and L.Edelstein, *Asclepius,* vol. 1, p. 239.

Lameness

Nicanor, the lame man

1.13. When a Boy Stole his Crutch, Nicanor Ran after Him and So Became Well

Inscriptiones Graecae, 4.1.121–122: Stele 1.16

Nicanor, a lame man. While he was sitting wide-awake, a boy snatched his crutch from him and ran away. But Nicanor got up, pursued him, and so became well.

The lame man from Epidaurus

1.14. A Cowardly Lame Man Fears to Follow Asclepius' Orders to Climb to the Top of the Sanctuary at Night; but When He Completes the Task in the Day, He is Cured

Inscriptiones Graecae 4.1.121–122: Stele 2.35

. . . from Epidaurus, lame. He came as a supplicant to the sanctuary on a stretcher. In his sleep he saw a vision. It seemed to him that the god broke his crutch and ordered him to go and get a ladder and to climb as high as possible up to the top of the sanctuary. The man tried it at first, then, however, lost his courage and rested up on the cornice; finally he gave up and climbed down the ladder little by little. Asclepius at first was angry about the deed, then he laughed at him because he was such a coward. He dared to carry it out after it had become daytime and walked out unhurt.

Cephisias, the man with the crippled foot

1.15. Cephisias Derided the Cures of Asclepius Until He Needed His Healing

Inscriptiones Graecae 4.1.121–122: Stele 2.36

Cephisias . . . with the foot. He laughed at the cures of Asclepius and said: "If the god says he has healed lame people he is lying; for, if he had the power to do so, why has he not healed Hephaestus?" But the god did not conceal that he was inflicting penalty for the insolence. For Cephisias, when riding, was stricken by his bullheaded horse which had been tickled in the seat, so that instantly his foot was crippled and on a stretcher he was carried into the Temple. Later on, after he had entreated him earnestly, the god made him well.

Paralysis

The man with paralyzed fingers is healed

1.16. To the Man with Paralyzed Fingers, Asclepius Said, "Since You Doubted the Cures, Your Name From Now On Will be 'Incredulous.'" Then in the Morning, He was Healed

Inscriptiones Graecae 4.1.121–122: Stele 1.3

A man whose fingers, with the exception of one, were paralyzed, came as a suppliant to the god. While looking at the tablets in the temple he expressed incredulity regarding the cures and scoffed at the inscriptions. But in his sleep he saw a vision. It seemed to him that, as he was playing at dice below the Temple and was about to cast the dice, the god appeared, sprang upon his hand, and stretched out his [the patient's] fingers. When the god had stepped aside it seemed to him [the patient] that he [the patient] bent his hand and stretched out all his fingers one by one. When he had straightened them all, the god asked him if he would still be incredulous of the inscriptions on the tablets in the Temple. He answered that he would not. "Since, then, formerly you were incredulous of the cures, though they were not incredible, for the future," he said, "your name will be 'Incredulous.'" When the day dawned he walked out sound.

The man who was paralyzed in his body is healed

1.17. When Asclepius Ordered Hermodicus to Bring to the Temple as Large a Stone as He Could, He Did and He Was Healed

Inscriptiones Graecae 4.1.121–122: Stele 1.15

Hermodicus of Lampsacus was paralyzed in body. This one, when he slept in the Temple, the god healed and he ordered him upon coming out to bring to the Temple as large a stone as he could. The man brought the stone which now lies before the Abaton.

Hermodicus leaves an inscription to Asclepius' honor

1.18. This Rock is an Evidence of Your Art

Inscriptiones Graecae 4.1.125 (circa third century BCE)

Hermodicus of Lampsacus

As an example of your power, Asclepius, I have put up this rock which I had lifted up, manifest for all to see, an evidence of your art. For before coming under your hands and those of your children I was stricken by a wretched illness, having an abscess in my chest and being paralyzed in my hands. But you, Paean, by ordering me to lift up this rock made me live free from disease.

Cleimenes of Argus, paralyzed in body

1.19. Asclepius Demands that the Cowardly Cleimenes be Full of Hope

Inscriptiones Graecae 4.1.121–122: Stele 2.37

Cleimenes of Argus, paralyzed in body. He came to the Abaton and slept there and saw a vision. It seemed to him that the god wound a red woolen fillet around his body and led him for a bath a short distance away from the Temple to a lake of which the water was exceedingly cold. When he behaved in a cowardly way Asclepius said he would not heal those people who were too cowardly for that, but those who came to him into his Temple, full of hope that he would do no harm to such a man, but would send him away well. When he woke up he took a bath and walked out unhurt.

Diaetus, paralyzed in the knees

1.20. Diaetus Dreamed that When Asclepius Drove His Horses over His Body, It was Then That He Got Control of His Knees Once More

Inscriptiones Graecae 4.1.121–122: Stele 2.38

Diaetus of Cirrha. He happened to be paralyzed in his knees. While sleeping in the Temple he saw a dream. It seemed to him that the god ordered his servants to lift him up and to carry him outside the Adyton and to lay him down in front of the Temple. After they had carried him outside, the god yoked his horses to a chariot and drove three times around him in a circle and trampled on him with his horses and he got control over his knees instantly. When day came he walked out sound.

Asclepius in dreams: Artemidorus (late second century CE)[13]

Artemidorus made a collection of dream interpretations based not only on former works already known to his own educated social circle, but also on research he conducted, gathering dream interpretations from the marketplaces all around the empire. Whether the interpretations are correct or not is completely beside the point, of course. The wonderful value of his collection is in its evidence of the most common associations of situations, objects and people with the cultural reality of the Greco-Roman Mediterranean world of the second century CE.

13 Artemidorus, *The Interpretation of Dreams: Oneirocritica* (trans. and commentary by Robert J. White; Park Ridge, NJ: Noyes Press, 1975).

Asclepius always indicates those who help in time of need

1.21. If You Dream that Asclepius Enters the House of One Sick, it Signifies Recovery

Artemidorus, *On the Interpretation of Dreams* 2.37

If Asclepios is set up in a temple and stands upon a pedestal, if he is seen and adored, it means good luck for all. But if he moves and approaches or goes into a house, it prophesies sickness and famine. But for those already sick, it signifies recovery. For the god is called Paean (the Healer). Asclepios always indicates those who help in time of need and those who manage the house of the dreamer.

Asclepius' healing as distinctive in the Greco-Roman period

Howard Kee provides this as an example of the main differences between the Greco-Roman attributions to Asclepius and those of Hellenistic times.

> The contrasts with the Iamata of Hellenistic times are striking: although the god is given ultimate credit for the cure, the therapy seems to have been largely self-administered. There is no mention of the sacred sleep or dream-visions. Rather, there are baths and strolls, presumably extending over a period of many days. The ailments are multiple: to heal them there is no lick by the tongue of a snake or a dog. The beneficiary is grateful for the improvement in his health, but there is no miraculous healing at a stroke. Significant, however, is the clear implication that the course of Apellas' life [see below] is under the guidance of the god. It is a factor which figures importantly in the evidence from Pergamum in the same period that Apellas was overcoming his maladies at Epidauros with the aid of the god.[14]

14 Howard Kee, *Miracle in the Early Christian World: A Study in Socio-historical Method* (New Haven and London: Yale University Press, 1983), 89.

1.22. A Devotee Receives General Healing of Stomach and Throat

Inscriptiones Graecae 4 Syll. 3.11170 (circa 160 CE)[15]
I, M. Julius Apellas, was sent forth by the god, since I fell sick often and was stricken with indigestion. On the journey to Aegina, not much happened to me. When I arrived at the sanctuary, it happened that my head was covered for two days during which there were torrents of rain. Cheese and bread were brought to me, celery and lettuce. I bathed alone without help; was forced to run; lemon rinds to take; soaked in water; at the *akoai* in the bath I rubbed myself on the wall; went for a stroll on the high road; swinging; smeared myself with dust; went walking barefoot; at the bath, poured wine over myself before entering the hot water; bathed alone and gave the bath-master an Attic drachma; made common offering to Asklepios, to Epion [his wife], to the Eleusinian goddess; took milk with honey. I used the oil and the headache was gone. I gargled with cold water against a sore throat, since this was another reason that I had turned to the god. The same remedy for swollen tonsils. I had occasion to write this out. With grateful heart and having become well, I took leave.

Raises the dead

1.23. Asclepius was requited with a thunderbolt for raising the dead

> Let your ancestor Asclepius be a warning to you
> in that he was requited with a thunderbolt
> for saving humankind.
>
> (Hippocrates)[16]

According to his legends, Asclepius was killed by Zeus for bringing the dead back to life. The most popular version explains the punishment in connection with the myth of Hippolytus. When Hippolytus, Theseus' son, discovered that his step-mother desired him, he violently upbraided her, after which she committed suicide, leaving a note which falsely accused Hippolytus of rape. Despite Hippolytus' pleas of his innocence, Theseus believed the suicide note and exiled Hippolytus. While the young man was driving his chariot by the sea, a monster came out of the waters and frightened the horses. Hippolytus was thrown from the chariot and died. Artemis, who loved Hippolytus, moved Asclepius to bring the young man

---

15 Translation is by Howard Kee, ibid., 88.
16 Hippocrates, *Epistulae* 17. Trans. E. and L. Edelstein, *Asclepius*, vol. 1, p. 463.

back to life. This act was sufficient to bring the wrath of Zeus against Asclepius and he sent lightning to strike and kill the physician.

The element that is of importance, then, as we see it, is the availability of the idea of a healer giving up his own life in return for raising the dead to life.

DIODORUS SICULUS (WROTE 60–30 BCE)

1.24. Asclepius is Slain by Zeus at the Complaint from Hades about the Diminishing Numbers of Dead because of the Healing God's Saving Them

Diodorus Siculus, *The Library of History* 4.71.1–3[17]

Asclepius was the son of Apollo and Coronis, and since he excelled in natural ability and sagacity of mind, he devoted himself to the science of healing and made many discoveries which contribute to the health of mankind. And so far did he advance along the road of fame that, to the amazement of all, he healed many sick whose lives had been despaired of, and for this reason it was believed that he had brought back to life many who had died. Consequently, the myth goes on to say, Hades brought accusation against Asclepius, charging him before Zeus of acting to the detriment of his own province, for, he said, the number of the dead was steadily diminishing, now that men were being healed by Asclepius. So Zeus, in indignation, slew Asclepius with his thunderbolt, but Apollo, indignant at the slaying of Asclepius, murdered the Cyclopes who had forged the thunderbolt for Zeus; but at the death of the Cyclopes Zeus was again indignant and laid a command upon Apollo that he should serve as a labourer for a human being and that this should be the punishment he should receive from him for his crimes.

VIRGIL (70–19 BCE)

1.25. The Father Omnipotent Hurled Down to Stygian Waters the Finder of Such Healing-Craft

Virgil, *Aeneid* 7.765–773[18]

For they tell how that Hippolytus, when he fell by his stepdame's craft, and slaked a sire's vengeance in blood, torn assunder by frightened steeds – came again to the starry firmament and heaven's upper air, recalled by

---

17 Diodorus Siculus, *The Library of History*, vol. 3 (trans. C. H. Oldfather; London: Heinemann, 1939), 4.71.1–3.
18 Virgil, *The Aeneid, Virgil*, vol. 2 (trans. H. Rushton Fairclough; London: Heinemann, 1918), 7.765–773.

the Healer's herbs and Diana's love. Then the Father omnipotent, wroth that any mortal should rise from the nether shades to the light of life, himself with his thunder hurled down to the Stygian waters the finder of such healing-craft, the Phoebus-born.

APOLLODORUS (CIRCA FIRST CENTURY CE)

1.26. Asclepius Raised Six Men: Capaneus, Lycurgus, Hippolytus, Tyndareus, Hymenaeus and Glaucus

Apollodorus, *The Library* 3.10.3–4[19]

I found some who are reported to have been raised by him, to wit, Capaneus and Lycurgus, as Stesichorus [645–555 BCE] says in the *Eriphyle*; Hippolytus, as the author of the *Naupactica* [sixth cntury BCE] reports; Tyndareus, as Panyasis [circa 500 BCE] says; Hymenaeus, as the Orphics report; and Glaucus, son of Minos, as Melasagoras [fifth century BCE] relates. But Zeus, fearing that men might acquire the healing art from him and so come to the rescue of each other, smote him with a thunderbolt.

PHILODEMUS (CIRCA FIRST CENTURY CE)

1.27. Was Asclepius Struck with Lightning for Raising Hippolytus, or Capaneus and Lycurgus?

Philodemus, *De Pietate* 52[20]

Zeus struck Asclepius by lightning, because according to the writer of the *Naupactica* [sixth century BCE] and the *Asclepius* of Telestes [fourth century BCE] and the (like-named work) of the lyric poet Cinesias [fourth century BCE] he raised Hippolytus from the dead at the instance of Artemis; but according to the *Eriphyle* of Stesichorus [circa 640–555 BCE] it was because he raised Capaneus and Lycurgus.

19 Apollodorus, *The Library*, vol. 2 (trans. Sir James George Frazer; London: Heinemann, 1921), 3.10.3–4.

20 Philodemus, *De Pietate*, in "The Poem of Cinesias," *Lyra Graeca*, vol. 3 (trans. J. M. Edmonds; London: Heinemann, 1927), 52.

1.28. Asclepius Was Killed for Raising Tyndareus to Life

Pliny the Elder, *Natural History* 29.1.3[21]
Then medicine became more famous even through sin, for legend said that Aesculapius was struck by lightning for bringing Tyndareus back to life.

1.29. Zeus Was Angry With Asclepius Over the Resurrection of Tyndareus

Lucian, *The Dance* 45[22]
Sparta, too, affords not a few stories of this sort . . . the resurrection of Tyndareus, and Zeus' anger at Asclepius over it.

1.30. Zeus Must Stop the Quarreling between Hercules and Asclepius Over Who Should Rank Above the Other

Lucian, *Dialogues of the Gods: Zeus, Asclepius and Heracles* 15(13)[23]

ZEUS Stop quarrelling, you two; you're just like a couple of men. It's quite improper and out of place at the table of the gods.

HERACLES But, Zeus, do you really mean this medicine man to have a place above me?

ASCLEPIUS He does, by Zeus, for I'm your better.

HERACLES How, you crackbrain? Because Zeus blasted you with his thunderbolt for your impious doings,[24] and now you've received immortality because he relented and pitied you?

ASCLEPIUS You must have forgotten, Heracles, how you too were scorched to death on Oeta,[25] that you taunt me with getting burned.

---

21 Pliny the Elder, *Natural History*, vol. 8 (trans. W. H. S. Jones; London: Heinemann, 1963), 29.1.3.

22 Lucian, *The Dance, Lucian*, vol. 5 (trans. A. M. Harmon; London: Heinemann, 1936), 45.

23 Lucian, *Dialogues of the Gods: Zeus, Asclepius and Heracles, Lucian*, vol. 7 (trans. M. D. Macleod; London: Heinemann, 1961), 15(13).

24 The reference is to Asclepius raising the dead, and here the allusion is probably to Hippolytus.

25 Hercules is said to have committed suicide by fire.

HERACLES That doesn't mean our lives were the same. I'm the son of Zeus, and performed all those labours cleaning up the world, by overcoming monsters, and punishing men of violence; but you're just a herb-chopper and quack, useful perhaps among suffering humanity for administering potions, but without one manly deed to show.

ASCLEPIUS Have you nothing to say of how I healed your burns when you came up half-scorched the other day? Between the tunic and the fire after it, your body was in a fine mess. Besides, if nothing else, I was never a slave like you, carding wool in Lydia, wearing purple, and being beaten with Omphale's golden sandal.[26] What's more, I never killed my wife and children in a fit of spleen.

HERACLES If you don't stop insulting me, you'll pretty soon find out that your immortality won't help you much. I'll pick you up and throw you head first out of heaven, so that you'll crack your skull, and not even Apollo the Healer will be able to do anything for you.

ZEUS Stop it, I say; don't disturb our dinner-party, or I'll send you both from the table. But its only reasonable, Heracles, that Asclepius should have a place above you, as he died before you.

Although the point Sextus Empiricus is trying to make is that popular myths are impossible to control, his review of scholarly stories about Asclepius' power to raise the dead only serves to underline how very closely this god is associated with this great miracle.

1.31. Asclepius Was Slain by Zeus for Raising the Dead: "Of a falsehood that is so multiform that it cannot be checked, and changes its shape at each man's fancy, there can be no technical treatment"

Sextus Empiricus, *Against the Professors* 1.260–262[27]
But particular histories are both infinite, because of their great number, and without fixity, because the same facts are not recorded by all respecting the same person. For instance (for it is not out of place to use familiar and

---

26 Hercules had to be a slave of the queen of Lydia, Omphale, for three years.
27 Sextus Empiricus, *Against the Professors* (trans. R. G. Bury; London: Heinemann, 1949), 260–262.

appropriate examples of the facts), the historians adopting a false assumption say that Asclepius, the founder of our science, was struck by lightning, and not content with this falsehood they invent many variations of it, Stesichorus [640–555 BCE] saying in *Eriphyle* that it was because he [Asclepius] had raised up some of the men who had fallen at Thebes, – Polyanthus of Cyrene [date unknown], in his work on the origin of the Asclepiades, that it was because he had cured the daughters of Proetus who had become mad owing to the wrath of Hera, – Panyasis [circa 500 BCE], that it was owing to his raising up the dead body of Tyndareos, Staphylus [circa 300 BCE], in his book about the Arcadians, that it was because he had healed Hippolytus when he was fleeing from Troezen, according to the reports handed down about him in the tragedies, – Phylarchus [third century BCE], in his ninth book, that it was because he restored their sight to the blinded sons of Phineus, as a favour to their mother Cleopatra, the daughter of Erechtheus, – Telesarchus [Hellenistic historian] in his *Argolicum*, that it was because he set himself to raise up Orion. Thus, of an assumption which begins with a falsehood and is so multiform that it cannot be checked, and changes its shape at each man's fancy, there can be no technical treatment.

PAUSANIAS (CIRCA 150 CE)

Pausanias was a geographer whose *Description of Greece* has proven to be quite accurate. He is particularly interested in recording historical and religious legends and traditions. In his treatment of Epidaurus he recounts the legend of Asclepius' birth, and his subsequent reputation for healings and raisings from the dead. He reports a second legend in which Asclepius is said to have raised Hippolytus from the dead after he was slain by Theseus.

1.32 Soon After Asclepius' Birth It Was Reported that He was Healing and Raising the Dead

Pausanias, *Corinth, Description of Greece* 1.26.4–5[28]
When he [Phlegyas, the greatest soldier of his time] went to the Peloponnesus, he was accompanied by his daughter, [Coronis] who all along had kept hidden from her father that she was with child by Apollo. In the country of the Epidaurians she bore a son, [Asclepius] and exposed him on the mountain called Nipple at the present day, but then named Myrtium. As the child lay exposed he was given milk by one of the goats

---

28 Pausanias, *Corinth, Description of Greece*, vol. 1 (trans. W.H.S. Jones; London: Heinemann, 1918), 1.26.4–5.

that pastured about the mountain, and was guarded by the watch-dog of the herd. And when Aresthanas (for this was the herdsman's name) discovered that the tale of the goats was not full, and that the watch-dog also was absent from the herd, he left, they say, no stone unturned, and on finding the child desired to take him up. As he drew near, he saw lightning that flashed from the child, and, thinking that it was something divine, as in fact it was, he turned away. Presently it was reported over every land and sea that Asclepius was discovering everything he wished to heal the sick, and that he was raising dead men to life.

1.33. Hippolytus Dedicated Twenty Horses to Asclepius in Thanksgiving

Pausanias, *Corinth, Description of Greece* 1.27.4–5

Apart from the others [stele thanking Asclepius for various cures] is an old slab, which declares that Hippolytus dedicated twenty horses to the god [Asclepius]. The Aricians tell a tale that agrees with the inscription of this slab, that when Hippolytus was killed, owing to the curses of Theseus, Asclepius raised him from the dead. On coming to life again he refused to forgive his father; rejecting his prayers, he went to the Aricians in Italy.

A foreign deity: Isis

Of the great goddesses of Greco-Roman antiquity, it is Isis who is most multivalent and mysterious. Most faithful wife and exquisite lover, she is also the tenderest mother, a protectress of the weak and vulnerable, whatever their social rank or class. The sacred mysteries associated with her cult were famous throughout the Mediterranean. Unlike the gods in the Olympian system, Isis is not subject to the Fates. She can countermand events in the future and will do so for her devotees. Thus in a broad sense Isis is a healer as part of her larger role as queen of the universe and goddess of cosmic good in every form. Plutarch's *Isis and Osiris* provides us with a Greco-Roman presentation of her myth and meaning.[29]

---

29 See Plutarch, *Isis and Osiris, Moralia*, vol. 5 (trans. Frank Cole Babbit; London: Heinemann, 1936).

Heals diseases

ISIDORUS (CIRCA 88 BCE)[30]

1.34.1. Isis, Manifold Miracles Were Your Care that You Might Bring Livelihood to Humankind and Morality to All

Isidorus, *Hymn to Isis* 1.1–5

O wealth-giver, Queen of the gods, Hermouthis, Lady,
Omnipotent Agathe Tyche, greatly renowned Isis,
Deo, highest Discoverer of all life,
manifold miracles were Your care that You might bring
livelihood to mankind and morality to all.

1.34.2. You, Being One, are All Other Goddesses Invoked by All the Races of Human Beings

Isidorus, *Hymn to Isis* 1.6–24

You taught customs that justice might in some measure
prevail;
You gave skills that men's life might be comfortable, and
You discovered the blossoms that produce edible vegetation.
Because of You heaven and the whole earth have their being;
And the gusts of the winds and the sun with its sweet light.
By Your power the channels of Nile are filled, every one,
At the harvest season and its most turbulent water is poured
On the whole land that produce may be unfailing.
All mortals who live on the boundless earth,
Thracians, Greeks and Barbarians,
Express Your fair Name, a Name greatly honoured among
all, (but)
Each (speaks) in his own language, in his own land.
The Syrians call You: Astarte, Artemis, Nanaia,
The Lycian tribes call You: Leto, the Lady,
The Thracians also name You as Mother of the gods,
And the Greeks (call You) Hera of the Great Throne,
Aphrodite,
Hestia the goodly, Rheia and Demeter.
But the Egyptians call You "Thiouis" (because they know)

---

30 All quotations are from Vera Frederika Vanderlip, *The Four Hymns of Isidorus and the Cult of Isis* (American Studies in Papyrology 12; Toronto: Hakkert, 1972).

that You, being One, are all
Other goddesses invoked by the races of men.

1.34.3. You Save All who are in Pain Through Long, Anguished, Sleepless Nights

Isidorus, *Hymn to Isis* 1.25–38

Mighty One, I shall not cease to sing of Your great Power,
Deathless Saviour, many-named, mightiest Isis,
Saving from war, cities and all their citizens;
Men, their wives, possessions, and children.
As many as are bound fast in prison, in the power of death,
As many as are in pain through long, anguished, sleepless nights,
All who are wanderers in a foreign land,
And as many as sail on the Great Sea in winter
When men may be destroyed and their ships wrecked and sunk . . .
All (these) are saved if they pray that you be present to help.
Hear my prayers, O One Whose Name has great Power;
Prove Yourself merciful to me and free me from all distress.
Isidorus
wrote (it).

DIODORUS SICULUS (WROTE 60–30 BCE)

1.35.1. Now That She is Immortal, Isis Finds Her Greatest Delight in the Healing of Humankind

Diodorus Siculus, *The Library of History* 1.25.2–3[31]
As for Isis, the Egyptians say that she was the discoverer of many health-giving drugs and was greatly versed in the science of healing; consequently, now that she has attained immortality, she finds her greatest delight in the healing of mankind and gives aid in their sleep to those who call upon her, plainly manifesting both her very presence and her beneficence towards men who ask her help.

31 Diodorus Siculus, *The Library of History*, vol. 1 (trans. C. H. Oldfather; London: Heinemann, 1933), 1.25.2–3.

1.35.2. Standing Above the Sick in their Sleep She Gives Them Aid for Their Disease and Works Remarkable Cures upon Such as Submit Themselves to Her

Diodorus Siculus, *The Library of History* 1.25.4–5

In proof of this, as they say, they advance, not legends, as the Greeks do, but manifest facts; for practically the entire inhabited world is their witness, in that it eagerly contributes to the honours of Isis because she manifests herself in healings. *For standing above the sick in their sleep she gives them aid for their diseases and works remarkable cures upon such as submit themselves to her;*[32] and many who have been despaired of by their physicians because of the difficult nature of their malady are restored to health by her, while numbers who have altogether lost the use of their eyes or of some other part of their body, wherever they turn for help to this goddess, are restored to their previous condition.

Raises the dead

1.36. Isis Discovered the Drug which Gives Immortality by Means of Which She Raised Her Persecuted Son from the Dead

Diodorus Siculus, *The Library of History* 1.25.6

Furthermore, she discovered also the drug which gives immortality, by means of which she not only raised from the dead her son Horus, who had been the object of plots on the part of the Titans and had been found dead under the water, giving him his soul again, but also made him immortal. And it appears that Horus was the last of the gods to be king after his father Osiris departed from among men.

1.37. Isis' Son, Horus, Is Now a Benefactor of the Human Race, through His Oracular Responses and His Healings

Diodorus Siculus, *The Library of History* 1.25.7

Moreover, they say that the name Horus, when translated, is Apollo, and that, having been instructed by his mother Isis in both medicine and divination, he is now a benefactor of the race of men through his oracular responses and his healings.

---

32 My italic. Notice that in Luke's version of the healing of Peter's mother-in-law (Luke 4:38–39) Jesus will stand above her and rebuke the fever.

1.38. "Whatsoever Laws I Have Established, These No One Can Make Void"

Diodorus Siculus, *The Library of History* 1.27.3–4

Now I am not unaware that some historians give the following account of Isis and Osiris: The tombs of these gods lie in Nyssa in Arabia, . . . and in that place there stands also a stele of each of the gods bearing an inscription in hieroglyphs. On the stele of Isis it runs: "I am Isis, the queen of every land, she who was instructed of Hermes, and whatsoever laws I have established, these no man can make void. I am the eldest daughter of the youngest god Cronus; I am the wife and sister of the king Osiris; I am she who first discovered fruits for mankind; I am the mother of Horus the king; I am she who riseth in the star that is in the Constellation of the Dog; by me was the city of Bubastus built. Farewell, farewell, O Egypt that nurtured me."

2

HEROES WHO HEAL

agent of God

INTRODUCTION

The most common way for a hero to be an agent in a miracle is by winning a god's favor to do it. In the Greco-Roman period we begin to see the kind of miracle story in which the hero works a miracle without prayers to a deity. Such stories invite speculation on the source of the power, of course. The narrators of this type of story sometimes offer the interpretation by an internal reference. That is, some allusion to a well-known text might be found in the story, or on the lips of some character.

My research revealed five classes of heroes who are attributed with miraculous healings, each type representing its own particular reason for the power. The five types or classes are presented in descending order of popular familiarity to the Greco-Roman world.

In the first category are the two Pythagoreans, Pythagoras himself and his famous disciple Empedocles. The lore that these Pythagoreans were able to "chase away pestilences" arises from the fact that Pythagoras and his disciples, like Empedocles, probed the secrets of Nature. It was only to be expected that Nature's intelligent entities would come to know these philosophers intimately. Thus, it is no surprise if Pythagoras and Empedocles could call upon their "insider" knowledge of Nature to chase off an epidemic. We need to remember that in the cosmology of Greco-Roman antiquity, the elements of creation are both living and rational entities.

A second category is that of three political rulers: one Greek king and two Roman emperors. Plutarch does not explain why it is that King Pyrrhus is able to heal the spleen just by touch. In a metaphor of praise, Philo gives to Caesar Augustus the power of healing the pestilences of trouble infecting the world. Vespasian's healings are interpreted by Suetonius as events designed to correct the new emperor's lack of "prestige and a certain divinity." Since it is the god Serapis who sends the two sick men to Vespasian, it is clear that the great god of the Egyptians will likewise give to Vespasian all manner of miraculous powers.

The itinerant philosopher and miracle worker Apollonius of Tyana occupies the third category. Although he is identified as a Neo-Pythagorean by Philostratus, the old legends about him date from the late first century and illustrate that he is better understood as a rather eclectic holy man rather than a Neo-Pythagorean. Apollonius' miracles seem to be the result of his personal holiness, and the forces of Nature as well as the daimon forces, seem to bow to him in deference to his total purity of life.

In the fourth category is the famous physician of Augustus, Asclepiades, who received many honors for his cure of the emperor's rheumatism. He is attributed with saving a girl from burial by recognizing that the force of life was still within her. His salvation of the girl belongs to his keen knowledge, that intelligence that understands Nature so very well. His story is mentioned here because, as Celsus remarks, conclusions that someone might be dead can be completely mistaken. Asclepiades is so revered because the wonders associated with him seem to mark him out as someone extraordinarily graced by the gods.

The fifth type of hero are the prophets of Jewish scripture, Moses, Elijah and Elisha. In the healing miracles attributed to them, the narrators sometimes include the significance to be drawn from the account, for example in Moses' dependence on God's instructions, or in the case of Elijah by the cry of the widow of Zarephath, "Now I know that you are a man of God, and the word in your mouth is truth" (1 Kgs. 17:24). Elisha's cure of Naaman the Syrian of leprosy (2 Kgs. 5:14) has no prayer to God, as even Naaman expected, but the prophet's order to wash in the Jordan. The divine power of Elisha is more heavily underlined. Jewish tradition in these prophetic stories is usually a guarantee of the reliability of the prophet as a spokesperson of God. Following the five types of heroes, I have presented the collection of the Jesus miracles, to invite the scholar to decide for him/herself which traditions from antiquity seem to find an "echo" in the accounts.

As a final word, it will be noted that as in the case of the gods of healing, so too several of the heroes who heal are also attributed with having raised someone from the dead. With the exception of Pythagoras, Moses and the political rulers, Pyrrhus, Augustus and

Vespasian, all the heroes, Empedocles, Apollonius, Elijah, Elisha and Jesus, raise the dead.

Greek classical philosophers

Pythagoras (582–500 BCE)

Heals diseases

PORPHYRY (222/3–305 CE)

1.39. Pythagoras Chases Away a Pestilence

Porphyry, *Life of Pythagoras* 29[1]

Verified predictions of earthquakes are handed down, also, that he immediately chased away a pestilence, suppressed violent winds and hail, calmed storms on both rivers and seas, for the comfort and safe passage of his friends.

1.40. Pythagoras Prepared Songs for the Diseases of the Body, by Singing by which He Cured the Sick

Porphyry, *Life of Pythagoras* 33[2]

His friends he loved exceedingly, being the first to declare that "The goods of friends are common," and that "A friend is another self." While they were in good health he always conversed with them; if they were sick, he nursed them; if they were afflicted in mind, he solaced them, some by incantations and magic charms, others by music. He had prepared songs for the diseases of the body, by singing which he cured the sick. He had also some that caused forgetfulness of sorrow, mitigation of anger, and destruction of lust.

1 Porphyry, *The Life of Pythagoras*, *The Pythagorean Sourcebook and Library: An Anthology of Ancient Writings Which Relate to Pythagoras and Pythagorean Philosophy* (compiled and translated by Kenneth Sylban Guthrie; Michigan: Phanes, 1987), 128–129.
2 Ibid., 129–130.

IAMBLICHUS (250–325 CE)

1.41. Pythagoras is Said to be Responsible for the Rapid Expulsions of Pestilences

Iamblichus, *Life of Pythagoras* 28[3]

Many other more admirable and divine particulars are likewise unanimously and uniformly related of *the man* [Pythagoras], such as infallible predictions of earthquakes, rapid expulsions of pestilences, and hurricanes, instantaneous cessations of hail, and tranquilizations of the waves of rivers and seas, in order that his disciples might the more easily pass over them.

Empedocles (484–424 BCE)

Heals diseases

DIOGENES LAERTIUS (CIRCA 250 CE)

1.42. Empedocles Saves a Woman from a Month-Long Trance

Diogenes Laertius, *Empedocles, Lives of Eminent Philosophers* 8.60–61[4]

Heraclides in his book *On Diseases* says that he [Empedocles] furnished Pausanias with the facts about the woman in a trance. This Pausanias, according to Aristippus and Satyrus, was his [Empedocles'] bosom-friend, to whom he dedicated his poem "On Nature." . . . At all events, Heraclides testifies that the case of the woman in a trance was such that for thirty days he [Empedocles] kept her body without pulsation although she never breathed; and for that reason Heraclides called him not merely a physician but a diviner as well, deriving titles from the following lines also.

1.43. All the Suffering Come to the New God, Empedocles

Diogenes Laertius, *Empedocles, Lives of Eminent Philosophers* 8.62

My friends, who dwell in the great city sloping down to yellow Acragas, hard by the citadel, busied with goodly works, all hail! I go about among you an immortal god, no more a mortal, so honoured of all, as is meet, crowned with fillets and flowery garlands. Straightway as soon as I enter with these, men and women, into flourishing towns, I am reverenced and tens of thousands follow, to learn where is the path which leads to welfare,

---

3 Iamblichus, *The Life of Pythagoras, The Pythagorean Sourcebook and Library*, 91.
4 All quotations are taken from Diogenes Laertius, *Empedocles, The Lives of Eminent Philosophers*, vol. 2 (trans. R. D. Hicks; London: Heinemann, 1925).

some desirous of oracles, others suffering from all kinds of diseases, desiring to hear a message of healing.

Raises the dead

Empedocles saves the life of Panthea, who was given up by doctors

1.44. Empedocles Cures Panthea, Who was Given up by Doctors

Diogenes Laertius, *Empedocles, Lives of Eminent Philosophers* 8.69
Hermippus tells us that Empedocles cured Panthea, a woman of Agrigentum, who had been given up by the physicians, and this was why he was offering sacrifice, and that those invited were about eighty in number.

Rulers who heal

A Greek king: King Pyrrhus of Epirus (319–272 BCE)

While the ancient Pythagoreans heal through an intimate knowledge of Nature and its forces, this king's power to heal is unexplained. Perhaps the fact that Pyrrhus was an enemy of Rome may account for Plutarch's portrait of him. Here, we can note that by the Greco-Roman period there are more stories of a king's power to heal. This power would be explained as one sign of the king's divine empowerment from heaven for his authoritative role on earth. This account by Plutarch may be a case of damning with faint praise.

Heals diseases

1.45. King Pyrrhus Healed Spleen Trouble of Even the Most Poor Simply by His Touch

Plutarch, *Pyrrhus, Lives* 3.4[5]
In the aspect of his countenance, Pyrrhus had more of the terror than of the majesty of kingly power. He had not many teeth, but his upper jaw was one continuous bone, on which the usual intervals between the teeth were indicated by slight depressions. People of a splenetic habit believed that he cured their ailment; he would sacrifice a white cock, and, while

---

5 Plutarch, *Pyrrhus, Lives*, vol. 9 (trans. Bernadotte Perrin; London: Heinemann, 1920), 3.4.

the patient lay flat upon his back, would press gently with his right foot against the spleen. Nor was nay one so obscure or poor as not to get this healing service from him if he asked it.

Roman emperors who heal

Augustus (63 BCE – 14 CE)

1.46. Augustus Heals the "Pestilences of the World" by the Pax

Philo, *The Embassy, To Gaius* 144–145[6]
The whole human race exhausted by mutual slaughter was on the verge of utter destruction, had it not been for one man and leader, Augustus whom men fitly call the averter of evil. This is the Caesar who calmed the torrential storms on every side, who healed pestilences common to Greeks and Barbarians, pestilences which descending from the south and east coursed to the west and north sowing seeds of calamity over the places and waters which lay between them.

Vespasian (9–79 CE)

TACITUS (56–115 [?] CE)

1.47. Vespasian's Cure of the Blind Man and the Restoration of a Man's Useless Hand Marked the Favor of Heaven and a Certain Partiality of the Gods Toward Him

Tacitus, *Histories* 4.81[7]
During the months while Vespasian was waiting at Alexandria for the regular season of the summer winds and a settled sea, many marvels occurred to mark the favour of heaven and a certain partiality of the gods toward him. One of the common people of Alexandria, well known for his loss of sight, threw himself before Vespasian's knees, praying him with groans to cure his blindness, being so directed by the god Serapis, whom this most superstitious of nations worships before all others; and he besought the emperor to deign to moisten his cheeks and eyes with his spittle. Another, whose hand was useless, prompted by the same god, begged Caesar to step

---

6 Philo, *The Embassy* to Gaius, *Philo*, vol. 10 (trans. F. H. Colson and J. W. Earp; London: Heinemann, 1962), 144–145.

7 All quotations are taken from Tacitus, *The Histories and the Annals*, vol. 2 (trans. Clifford H. Moore; London: Heinemann, 1931), 4.81.

and trample on it. Vespasian at first ridiculed these appeals and treated them with scorn; then, when the men persisted, he began at one moment to fear the discredit of failure, at another to be inspired with hopes of success by the appeals of the suppliants and the flattery of his courtiers; finally he directed the physicians to give their opinion whether such blindness and infirmity could be overcome by human aid. Their reply treated the two cases differently: they said that in the first [the case of the blind man] the power of sight had not been completely eaten away and it would return if the obstacles were removed; in the other [the useless hand], the joints had slipped and become displaced, but they could be restored if a healing pressure were applied to them. *Such perhaps was the wish of the gods, and it might be that the emperor had been chosen for this divine service; in any case, if a cure were obtained, the glory would be Caesar's, but in the event of failure, ridicule would fall only on the poor supplicants. So Vespasian, believing that his good fortune was capable of anything and that nothing was any longer incredible,*[8] with a smiling countenance, and amid intense excitement on the part of the bystanders, did as he was asked to do. The hand was instantly restored to use, and the day again shone for the blind man. Both facts are told by eye-witnesses even now when falsehood brings no reward.

1.48. Vespasian Understands his Healings from a Vision in the Temple: he is Royalty

Tacitus, *Histories* 4.82

These events [the healing of the blind man and the cure of the useless hand] gave Vespasian a deeper desire to visit the sanctuary of the god [Serapis] to consult him with regard to his imperial fortune: he ordered all to be excluded from the temple. Then after he had entered the temple and was absorbed in contemplation of the god, he saw behind him one of the leading men of Egypt, named Basilides, who he knew was detained by sickness in a place many days' journey distant from Alexandria. He asked the priests whether Basilides had entered the temple on that day; he questioned the passers-by whether he had been seen in the city; finally, he sent some cavalry and found that at that moment he had been eighty miles away: *then he concluded that this was a supernatural vision and drew a prophecy from the name Basilides.*[9]

8 My italic.
9 My italic.

SUETONIUS (WROTE 41–69 CE)

1.49. Vespasian's Miracle Gives him the Prestige and Divinity he Lacked

Suetonius, *Divine Vespasian, Lives of the Caesars* 7.2[10]

Vespasian as yet lacked prestige and a certain divinity, so to speak, since he was an unexpected and still new-made emperor; but these also were given him. A man of the people [i.e. in Alexandria] who was blind, and another who was lame, came to him together as he sat on the tribunal, begging for the help for their disorders which Serapis had promised in a dream; for the god declared that Vespasian would restore the eyes, if he would spit upon them, and give strength to the leg, if he would deign to touch it with his heel. Though he had hardly any faith that this could possibly succeed, and therefore shrank even from making the attempt, he was at last prevailed upon by his friends and tried both things in public before a large crowd; and with success.

DIO CASSIUS (WROTE 194–229 CE)

1.50. Heaven was Magnifying Vespasian by Miracles, but the Alexandrians Detested him

Dio Cassius, *Roman History* 65.8[11]

Following Vespasian's entry into Alexandria the Nile overflowed, having in one day risen a palm higher than usual; such an occurrence, it was said, had taken place only once before. Vespasian himself healed two persons, one having a withered hand, the other being blind, who had come to him because of a vision seen in dreams; he cured the one by stepping on his hand and the other by spitting upon his eyes. Yet, though Heaven was thus magnifying him, the Alexandrians, far from delighting in his presence, detested him so heartily that they were for ever mocking and reviling him. For they had expected to receive from him some great reward because they had been the first to make him emperor, but instead of securing anything they had additional contributions levied upon them.

---

10 Suetonius, *Divine Vespasian, The Lives of the Ceasars*, vol. 2 (trans. J. C. Rolfe; London: Heinemann, 1914).

11 Dio Cassius, *Roman History*, vol. 8 (trans. Earnest Cary; London: Heinemann, 1925), 65.8.

The Itinerant Philosopher of Imperial Times:
Apollonius of Tyana (d. circa 98 CE)

The only extant "biography" of the itinerant holy man Apollonius of Tyana is that of Flavius Philostratus (170–249 [?]), who compiled the work for the wife of the emperor Septimus Severus, the empress Julia Domna. She had a special regard for Apollonius and wanted to refute the charges that he was really only a magician. The reliability of the work has always been questioned. Even though the figure of Damis, a supposed disciple of Apollonius who wrote the first biography, is judged to be purely fictitious, the miracle stories themselves are less easy to dismiss as fabrications of Philostratus. As a Neo-Pythagorean himself, he would have been caused no little embarrassment by the miracle stories. If Apollonius was a member of the Neo-Pythagorean school, as Philostratus grants, it would have been extremely unlikely that he would have proceeded to create these miracle stories, so very foreign to his own philosophical perspective.

Heals diseases

1.51. Apollonius Cures a Lame Man and a Blind Man

(See Mark 8:22–26//; Mark 10:46–52//; and Luke 4:16–30.)

Philostratus, *Life of Apollonius of Tyana* 3.39[12]
There also arrived a man who was lame. He was already thirty years old and was a keen hunter of lions; but a lion had sprung upon him and dislocated his hip so that he limped with one leg. However when they massaged with their hands his hip, the man immediately recovered his upright gait. And another man had had his eyes put out, and he went away having recovered the sight of both of them.

1.52. Apollonius Cures a Paralyzed Hand

Philostratus, *Life of Apollonius of Tyana* 3.39
Yet another man had his hand paralysed, but left their presence in full possession of his limb.

---

12 The quotations here and in 1.52, 1.53 and 1.55 are taken from Philostratus, *The Life of Apollonius of Tyana*, vol. 1 (trans. F. C. Conybeare; London: Heinemann, 1912).

1.53. Apollonius is Responsible for a Woman's Successfully Giving Birth

Philostratus, *Life of Apollonius of Tyana* 3.39

And a certain woman had suffered in labour already seven times, but was healed in the following way through the intercession of her husband. He bade the man whenever his wife should be about to bring forth her next child, to enter her chamber carrying in his bosom a live hare; then he was to walk once round her and at the same moment to release the hare; for that the womb would be extruded together with the foetus, unless the hare was at once driven out.

1.54. Apollonius Heals a Boy Bitten by a Mad Dog

Philostratus, *Life of Apollonius of Tyana* 6.43[13]

Here too is a story which they tell of him in Tarsus. A mad dog had attacked a lad, and as a result of the bite the lad behaved exactly like a dog, for he barked and howled and went on all four feet using his hands as such, and ran about in that manner. And he had been ill in this way for thirty days, when Apollonius, who had recently come to Tarsus, met him and ordered a search to be made for the dog which had done the harm. But they said that the dog had not been found, because the youth had been attacked outside the wall when he was practising with javelins, nor could they learn from the patient what the dog was like, for he did not even know himself any more. Then Apollonius reflected a moment and said: "O Damis, the dog is a white shaggy sheep-dog, as big as an Amphilochian hound, and he is standing at a certain fountain trembling all over, for he is longing to drink the water, but at the same time is afraid of it. Bring him to me to the bank of the river, where there are the wrestling grounds, merely telling him that it is I who call him." So Damis dragged the dog along, and it crouched at the feet of Apollonius, crying out as a supplicant might do before an altar. But he quite tamed it by stroking it with his hand, and then he stood the lad close by, holding him with his hand; and in order that the multitude might be cognisant of so great a mystery, he said: "The soul of Telephus of Mysia has been transferred into this boy, and the Fates impose the same things upon him as upon Telephus." And with these words he bade the dog lick the wound all round where he had bitten the boy, so that the agent of the wound might in turn be its physician and healer. After that the boy returned to his father and recognised his mother, and saluted his comrades as before, and drank of the waters of the Cydnus. Nor did the sage neglect the dog either, but after offering a prayer to the river he sent the dog across it;

13 Philostratus, *The Life of Apollonius of Tyana*, vol. 2 (trans. F. C. Conybeare; London: Heinemann, 1912, revised 1950), 6.43.

and when the dog had crossed the river, he took his stand on the opposite bank, and began to bark, a thing which mad dogs rarely do, and he folded back his ears and wagged his tail, because he knew that he was all right again, for a draught of water cures a mad dog, if he has only the courage to take it.

Raises the dead

Apollonius raises from the dead a young bride

1.55. Apollonius Said to the People, "Put Down the Bier, for I will Stay your Tears"

Philostratus, *Life of Apollonius of Tyana* 4.45

Here too is a miracle which Apollonius worked: A girl had died just in the hour of her marriage, and the bridegroom was following her bier lamenting as was natural his marriage left unfulfilled, and the whole of Rome was mourning with him, for the maiden belonged to a consular family. Apollonius then witnessing their grief, said: "Put down the bier, for I will stay the tears that you are shedding for this maiden." And withal he asked what was her name. The crowd accordingly thought that he was about to deliver such an oration as is commonly delivered as much to grace the funeral as to stir up lamentation; but he did nothing of the kind, but merely touching her and whispering in secret some spell over her, at once woke up the maiden from her seeming death; and the girl spoke out loud, and returned to her father's house, just as Alcestis did when she was brought back to life by Hercules. And the relations of the maiden wanted to present him with the sum of 150,000 sesterces, but he said that he would freely present the money to the young lady by way of a dowry. Now, whether he detected some spark of life in her, which those who were nursing her had not noticed, – for it is said that although it was raining at the time, a vapour went up from her face – or whether life was really extinct, and he restored it by the warmth of his touch, is a mysterious problem which neither I myself nor those who were present could decide.

The Physician Asclepiades (first century BCE)

Asclepiades was a prominent physician in the Augustan era. He was honored by Augustus for curing his bouts of rheumatism with cold treatments where the conventional hot-water baths prescribed by his own doctors had proved incapacitating. His methods were based on Epicurean philosophy, quite unlike Hippocrates. Rejecting the notion of bodily humors and "Natural Law," Asclepiades emphasized the importance of immediate maintenance of atomic stability in the patient through diet, environment and emotional calm.

Raises the dead

1.56. Asclepiades' Revival of a Girl Thought Dead Proves how Deceiving the Signs of Death Often are

Celsus, *On Medicine* 2.6.16–18[14]

Asclepiades, when he met a funeral procession, recognized that a man who was being carried out to burial was alive; and it is not primarily a fault of the art if there is a fault on the part of its professor. But I shall more modestly suggest that the art of medicine is conjectural, and such is the characteristic of a conjecture, that though it answers more frequently, yet it sometimes deceives. A sign therefore is not to be rejected if it is deceptive in scarcely one out of a thousand cases, since it holds good in countless patients. I state this, not merely in connexion with noxious signs, but as to salutary signs as well; seeing that hope is disappointed now and again, and that the patient dies whom the practitioner at first deemed safe; and further that measures proper for curing now and again make a change into something worse. Nor, in the face of such a variety of temperaments, can human frailty avoid this. Nevertheless the medical art is to be relied upon, which more often, and in by far the greater number of patients, benefits the sick. It should not be ignored, however, that it is rather in acute diseases that signs, whether of recovery or of death, may be fallacious.

APULEIUS (123–170 [?] CE)

1.57. Asclepiades Examined the "Corpse" and Cried "He Lives!"; He Brought Back the Life that Still Lay Hidden in the Secret Places of the Body

Apuleius, *Florida* 19[15]

The famous Asclepiades, who ranks among the greatest of doctors, indeed, if you except Hippocrates, as the very greatest, was the first to discover the use of wine as a remedy. It requires, however, to be administered at the proper moment, and it was in the discovery of the right moment that he showed special skill, noting most carefully the slightest symptom of

14 Celsus, *On Medicine*, vol. 1 (trans. W. G. Spencer; London: Heinemann, 1935), 2.6.16–18.
15 Apuleius, *Florida, Apologia and Florida* (trans. H. E. Butler; Oxford: Clarendon Press, 1909), 19.

disorder or undue rapidity of the pulse. It chanced that once, when he was returning to town from his country house, he observed an enormous funeral procession in the suburbs of the city. A huge multitude of men who had come out to perform the last honours stood round about the bier, all of them plunged in deep sorrow and wearing worn and ragged apparel. He asked whom they were burying, but no one replied; so he went nearer to satisfy his curiosity and to see who it might be that was dead, or, it may be, in the hope to make some discovery in the interests of his profession. Be this as it may, he certainly snatched the man from the jaws of death as he lay there on the verge of burial. The poor fellow's limbs were already covered with spices, his mouth filled with sweet-smelling unguent. He had been anointed and was all ready for the pyre. But Asclepiades looked upon him, took careful note of certain signs; handled his body again and again, and perceived that the life was still in him, though scarcely to be detected. Straightway he cried out, "He lives! Throw down your torches, take away your fire, demolish the pyre, take back the funeral feast and spread it on his board at home." While he spoke, a murmur arose: some said that they must take the doctor's word, others mocked at the physician's skill. At last, in spite of the opposition offered even by his relations, perhaps because they had already entered into possession of the dead man's property, perhaps because they did not yet believe his words, Asclepiades persuaded them to put off the burial for a brief space. Having thus rescued him from the hands of the undertaker, he carried the man home, as it were from the very mouth of hell, and straightaway revived the spirit within him, and by means of certain drugs[16] called forth the life that still lay hidden in the secret places of the body.

Ancient Heroes from the Jewish Scriptures

Moses (circa 1200 BCE)

In the story of the people's cure of snake bites, it is God who heals them, but Moses who is their advocate. The people do not see God, but they do see Moses, his designated leader of these people. Thus, Moses' role is that of God's agent, but it is clear from the story that it is God who is responsible for the salvation.

---

16 Although Asclepiades was known to feature diet over drugs, his resort to them here is a result of special circumstances.

Heals people of snake bites

1.58. Moses Intercedes for the People and Follows the Lord's Commands for their Healing

Num. 21:4–9

4. From Mount Horeb they [the escaping Israelites] set out by the way to the Red Sea, to go around the land of Edom; and the people became impatient on the way. 5. The people spoke against God and against Moses, "Why have you brought us up out of Egypt to die in the wilderness? For there is no food and no water, and we detest this miserable food [manna]." 6. Then the Lord sent poisonous serpents among the people and they bit the people, so that many Israelites died. 7. The people came to Moses, and said, "We have sinned by speaking against the Lord and against you; pray to the Lord to take away the serpents from us." So Moses prayed for the people. 8. And the Lord said to Moses, "Make a poisonous serpent, and set it on a pole; and every one who is bitten shall look at it and live." 9. So Moses made a serpent of bronze, and put it upon a pole; and whenever a serpent bit someone, that person would look at the serpent of bronze and live.

Elijah (circa 900 BCE)

Raises the dead

Elijah's prayer wins back the life of the widow's dead son
This story and the one that follows about Elisha again engage the idea that a man empowered with authority from God will be able to call back the dead. In this case, Elijah's miracle is interpreted for us by the widow.

1.59. And the Woman said to Elijah, "Now I know that you are a man of God, and that the word of the Lord in your mouth is truth"

(See Mark 5:21–43 and John 11:1–46 below.)

1 Kgs. 17:17–24

17. After this the son of the woman, the mistress of the house, became ill; his illness was so severe that there was no breath left in him. 18. She then said to Elijah, "What have you against me, O man of God? You have come to me to bring my sin to remembrance, and to cause the death of my son!" 19. But he said to her, "Give me your son." He took him from her bosom, carried him up into the upper chamber where he was lodging, and laid him on his own bed. 20. He cried out to the Lord, "O

Lord my God, have you brought calamity even upon the widow with whom I am staying, by killing her son?" *21.* Then he stretched himself upon the child three times, and cried out to the Lord, "O Lord my God, let this child's life come into him again." *22.* The Lord listened to the voice of Elijah; the life of the child came into him again, and he revived. *23.* Elijah took the child, brought him down from the upper chamber into the house, and gave him to his mother; then Elijah said, "See, your son is alive." *24.* So the woman said to Elijah, "Now I know that you are a man of God, and that the word of the Lord in your mouth is truth."

JOSEPHUS (WROTE 63–79 CE): A RETELLING OF THE
ELIJAH MIRACLE

1.60. The Mother Thanked the Prophet and Said that Now she Clearly Realized that the Deity Spoke with him

Josephus, *Jewish Antiquities* 8.325–327[17]

Now the woman of whom we spoke above [the widow of Sarephtha], who gave food to the prophet – her son fell ill so seriously that he ceased to breathe and seemed to be dead, whereupon she wept bitterly, injuring herself with her hands and uttering such cries as her grief prompted;[18] and she reproached the prophet for having come to her to convict her of sin and on that account causing the death of her son. But he urged her to take heart and give her son over to him, for he would, he said, restore him to her alive. So she gave him over, and he carried him into the chamber in which he himself lived, and placed him on the bed; then he cried aloud to God, saying that He would ill requite the woman who had received him and nourished him, if He took her son from her, and he prayed God to send the breath into the child again and give him life.[19] Thereupon God, because He took pity on the mother and also because He wished graciously to spare the prophet from seeming to have come to her for the purpose of harming her,[20] beyond all expectation brought the child back to life. Then the mother thanked the prophet and said that now she clearly realized that the Deity spoke with him.

17 Josephus, *Jewish Antiquities, Josephus*, vol. 5 (trans. H. St. J. Thackeray and Ralph Marcus; London: Heinemann, 1934).
18 Here Josephus seems to incorporate the mourning customs of his own day, as set forth in the satire of Lucian *On funerals*, in *Lucian*, vol. 4 (trans. A. M. Harmon; London: Heinemann, 1925), pp. 112–131.
19 Notice that Josephus refrains from recounting the prophet lying on the child. This is surely no oversight on the part of Josephus but evidence of his own judgment. It might be that such conduct would give rise to criticism of ignoble intentions or more seriously yet, a resort to magical rites.
20 "This explanation of God's motive is an addition to Scripture" is the translator's note, p. 749. But here Josephus is referring to the woman's charge that

Elisha (900 BCE)

Heals diseases

Elisha cures Naaman the leper

1.61.1. And When the King of Israel Read the Letter, he Rent his Clothes and Said, "Am I God to Kill and to Make Alive, that this Man Sends Word to me to Cure a Man of his Leprosy?"

2 Kgs. 5:1–19

1. Naaman, commander of the army of the king of Aram, was a great man and in high favor with his master, because by him the Lord had given victory to Aram. The man, though a mighty warrior, suffered from leprosy. 2. Now the Arameans on one of their raids had taken a young girl captive from the land of Israel, and she served Naaman's wife. 3. She said to her mistress, "If only my lord were with the prophet who is in Samaria! He would cure him of his leprosy." 4. So Naaman went in and told his lord just what the girl from the land of Israel had said. 5. And the king of Aram said, "Go, then, and I will send along a letter to the king of Israel."

He went, taking with him ten talents of silver, six thousand shekels of gold, and ten sets of garments. 6. He brought the letter to the king of Israel, which read, "When this letter reaches you, know that I have sent to you my servant Naaman, that you may cure him of his leprosy." 7. When the king of Israel read the letter, he tore his clothes and said, "Am I God, to give death or life, that this man sends word to me to cure a man of his leprosy? Just look and see how he is trying to pick a quarrel with me."

8. But when Elisha the man of God heard that the king of Israel had torn his clothes, he sent a message to the king, "Why have you torn your clothes? Let him come to me, that he may learn that there is a prophet in Israel." 9. So Naaman came with his horses and chariots, and halted at the entrance of Elisha's house. 10. Elisha sent a messenger to him, saying, "Go, wash in the Jordan seven times, and your flesh shall be restored and you shall be clean." 11. But Naaman became angry and went away, saying, "I thought that for me he would surely come out, and stand and call on the name of the Lord his God, and would wave his hand over the spot, and cure the leprosy! 12. Are not Abana and Pharphar, the rivers of Damascus, better than all the waters of Israel? Could I not wash in them and be clean?" He turned and went away in a rage.

the holiness of the prophet in her home serves to emphasize her sinfulness in comparison to Elijah's holiness.

13. But his servants approached and said to him, "Father, if the prophet had commanded you to do something difficult, would you not have done it? How much more, when all he said to you was, 'Wash and be clean'?" *14.* So he went down and immersed himself seven times in the Jordan, according to the word of the man of God; his flesh was restored like the flesh of a young boy, and he was clean.

15. Then he returned to the man of God, he and all his company; he came and stood before him and said, "Now I know that there is no God in all the earth except in Israel; please accept a present from your servant." *16.* But he said, "As the Lord lives, whom I serve, I will accept nothing!" He urged him to accept, but he refused. *17.* Then Naaman said, "If not, please let two mule-loads of earth be given your servant; for your servant will no longer offer burnt offering or sacrifice to any god except the Lord. *18.* But may the Lord pardon your servant on one count: when my master goes into the house of Rimmon to worship there, leaning on my arm, and I bow down in the house of Rimmon, may the Lord pardon your servant on this one count." *19.* He said to him, "Go in peace."

1.61.2. To Punish Gehazi's Sacrilegious Greed, Elisha Causes Naaman's Leprosy to Fall upon Him and His Family Forever

2 Kgs. 19–27

But when Naaman had gone from him a short distance, *20.* Gehazi, the servant of Elisha the man of God, thought, "My master has let that Aramean Naaman off too lightly by not accepting from him what he offered. As the Lord lives, I will run after him and get something out of him." *21.* So Gehazi went after Naaman. When Naaman saw someone running after him, he jumped down from the chariot to meet him and said, "Is everything all right?" *22.* He replied, "Yes, but my master sent me to say, 'Two members of a company of prophets have just come to me from the hill country of Ephraim; please give them a talent of silver and two changes of clothing.'" *23.* Naaman said, "Please accept two talents." He urged him, and tied up two talents of silver in two bags, with two changes of clothing, and gave them to two of his servants, who carried them in front of Gehazi. *24.* When he came to the citadel, he took the bags from them, and stored them inside; he dismissed the men, and they left.

25. He went in and stood before his master; and Elisha said to him, "Where have you been, Gehazi?" He answered, "Your servant has not gone anywhere at all." *26.* But he said to him, "Did I not go with you in spirit when someone left his chariot to meet you? Is this a time to accept money and to accept clothing, olive orchards and vineyards, sheep and oxen, and male and female slaves? *27.* Therefore, the leprosy of Naaman shall cling to you, and to your descendants forever." So he left his presence leprous, as white as snow.

Note

Although some scholars have suggested that the healing of the leper is built on the Elijah story, we do not see the necessary clues. In the Elisha story, Naaman complains that he expected the prophet to pass his hand over him, not order him to wash in the Jordan. This expectation of Naaman is likely because the passing of the hand over the sick was a conventional action. For the Jesus story to signal a deliberate association with the Elisha account, the leper should have been asked to wash himself in the Jordan or in some stream, for example. Moreover, in the Elisha story, the prophet does not meet Naaman but sends a messenger. In the Jesus story, Jesus reaches out his hand and grasps the leper, assuring him of his desire to see him clean of the disease. Finally, the tension in the Elisha story involves Jewish–gentile relationships. In the Jesus story, the fact that the leper is told to go show himself to the priest and make the offering prescribed by Moses makes it clear that Jesus thinks that the man is Jewish.

Raises the dead

Elisha's prayer wins the life of the woman's dead son
It is clear to anyone familiar with the Elijah account that this story is an expansion upon it. In both cases the petitioner is a non-Jewish woman who has offered hospitality to a Jewish prophet. The prophet is recognized as holy by the strength of his prayers. We can expect that this story was taught to early Christians as they became more and more familiar with the heroes of the Jewish tradition.

1.62. She Came and Fell at his Feet, Bowing to the Ground; Then she Took her {Restored} Son and Left

2 Kgs. 4:18–37
18. When the child [whom Elisha had promised God would grant to a woman who was kind to him] was older, he went out one day to his father among the reapers. 19. He complained to his father, "Oh my head, my head!" The father said to his servant, "Carry him to his mother." 20. He carried him and brought him to his mother; the child sat on her lap until noon, and he died. 21. She went up and laid him on the bed of the man of God, closed the door on him, and left. 22. Then she called to her husband, and said, "Send me one of the servants and one of the donkeys, so that I may quickly go to the man of God and come back again." 23. He said, "Why go to him today? It is neither new moon nor sabbath."

She said, "It will be all right." *24*. Then she saddled the donkey and said to her servant, "Urge the animal on; do not hold back for me unless I tell you." *25*. So she set out, and came to the man of God at Mount Carmel.

When the man of god saw her coming, he said to Gehazi his servant, "Look, there is the Shunammite woman; *26*. run at once to meet her, and say to her, 'Are you all right? Is your husband all right? Is the child all right?'" She answered, "It is all right." *27*. When she came to the man of God at the mountain, she caught hold of his feet. Gehazi approached to push her away. But the man of God said, "Let her alone, for she is in bitter distress; the Lord has hidden it from me and has not told me." *28*. Then she said, "Did I ask my lord for a son? Did I not say, 'Do not mislead me'?" *29*. He said to Gehazi, "Gird up your loins, and take my staff in your hand, and go. If you meet anyone, give no greeting and if anyone greets you, do not answer; and lay my staff on the face of the child." *30*. Then the mother of the child said, "As the Lord lives, and as you yourself live, I will not leave without you." So he rose up and followed her. *31*. Gehazi went on ahead and laid the staff on the face of the child, but there was no sound or sign of life. He came back to meet him and told him, "The child has not awakened."

32. When Elisha came into the house, he saw the child lying dead on his bed. *33*. So he went in and closed the door on the two of them, and prayed to the Lord. *34*. Then he got up on the bed and lay upon the child, putting his mouth upon his mouth, his eyes upon his eyes, and his hands upon his hands; and while he lay bent over him, the flesh of the child became warm. *35*. He got down, walked once to and fro in the room, then got up again and bent over him; the child sneezed seven times, and the child opened his eyes. *36*. Elisha summoned Gehazi and said, "Call the Shunammite woman." So he called her. When she came to him, he said, "Take your son." *37*. She came and fell at his feet, bowing to the ground; then she took her son and left.

3

THE HEALING MIRACLES OF JESUS

Heals diseases

Jesus heals Simon's mother-in-law of a fever

1.63. He Came and Took Her by the Hand and Lifted Her up. Then the Fever Left Her, and She Began to Serve Them

Mark 1:29–31 (Matt. 4:1–11; Luke 4:1–13)

29. As soon as they left the synagogue, they entered the house of Simon and Andrew, with James and John. *30.* Now Simon's mother-in-law was in bed with a fever, and they told him about her at once. *31.* He came and took her by the hand and lifted her up. Then the fever left her, and she began to serve them.

Jesus heals a leper

1.64. Moved with Pity, Jesus Stretched Out His Hand and Touched Him, and Said to Him, "I Do Choose. Be Made Clean"

Mark 1:40–45 (Matt. 8:1–4; Luke 5:12–16)

40. A leper came to him begging him, and kneeling he said to him, "If you choose, you can make me clean." *41.* Moved with pity, Jesus stretched out his hand and touched him, and said to him, "I do choose. Be made clean." *42.* Immediately the leprosy left him, and he was made clean. *43.* After sternly warning him, he sent him away at once, *44.* saying to him, "See that you say nothing to anyone; but go, show yourself to the priest, and offer for your cleansing what Moses commanded, as a testimony to them." *45.* But he went out and began to proclaim it freely, and to spread the word, so that Jesus could no longer go into a town openly, but stayed out in the country; and people came to him from every quarter.

Jesus heals ten lepers

1.65. Then Jesus Asked, "Were Not Ten Made Clean? But the Other Nine, Where are They? Was None of Them Found to Return and Give Praise to God Except This Foreigner?"

Luke 17: 11–19

11. On the way to Jerusalem Jesus was going through the region between Samaria and Galilee. *12.* As he entered a village, ten lepers approached him. Keeping their distance, *13.* they called out, saying, "Jesus, Master, have mercy on us." *14.* When he saw them he said to them, "Go and show yourselves to the priests." And as they went, they were made clean. *15.* Then one of them, when he saw that he was healed, turned back, praising God with a loud voice. *16.* He prostrated himself at Jesus' feet and thanked him. And he was a Samaritan. *17.* Then Jesus asked, "Were not ten made clean? But the other nine, where are they? *18.* Was none of them found to return and give praise to God except this foreigner?" *19.* Then he said to him, "Get up and go on your way; your faith has made you well."

Jesus heals a man who is paralyzed[1]

1.66. "But So That You May Know that the Son of Man has Power on Earth to Forgive Sins" – and He Said to the Paralytic, "I Say to You, Stand Up, Take Your Mat and Go to Your Home"

Mark 2:1–12 (Matt. 9:1–8; Luke 5:17–26)

1. And when he returned to Capernaum after some days, it was reported that he was at home. *2.* So many gathered around that there was no longer room for them, not even in front of the door; and he was speaking the word to them. *3.* Then some people came, bringing to him a paralyzed man, carried by four of them. *4.* And when they could not bring him to Jesus because of the crowd, they removed the roof above him; and after having dug through it, they let down the mat on which the paralytic lay. *5.* And when Jesus saw their faith, he said to the paralytic, "Son, your sins are forgiven." *6.* Now some of the scribes were sitting there, questioning in their hearts, *7.* "Why does this fellow speak in this way? It is

---

1 This story is classified as a "controversy story" because the miracle is really serving to defend Jesus' forgiveness of sins. It is listed here because for the earliest Christians, such distinctions would have been quite artificial, and the care of Jesus for the man, body and soul, testifies to his depth as a healer.

blasphemy! Who can forgive sins but God alone?" *8.* At once, Jesus perceived in his spirit that they were discussing these questions among themselves; and he said to them, "Why do you raise such questions in your hearts? *9.* Which is easier, to say to the paralytic, 'Your sins are forgiven,' or to say, 'Stand up and take your mat and walk'? *10.* But so that you may know that the Son of Man has power on earth to forgive sins" – and he said to the paralytic – *11.* "I say to you, stand up, take your mat and go to your home." *12.* And he stood up, and immediately took the mat and went out before all of them; so that they were all amazed and glorified God, saying, "We have never seen anything like this!"

Jesus heals the paralyzed servant of a centurion[2]

1.67. And to the Centurion Jesus Said, "Go; Let it be Done for you According to your Faith." And the Servant was Healed in that Hour

Matt. 8:5–13 (Luke 7:1–10)

5. When he entered Capernaum, a centurion came to him, appealing to him and *6.* saying, "Lord, my servant is lying at home paralyzed, in terrible distress." *7.* And he said to him, "I will come and cure him." *8.* The centurion answered, "Lord, I am not worthy to have you come under my roof; but only speak the word, and my servant will be healed. *9.* For I also am a man under authority, with soldiers under me; and I say to one, 'Go,' and he goes, and to another, 'Come,' and he comes, and to my slave, 'Do this,' and the slave does it." *10.* When Jesus heard him, he was amazed and said to those who followed him, "Truly I tell you, in no one in Israel have I found such faith. *11.* I tell you, many will come from east and west and will eat with Abraham and Isaac and Jacob in the kingdom of heaven, *12.* while the heirs of the kingdom will be thrown into the outer darkness, where there will be weeping and gnashing of teeth." *13.* And to the centurion Jesus said, "Go; let it be done for you according to your faith." And the servant was healed in that hour.

---

2 This story would not be classified as a miracle story because according to form criticism the focus is on the faith exchange of the soldier and Jesus. But as far as content is concerned, Jesus is being approached by the centurion precisely because the soldier sees him as a healer with heavenly authority. Moreover, the fact that the centurion's servant is healed from a distance emphasized Jesus' empowerment from heaven, which demonstrates itself in the most compassionate ways.

Jesus heals the sick child of a royal official[3]

1.68. Jesus Said to Him, "Go; Your Son will Live." The Man Believed the Word that Jesus Spoke to Him ... As he was Going Down His Slaves Met Him and Told Him that His Child was Alive

John 4:46–54

46. Then he came again to Cana in Galilee where he had changed the water into wine. Now there was a royal official whose son lay ill in Capernaum. 47. When he heard that Jesus had come from Judea to Galilee, he went and begged him to come down and heal his son, for he was at the point of death. 48. Then Jesus said to him, "Unless you see signs and wonders you will not believe." 49. The official said to him, "Sir, come down before my little boy dies." 50. Jesus said to him, "Go; your son will live." The man believed the word that Jesus spoke to him and started on his way. 51. As he was going down, his slaves met him and told him that his child was alive. 52. So he asked them the hour when he began to recover, and they said to him, "Yesterday at one in the afternoon the fever left him." 53. The father realized that this was the hour when Jesus had said to him, "Your son will live." So he himself believed, along with his whole household. 54. Now this was the second sign that Jesus did after coming from Judea to Galilee.

Jesus heals the man by the pool called Bethzatha[4]

1.69. Jesus Said to him, "Stand up, Take your Mat and Walk." At Once the Man was Made Well, and he Took up his Mat and Began to Walk

John 5:1–18

1. After this there was a festival of the Jews, and Jesus went up to Jerusalem. 2. Now in Jerusalem by the Sheep Gate there is a pool, called in Hebrew Beth-zatha, which has five porticoes. 3. In these lay many invalids – blind, lame, and paralyzed. 5. One man was there who had been ill for thirty-eight years. 6. When Jesus saw him lying there and knew that he had been there a long time, he said to him, "Do you want

---

3 This story is very close to the Q story of the centurion's servant (Matt. 8:5–13//Luke 7:1–10). As in that account, the focus of the story is on the exchange between Jesus and the official. The healing is accomplished from a distance, which serves to reinforce the importance of faith without actually seeing results, as it confirms to the listener, despite Jesus' warning about signs, the power of Jesus as manifest in this miracle.

4 This is another example of a miracle story being used for a controversy story.

to be made well?" 7. The sick man answered him, "Sir, I have no one to put me into the pool when the water is stirred up; and while I am making my way, someone else steps down ahead of me." 8. Jesus said to him, "Stand up, take your mat and walk." 9. At once the man was made well, and he took up his mat and began to walk.

10. Now that day was a sabbath. So the Jews said to the man who had been cured, "It is the sabbath; it is not lawful for you to carry your mat." 11. But he answered them, "The man who made me well said to me, 'Take up your mat and walk.'" 12. They asked him, "Who is the man who said to you, 'Take it up and walk'?" 13. Now the man who had been healed did not know who it was, for Jesus had disappeared in the crowd that was there. 14. Later Jesus found him in the temple and said to him, "See, you have been made well! Do not sin any more, so that nothing worse happens to you." 15. The man went away and told the Jews that it was Jesus who had made him well. 16. Therefore the Jews started persecuting Jesus, because he was doing such things on the sabbath. 17. But Jesus answered them, "My Father is still working, and I also am working." 18. For this reason the Jews were seeking all the more to kill him, because he was not only breaking the sabbath, but was also calling God his own Father, thereby making himself equal to God.

Jesus heals a man's withered hand on the sabbath[5]

1.70. He Looked Around at Them with Anger; He was Grieved at their Hardness of Heart, and Said to the Man, "Stretch Out Your Hand." He Stretched It Out, and His Hand was Restored

Mark 3:1–6 (Matt. 12:9–14// Luke 6:17–19)

1. Again he entered the synagogue, and a man was there who had a withered hand. 2. They watched him to see whether he would cure him on the sabbath, so that they might accuse him. 3. And he said to the man who had the withered hand, "Come forward." 4. Then he said to them, "Is it lawful to do good or to do harm on the sabbath, to save life or to kill?" But they were silent. 5. He looked around at them with anger; he was grieved at their hardness of heart, and said to the man, "Stretch out your hand." He stretched it out and his hand was restored. 6. The Pharisees went out, and immediately conspired with the Herodians against him, how to destroy him.

---

5   According to form criticism, this unit of tradition is categorized as a "controversy story" because the healing is subordinated to the healing. However, I include it here because it is very doubtful that earliest Christian listeners would have made such distinctions. In the story, Jesus stands up to the authorities to restore this man's hand, and for many a working person, this story would have emphasized Jesus' great *humanitas* as a healer.

Jesus heals a woman from her eighteen-year infirmity on the sabbath

1.71. When Jesus Saw Her, He Called Her Over and Said to Her, "Woman, You are Set Free from Your Ailment." ... Immediately She Stood up Straight and Began Praising God

Luke 13:10–17

10. Now he was teaching in one of the synagogues on the sabbath. *11.* And just then there appeared a woman with a spirit that had crippled her for eighteen years. She was bent over and was quite unable to stand up straight. *12.* When Jesus saw her, he called her over and said, "Woman, you are set free from your ailment." *13.* When he laid his hands on her, immediately she stood up straight and began praising God. *14.* But the leader of the synagogue, indignant because Jesus had cured on the sabbath, kept saying to the crowd, "There are six days on which work ought to be done; come on those days and be cured, and not on the sabbath day." *15.* But the Lord answered him, "You hypocrites! Does not each of you on the sabbath untie his ox or his donkey from the manger, and lead it away to give it water? *16.* And ought not this woman, a daughter of Abraham whom Satan bound for eighteen long years, be set free from this bondage on the sabbath day?" *17.* When he said this, all his opponents were put to shame; and the entire crowd was rejoicing at all the wonderful things that he was doing.

Jesus heals a man with dropsy on the sabbath

1.72. Jesus Said, "Is it Lawful to Cure People on the Sabbath or Not?" But They were Silent. So Jesus Took Him and Healed Him, and Sent Him Away

Luke 14:1–6

1. On one occasion when Jesus was going to the house of a leader of the Pharisees to eat a meal on the sabbath, they were watching him closely. *2.* Just then, in front of him, there was a man who had dropsy. *3.* And Jesus asked the lawyers and Pharisees, "Is it lawful to cure people on the sabbath or not?" *4.* But they were silent. So Jesus took him and healed him, and sent him away. *5.* Then he said to them, "If one of you has a child or an ox that has fallen into a well, will you not immediately pull it out on the sabbath day?" *6.* And they could not reply to this.

Jesus heals a woman suffering from hemorrhage for twelve years

1.73. She Said, "If I but Touch His Clothes, I Will Be Made Well." Immediately Her Hemorrhage Stopped; and She Felt in Her Body that She was Healed of Her Disease

Mark 5:21–34 (Matt. 9:18–26; Luke 8:40–48)

21. When Jesus had crossed again in the boat to the other side, a great crowd gathered around him; and he was by the sea. *22.* Then one of the leaders of the synagogue named Jairus came and when he saw him, fell at his feet *23.* and begged him repeatedly, "My little daughter is at the point of death. Come and lay your hands on her, so that she may be made well, and live." *24.* So he went with him.

And a large crowd followed him and pressed in on him. *25.* Now there was a woman who had been suffering from hemorrhages for twelve years. *26.* She had endured much under many physicians, and had spent all that she had; and she was no better but rather grew worse. *27.* She had heard about Jesus, and came up behind him in the crowd and touched his cloak, *28.* for she said, "If I but touch his clothes, I will be made well." *29.* Immediately her hemorrhage stopped; and she felt in her body that she was healed of her disease. *30.* Immediately aware that power had gone forth from him, Jesus turned about in the crowd and said, "Who touched my clothes?" *31.* And his disciples said to him, "You see the crowd pressing in on you; how can you say, 'Who touched me?'" *32.* He looked all around to see who had done it. *33.* But the woman, knowing what had happened to her, came in fear and trembling, fell down before him, and told him the whole truth. *34.* He said to her, "Daughter, your faith has made you well; go in peace, and be healed of your disease."

Jesus heals a man who is deaf and has a speech impediment

1.74. Then Looking up to Heaven, He Sighed and Said to Him, "Ephphatha," that is, "Be Opened." And Immediately His Ears were Opened, His Tongue was Released, and He Spoke Plainly

Mark 7:31–37 (Matt. 15:29–31)

31. Then he returned from the region of Tyre, and went by way of Sidon towards the Sea of Galilee, in the region of the Decapolis. *32.* They brought to him a deaf man who had an impediment in his speech; and they begged him to lay his hand on him. *33.* He took him aside in private, away from the crowd, and put his fingers into his ears, and he spat and touched his tongue. *34.* Then looking up to heaven, he sighed and said to him, "Ephphatha," that is, "Be opened." *35.* And immediately his ears were opened, his tongue was released, and he spoke plainly. *36.* Then Jesus ordered them to tell no one; but the more he ordered them, the more zealously they proclaimed it. *37.* They were astounded beyond measure, saying, "He has done everything well; he even makes the deaf to hear and the mute to speak."

Jesus heals the blind man of Bethsaida

1.75. Jesus Laid His Hands on His Eyes Again; and He Looked Intently and His Sight was Restored, and He Saw Everything Clearly

Mark 8:22–26

22. They came to Bethsaida. Some people brought a blind man to him, and begged him to touch him. *23.* He took the blind man by the hand and led him out of the village; and when he had put saliva on his eyes and laid his hands on him, he asked him, "Can you see anything?" *24.* And the man looked up and said, "I can see people, but they look like trees, walking." *25.* Then Jesus laid his hands on his eyes again; and he looked intently and his sight was restored, and he saw everything clearly. *26.* Then he sent him away to his home, saying, "Do not even go into the village."

Jesus heals the blind man Bartimaeus

1.76. The Blind Man Said to Jesus, "Master, Let me See Again." Jesus Said to him, "Go; Your Faith has Made You Well." Immediately He Regained His Sight and Followed Him on the Way

Mark 10:46–52 (//Matt. 20:29–34//Luke 18:35–43)

46. They came to Jericho. As he and his disciples and a large crowed were leaving Jericho, Bartimaeus son of Timaeus, a blind beggar, was sitting by the roadside. *47.* When he heard that it was Jesus of Nazareth, he began to shout out and say, "Jesus, Son of David, have mercy on me!" *48.* Many sternly ordered him to be quiet, but he cried out even more loudly, "Son of David, have mercy on me!" *49.* Jesus stood still and said, "Call him here." And they called the blind man, saying to him, "Take heart; get up, he is calling you." *50.* So throwing off his cloak, he sprang up and came to Jesus. *51.* Then Jesus said to him, "What do you want me to do for you?" The blind man said to him, "My teacher, let me see again." *52.* Jesus said to him, "Go; your faith has made you well." Immediately he regained his sight and followed him on the way.

Jesus heals a man born blind

1.77. Jesus Spat on the Ground and Made Mud with Saliva and Spread the Mud on the Man's Eyes, Saying to Him, "Go, Wash in the Pool of Siloam." . . . Then He Went and Washed and Came Back Able to See

John 9:1–41

1. As he walked along, he saw a man blind from birth. *2.* His disciples asked him, "Rabbi, who sinned, this man or his parents, that he was born blind?" *3.* Jesus answered, "Neither this man nor his parents sinned; he was born blind so that God's works might be revealed in him. *4.* We must work the works of him who sent me while it is day; night is coming when no one can work. *5.* As long as I am in the world, I am the light of the world. *6.* When he had said this, he spat on the ground and made mud with the saliva and spread the mud on the man's eyes, *7.* saying to him, "Go, wash in the pool of Siloam" (which means Sent). Then he went and washed and came back able to see. *8.* The neighbors and those who had seen him before as a beggar began to ask, "Is this not the man who used to sit and beg?" *9.* Some were saying, "It is he." Others were saying, "No, but it is someone like him." He kept saying, "I am the man." *10.* But they kept asking him, "Then how were your eyes opened?" *11.* He answered, "The man called Jesus made mud, spread it on my eyes, and said to me, 'Go to Siloam and wash.' Then I went and washed and received my sight." *12.* They said to him, "Where is he?" He said, "I do not know."

13. They brought to the Pharisees the man who had formerly been blind. *14.* Now it was a sabbath day when Jesus made the mud and opened his eyes. *15.* Then the Pharisees also began to ask him how he had received his sight. He said to them, "He put mud on my eyes. Then I washed, and now I see." *16.* Some of the Pharisees said, "This man is not from God, for he does not observe the sabbath." But others said, "How can a man who is a sinner perform such signs?" And they were divided. *17.* So they said again to the blind man, "What do you say about him? It was your eyes he opened." He said, "He is a prophet."

18. The Jews did not believe that he had been blind and had received his sight until they called the parents of the man who had received his sight *19.* and asked them, "Is this your son, who you say was born blind? How then does he now see?" *20.* His parents answered, "We know that this is our son, and that he was born blind; *21.* but we do not know how it is that now he sees, nor do we know who opened his eyes. Ask him; he is of age. He will speak for himself." *22.* His parents said this because they were afraid of the Jews; for the Jews had already agreed that anyone who confessed Jesus to be the Messiah would be put out of the synagogue. *23.* Therefore his parents said, "He is of age; ask him."

24. So for the second time they called the man who had been blind, and they said to him, "Give glory to God! We know that this man is a sinner." *25.* He answered, "I do not know whether he is a sinner. One thing I know, that though I was blind, now I see." *26.* They said to him, "What did he do to you? How did he open your eyes?" *27.* He answered them, "I have told you already, and you would not listen. Why do you want to hear it again? Do you also want to become his disciples? *28.* Then they reviled him, saying, "You are his disciple, but we are disciples of Moses. *29.* We know that God has spoken to Moses, but as for this man, we do not know where he comes from." *30.* The man answered, "Here is an astonishing thing! You do not know where he comes from, and yet he opened my eyes. *31.* We know that God does not listen to sinners, but he does listen to one who worships him and obeys his will. *32.* Never since the world began has it been heard that anyone opened the eyes of a person born blind. *33.* If this man were not from God, he could do nothing." *34.* They answered him, "You were born entirely in sins, and are you trying to teach us?" And they drove him out.

35. Jesus heard that they had driven him out, and when he found him, he said, "Do you believe in the Son of Man?" *36.* He answered, "And who is he, sir? Tell me, so that I may believe in him." *37.* Jesus said to him, "You have seen him, and the one speaking with you is he." *38.* He said, "Lord, I believe." And he worshiped him. *39.* Jesus said, "I came into this world for judgment so that those who do see may see, and those who do not see may become blind." *40.* Some of the Pharisees near him heard this and said to him, "Surely we are not blind, are we?" *41.* Jesus said to them, "If you were blind, you would not have sin. But now that you say, 'We see,'" your sin remains.

Jesus' miracles fulfill the prophet Isaiah

1.78. "No Prophet is Acceptable in his Own Country"

Luke 4:16–30

16. When he came to Nazareth, where he had been brought up, he went to the synagogue on the sabbath day, as was his custom. He stood up to read, *17.* and the scroll of the prophet Isaiah was given to him. He unrolled the scroll and found the place where it was written:
18. "The Spirit of the Lord is upon me,
because he has anointed me to bring good news to the poor.
He sent me to proclaim release to the captives
and recovering of sight to the blind,
to let the oppressed go free,
19. to proclaim the year of the Lord's favor."
20. And he rolled up the scroll, gave it to the attendant, and sat down. The eyes of all in the synagogue were fixed on him. *21.* Then he began to say to them, "Today this scripture has been fulfilled in your hearing." *22.* All spoke well of him and were amazed at the gracious words that came from his mouth. They said, "Is not this Joseph's son?" *23.* He said

to them, "Doubtless you will quote to me this proverb, 'Doctor, cure your-self!' And you will say, 'Do here also in your hometown the things that we have heard you did at Capernaum.'" *24.* And he said, "Truly I tell you, no prophet is accepted in the prophet's hometown. *25.* But the truth is, there were many widows in Israel in the time of Elijah, when the heaven was shut up three years and six months, and there was a severe famine over all the land; *26.* yet Elijah was sent to none of them except to a widow at Zarephath in Sidon. *27.* There were also many lepers in Israel in the time of the prophet Elisha, and none of them was cleansed except Naaman the Syrian." *28.* When they heard this, all in the syna-gogue were filled with rage. *29.* They got up, drove him out of the town, and led him to the brow of the hill on which their town was built, so that they might hurl him off the cliff. *30.* But he passed through the midst of them and went on his way.

Raises from the dead

Jesus raises a twelve-year-old girl from the dead

1.79. Some People Came from the Leader's House to Say, "Your Daughter is Dead. Why Trouble the Teacher any Further?" But Overhearing What They Said, Jesus Said to the Leader of the Synagogue, "Do Not Fear, Only Believe"

Mark 5:21–43 (Matt. 9:18–26; Luke 8:40–56)
21. When Jesus had crossed again in the boat to the other side, a great crowd gathered around him; and he was by the sea. *22.* Then one of the leaders of the synagogue named Jairus came and, when he saw him, fell at his feet *23.* and begged him repeatedly, "My little daughter is at the point of death. Come and lay your hands on her, so that she may be made well, and live." *24.* So he went with him.

And a large crowd followed him and pressed in on him. *25.* Now there was a woman who had been suffering from hemorrhages for twelve years. *26.* She had endured much under many physicians, and had spent all that she had; and she was no better but rather grew worse. *27.* She had heard about Jesus, and came up behind him in the crowd and touched his cloak, *28.* for she said, "If I but touch his clothes, I will be made well." *29.* Immediately her hemorrhage stopped; and she felt in her body that she was healed of her disease. *30.* Immediately aware that power had gone forth from him, Jesus turned about in the crowd and said, "Who touched my clothes?" *31.* And his disciples said to him, "You see the crowd pressing in on you; how can you say, 'Who touched me?'" *32.* He looked all around to see who had done it. *33.* But the woman, knowing what had happened to her, came in fear and trembling, fell down before him, and told him the whole truth. *34.* He said to her, "Daughter, your faith has made you well; go in peace, and be healed of your disease."

35. While he was still speaking, some people came from the leader's house to say, "Your daughter is dead. Why trouble the teacher any further?" 36. But overhearing what they said, Jesus said to the leader of the synagogue, "Do not fear, only believe." 37. He allowed no one to follow him except Peter, James and John, the brother of James. 38. When they came to the house of the leader of the synagogue, he saw a commotion, people weeping and wailing loudly. 39. When he had entered, he said to them, "Why do you make a commotion and weep? The child is not dead but sleeping." 40. And they laughed at him. Then he put them all outside, and took the child's father and mother and those who were with him, and went in where the child was. 41. He took her by the hand and said to her, "Talitha cum" which means, "Little girl, get up!" 42. And immediately the girl got up and began to walk about (she was twelve years of age). At this they were overcome with amazement. 43. He strictly ordered them that no one should know this, and told them to give her something to eat.

Jesus raises the only son of a widow from the dead

1.80. When the Lord Saw Her, He had Compassion on Her and Said to Her, "Do Not Weep." Then He Came Forward and Touched the Bier, and the Bearers Stood Still. And He Said, "Young Man, I Say to You, Rise!"

Luke 7:11–17

11. Soon afterwards he went to a town called Nain, and his disciples and a large crowd went with him. 12. As he approached the gate of the town, a man who had died was being carried out. He was his mother's only son, and she was a widow; and with her was a large crowd from the town. 13. When the Lord saw her, he had compassion on her and said to her, "Do not weep." 14. Then he came forward and touched the bier, and the bearers stood still. And he said, "Young man, I say to you, rise!" 15. The dead man sat up and began to speak, and Jesus gave him to his mother. 16. Fear seized all of them; and they glorified God, saying, "A great prophet has risen among us!" and "God has looked favorably on his people!" 17. This word about him spread throughout Judea and all the surrounding country.

Jesus raises his friend Lazarus from the dead

1.81. "Father, I Thank You for Having Heard Me. I Knew that You Always Hear Me, but I Have Said This for the Sake of the Crowd Standing Here, So That They May Believe That You Sent Me." When He had Said This, He Cried with a Loud Voice, "Lazarus, Come Out"

John 11:1–46

1. Now a certain man was ill, Lazarus of Bethany, the village of Mary and her sister Martha. *2*. Mary was the one who anointed the Lord with perfume and wiped his feet with her hair; her brother Lazarus was ill. *3*. So the sisters sent a message to Jesus, "Lord, he whom you love is ill." *4*. But when Jesus heard it, he said, "This illness does not lead to death; rather it is for God's glory, so that the Son of God may be glorified through it." *5*. Accordingly, though Jesus loved Martha and her sister and Lazarus, *6*. after having heard that Lazarus was ill, he stayed two days longer in the place where he was.

7. Then after this he said to the disciples, "Let us go to Judea again." *8*. The disciples said to him, "Rabbi, the Jews were just now trying to stone you, and are you going there again?" *9*. Jesus answered, "Are there not twelve hours of daylight? Those who walk during the day do not stumble, because they see the light of this world. *10*. But those who walk at night stumble, because the light is not in them." *11*. After saying this, he told them, "Our friend Lazarus has fallen asleep, but I am going there to awaken him." *12*. The disciples said to him, "Lord, if he has fallen asleep, he will be all right." *13*. Jesus, however, had been speaking about his death, but they thought that he was referring merely to sleep. *14*. Then Jesus told them plainly, "Lazarus is dead; *15*. For your sake I am glad I was not there, so that you may believe. But let us go to him." *16*. Thomas, who was called the Twin, said to his fellow disciples, "Let us also go, that we may die with him."

17. When Jesus arrived, he found that Lazarus had already been in the tomb four days. *18*. Now Bethany was near Jerusalem, some two miles away, *19*. and many of the Jews had come to Martha and Mary to console them about their brother. *20*. When Martha heard that Jesus was coming, she went and met him, while Mary stayed at home. *21*. Martha said to Jesus, "Lord, if you had been here, my brother would not have died. *22*. But even now I know that God will give you whatever you ask of him." *23*. Jesus said to her, "Your brother will rise again." *24*. Martha said to him, "I know that he will rise again in the resurrection on the last day." *25*. Jesus said to her, "I am the resurrection and the life. Those who believe in me, even though they die, will live, *26*. and everyone who lives and believes in me will never die. Do you believe this?" *27*. She said to him, "Yes, Lord, I believe that you are the Messiah, the Son of God, the one coming into the world."

28. When she had said this, she went back and called her sister Mary, and told her privately, "The Teacher is here and is calling for you." 29. And when she heard it, she got up quickly and went to him. 30. Now Jesus had not yet come to the village, but was still at the place where Martha had met him. 31. The Jews who were with her in the house, consoling her, saw Mary get up quickly and go out. They followed her because they thought that she was going to the tomb to weep there. 32. When Mary came where Jesus was and saw him, she knelt at his feet and said to him, "Lord, if you had been here, my brother would not have died." 33. When Jesus saw her weeping, and the Jews who came with her also weeping, he was greatly disturbed in spirit and deeply moved. 34. He said, "Where have you laid him?" They said to him, "Lord, come and see." 35. Jesus began to weep. 36. So the Jews said, "See how he loved him!" 37. But some of them said, "Could not he who opened the eyes of the blind man have kept this man from dying?"

38. Then Jesus, again greatly disturbed, came to the tomb. It was a cave, and a stone was lying against it. 39. Jesus said, "Take away the stone." Martha, the sister of the dead man, said to him, "Lord, already there is a stench because he has been dead four days." 40. Jesus said to her, "Did I not tell you that if you believed, you would see the glory of God?" 41. So they took away the stone. And Jesus looked upward and said, "Father, I thank you for having heard me. 42. I knew that you always hear me, but I have said this for the sake of the crowd standing here, so that they may believe that you sent me." 43. When he had said this, he cried with a loud voice, "Lazarus, come out!" 44. The dead man came out, his hands and feet bound with strips of cloth, and his face wrapped in a cloth. Jesus said to them, "Unbind him, and let him go."

45. Many of the Jews therefore, who had come with Mary and had seen what Jesus did, believed in him. 46. But some of them went to the Pharisees and told them what he had done.

THE HEALING MIRACLES IN JESUS' NAME

Acts of the Apostles

The healings in Jesus' name that would find their way to the Acts of the Apostles provide more evidence about the significance of Jesus' own miracles for these communities. Both the actual miracle story and the interpretation attached to it, where one occurs, are included.

Peter

Heals the infirm

Peter heals a crippled beggar in Jesus' name

1.82. "By Faith in His Name, His Name Itself Has Made This Man Strong, Whom You See and Know; and the Faith That is Through Jesus Has Given Him This Perfect Health In the Presence of All of You"

Acts 3:1–16

1. One day Peter and John were going up to the temple at the hour of prayer, at three o'clock in the afternoon. *2.* And a man lame from birth was being carried in. People would lay him daily at the gate of the temple called the Beautiful Gate so that he could ask for alms from those entering the temple. *3.* When he saw Peter and John about to go into the temple, he asked them for alms. *4.* Peter looked intently at him, as did John, and said, "Look at us." *5.* And he fixed his attention on them, expecting to receive something from them. *6.* But Peter said, "I have no silver or gold, but what I have I give you; in the name of Jesus Christ of Nazareth, stand up and walk." *7.* And he took him by the right hand and raised him up; and immediately his feet and ankles were made strong. *8.* Jumping up, he stood and began to walk, and he entered the temple with them, walking and leaping and praising God. *9.* All the people saw him walking and praising God, *10.* and they recognized him as the one who used to sit and ask for alms at the Beautiful Gate of the temple; and they were filled with wonder and amazement at what had happened to him.

11. While he clung to Peter and John, all the people ran together to them in the portico called Solomon's Portico, utterly astonished. *12.* When Peter saw it, he addressed the people, "You Israelites, why do you wonder at this, or why do you stare at us, as though by our own power or piety we had made him walk? *13.* The God of Abraham, the God of Isaac, and the God of Jacob, the God of our ancestors has glorified his servant Jesus, whom you handed over and rejected in the presence of Pilate, though he had decided to release him. *14.* But you rejected the Holy and Righteous One and asked to have a murderer given to you, *15.* and you killed the Author of life, whom God raised from the dead. To this we are witnesses. *16.* And by faith in his name, his name itself has made this man strong, whom you see and know; and the faith that is through Jesus has given him this perfect health in the presence of all of you."

Peter heals the paralyzed Aeneas in Jesus' name

1.83. Peter Said to him, "Aeneas, Jesus Christ Heals You; Get Up and Make Your Bed!" And Immediately He Got Up

Acts 9:32–35

32. Now as Peter went here and there among all the believers, he came down also to the saints living in Lydda. *33.* There he found a man named Aeneas, who had been bedridden for eight years, for he was paralyzed. *34.* Peter said to him, "Aeneas, Jesus Christ heals you; get up and make your bed!" And immediately he got up. *35.* And all the residents of Lydda and Sharon saw him and turned to the Lord.

Raises the dead

Peter raises Tabitha from the dead in Jesus' name

1.84. Peter Put All of Them Outside, and then He Knelt Down and Prayed. He Turned to the Body and Said, "Tabitha, Get Up." Then She Opened her Eyes, and Seeing Peter, She Sat Up. He Gave Her His Hand and Helped Her Up

Acts 9:36–42

36. Now in Joppa there was a disciple whose name was Tabitha, which in Greek is Dorcas. She was devoted to good works and acts of charity. *37.* At that time she became ill and died. When they had washed her, they laid her in a room upstairs. *38.* Since Lydda was near Joppa, the disciples, who heard that Peter was there, sent two men to him with the request, "Please come to us without delay." *39.* So Peter got up and went with them; and when he arrived, they took him to the room upstairs. All the widows stood beside him, weeping and showing tunics and other clothing that Dorcas had made while she was with them. *40.* Peter put all of them outside, and then he knelt down and prayed. He turned to the body and said, "Tabitha, get up." Then she opened her eyes, and seeing Peter, she sat up. *41.* He gave her his hand and helped her up. Then calling the saints and widows, he showed her to be alive. *42.* This became known throughout Joppa, and many believed in the Lord.

Paul

Heals the infirm

Paul is given his sight by Ananias in Jesus' name

1.85.1. Saul is Blinded by the Light from Heaven

Acts 9:1–9

1. Meanwhile Saul, still breathing threats and murder against the disciples of the Lord, went to the high priest *2*. and asked him for letters to the synagogues at Damascus, so that if he found any who belonged to the Way, men or women, he might bring them bound to Jerusalem. *3*. Now as he was going along and approaching Damascus, suddenly a light from heaven flashed around him. *4*. He fell to the ground and heard a voice saying to him, "Saul, Saul, why do you persecute me?" *5*. He asked, "Who are you, Lord?" The reply came, "I am Jesus, whom you are persecuting. *6*. But get up and enter the city, and you will be told what you are to do." *7*. The men who were traveling with him stood speechless because they heard the voice but saw no one. *8*. Saul got up from the ground, and though his eyes were open, he could see nothing; so they led him by the hand and brought him into Damascus. *9*. For three days he was without sight, and neither ate nor drank.

1.85.2. Saul Receives His Sight from Ananias in Jesus' Name

Acts 9:10–19

10. Now there was a disciple in Damascus named Ananias. The Lord said to him in a vision, "Ananias." He answered, "Here I am, Lord." *11*. The Lord said to him, "Get up and go to the street called Straight, and at the house of Judas look for a man of Tarsus named Saul. At this moment he is praying *12*. and he has seen in a vision a man named Ananias come in and lay his hands on him so that he might regain his sight." *13*. But Ananias answered, "Lord, I have heard from many about this man, how much evil he has done to your saints in Jerusalem; *14*. and here he has authority from the chief priests to bind all who invoke your name." *15*. But the Lord said to him, "Go, for he is an instrument whom I have chosen to bring my name before Gentiles and kings and before the people of Israel; *16*. I myself will show him how much he must suffer for the sake of my name." *17*. So Ananias went and entered the house. He laid his hands on Saul and said, "Brother Saul, the Lord Jesus, who appeared to you on your way here, has sent me so that you may regain your sight and be filled with the Holy Spirit." *18*. And immediately something like scales fell from his eyes, and his sight was restored. Then he got up and was baptized, *19*. and after taking some food, he regained his strength.

Paul cures a lame man

1.86. When the Crowds Saw What Paul had Done, They Shouted in the Lycaonian Language, "The Gods Have Come Down to Us in Human Form!"

Acts 14:8–18

8. In Lystra there was a man sitting who could not use his feet and had never walked, for he had been crippled from birth. 9. He listened to Paul as he was speaking. And Paul, looking at him intently and seeing that he had faith to be healed, 10. said in a loud voice, "Stand upright on your feet." And the man sprang up and began to walk. 11. When the crowds saw what Paul had done, they shouted in the Lycaonian language, "The gods have come down to us in human form!" 12. Barnabas they called Zeus, and Paul they called Hermes, because he was the chief speaker. 13. The priest of Zeus, whose temple was just outside the city, brought oxen and garlands to the gates; he and the crowds wanted to offer sacrifice. 14. When the apostles Barnabas and Paul heard of it, they tore their clothes and rushed out into the crowd, shouting, 15. "Friends, why are you doing this? We are mortals just like you, and we bring you good news, that you should turn from these worthless things to the living God, who made the heaven and the earth and the sea and all that is in them. 16. In past generations he allowed all the nations to follow their own ways; 17. yet he has not left himself without a witness in doing good – giving you rains from heaven and fruitful seasons, and filling you with food and your hearts with joy." 18. Even with these words, they scarcely restrained the crowds from offering sacrifice to them.

Raises the dead

Paul raises a boy from the dead by holding him in his arms

1.87. But Paul Went Down, and Bending Over Him, Took Him in His Arms and Said, "Do Not Be Alarmed, for His Life is in Him"

Acts 20:7–12

7. On the first day of the week, when we met to break bread, Paul was holding a discussion with them; since he intended to leave the next day, he continued speaking until midnight. 8. There were many lamps in the room upstairs where we were meeting. 9. A young man named Eutychus, who was sitting in the window, began to sink off into a deep sleep while Paul talked still longer. Overcome by sleep, he fell to the ground three floors below and was picked up dead. 10. But Paul went down, and bending over him took him in his arms, and said, "Do not be alarmed, for his life is in

him." *11*. Then Paul went upstairs, and after he had broken bread and eaten, he continued to converse with them until dawn; then he left. *12*. Meanwhile they had taken the boy away alive and were not a little comforted.

Part II

EXORCISTS AND
EXORCISMS

4

DAIMONS/DEMONS IN
GRECO-ROMAN ANTIQUITY

And they were all amazed, so that they questioned among themselves, saying, "What is this? A new teaching! With authority
he commands even the unclean spirits, and they obey him." And
at once his fame spread everywhere throughout all the
surrounding region of Galilee.

(Mark 1:27)

INTRODUCTION

The meaning of an exorcism is dependent on the interpreter's lens
and not on an objective set of criteria.[1] Harold Remus makes this
point in his *Pagan–Christian Conflict over Miracle in the Second
Century*.[2] Jesus' exorcisms are examples of his saving power, but for
those opposed to him, they may be examples of magic, of collusion with the world of demons or of quackery. So, of first importance
is the disposition of the narrator about the exorcist.

Where the exorcism is granted to be authentic and a positive act
of salvation, its meaning for the hero's identity is open to several
interpretations. The most basic consideration is the cosmological

---

1 I am greatly indebted to Graham H. Twelftree for his erudite monograph
Jesus the Exorcist: A Contribution to the Study of the Historical Jesus (WUNT 54;
Tübingen: J. C. B. Mohr [Paul Siebeck], 1993). Although this book is directed
to the question of the historical probability of Jesus' exorcisms, the meticulous research into ancient sources as well as the perceptive precision of the
redaction criticism renders it indispensable for any scholar intent on recovering the meaning of the pre-gospel exorcism account.
2 Harold Remus, *Pagan–Christian Conflict over Miracle in the Second Century*
(Patristic Monograph Series 10; Cambridge, MA: The Philadelphia Patristic
Foundation, 1983).

backdrop presupposed for the hero's action. If the narrator signals to us that an apocalyptic eschatology is being presumed, then the exorcism will be seen in that light. For example, seen against apocalyptic expectations, an exorcism of Jesus will be interpreted as the in-breaking of the final age and the coming overthrow of Satan's control of the world. But if the Jesus exorcism carries no signal that apocalyptic expectations are explicit, then that story must be interpreted and contextualized by the ordinary Greco-Roman cosmology, and other exorcism stories that assume a cosmological backdrop.

To understand the range of meanings possible for an exorcism story, it is also important to know the various ideas extant about the nature and identity of daimons/demons, as they are found in non-apocalyptic/eschatological stories of the ordinary Greco-Roman world, as well as in Jewish apocalyptic texts.

Part 2 will treat each cosmology separately. In Chapter 4, the ideas about daimons that would be available to the ordinary person of Greco-Roman antiquity will be presented, followed by exorcism stories belonging to that cosmology. Then, in Chapter 5, the most common traditions about demons as found in the two Jewish apocalyptic texts 1 Enoch and Jubilees will be presented. The chapter closes with a collection of the Jesus exorcisms in the gospels and those done in his name in Acts of the Apostles.

THE NATURE AND IDENTITY OF
DAIMONS IN NON-JEWISH SOURCES
OF GRECO-ROMAN ANTIQUITY

The impressive essay of Frederick E. Brenk, SJ, "In the Light of the Moon: Demonology in the Early Imperial Period," provides a detailed description of the various ideas of the "daimon" from the earliest folk traditions through to the third century CE.[3] The most pertinent conclusion of his work is the proof that no one meaning can be presumed for the term "daimon," but rather, the context dictates its intended significance.

Plutarch (45–125 CE) names Hesiod as the first to separate the daimons from the gods, assigning them a limitation to their life \

---

3 Frederick E. Brenk, SJ, "In the Light of the Moon: Demonology in the Early Imperial Period," *ANRW* II 16/3 (1986) 2068–2145.

(9,720 years).[4] But beyond this basic distinction, a variety of usage characterizes the term. The best notion to sum up these roles would seem to be "spirit." This idea allows for their role as messengers or agents of the gods, or spirits in opposition to the gods, guardian spirits of people or troublers of people, happy souls or spirits of the dead who are embittered and vengeful toward the living.

Plutarch (circa 50–120 CE)

A fine presentation of ideas available to a large range of the Mediterranean population in Imperial times is provided in Plutarch's *De Defectu Oraculorum* (415A–418D).[5] We also find reference to the daimons in his *Moralia* (350E), and to the effects of their possession in his *Lives: Marcellus* (20.5f.)

In the *De Defectu Oraculorum* a group of educated friends meet at the baths in the temple and find themselves discussing the reasons why the oracles like these at Delphi where they are staying are so devoid of the divine communications that made them so famous in the past. Cleombrotus of Sparta, a wealthy world traveler who is constantly searching for knowledge, offers this answer.

2.1. Many Perplexities are Explained by the Teaching that a Race of Demigods Exists between the Gods and Humanity

Plutarch, *De Defectu Oraculorum* 415A[6]

They put the case well who say that Plato, by his discovery of the element underlying all created qualities, which is now called "Matter" and "Nature," has relieved philosophers of many perplexities; but, as it seems to me, those persons have resolved more and greater perplexities who have set the race of demigods midway between gods and men, and have discovered a force to draw together, in a way, and to unite our common fellowship – whether this doctrine comes from the wise men of the cult of Zoroaster, or whether it is Thracian and harks back to Orpheus, or is Egyptian or Phrygian, as we may infer from observing that many things connected with death and mourning in the rites of both lands are combined in the ceremonies so fervently celebrated there.

---

4 Plutarch, *De Defectu Oraculorum* 415D.
5 I am grateful to Everett Ferguson for this excellent example, from his work *Demonology of the Early Christian World* (Symposium Series 12; Lewiston/Queenston: Edwin Mellen Press, 1984), 33–35.
6 All quotations are taken from Plutarch, *De Defectu Oraculorum*, *Moralia*, vol. 5 (trans. Frank Cole Babbitt; London: Heinemann, 1936), 2068–2145.

2.2. Heroes who Die can become Demigods and Demigods Heroes

Plutarch, *De Defectu Oraculorum* 415B

Among the Greeks, Homer, moreover, appears to use both names in common and sometimes to speak of the gods as demigods [*daimonas*]; but Hesiod was the first to set forth clearly and distinctly four classes of rational beings: gods, demigods, heroes, in this order, and last of all, men; and as a sequence to this, apparently, he postulates his transmutation, the golden race passing selectively into many good divinities, and the demigods into heroes.

Others postulate a transmutation for bodies and souls alike; in the same manner in which water is seen to be generated from earth, air from water, and fire from air, as their substance is borne upward, even so from men into heroes and from heroes into demigods the better souls obtain their transmutation. But from the demigods a few souls still, in the long reach of time, because of supreme excellence, come, after being purified, to share completely in divine qualities.

2.3. If Souls Lose Control of Themselves, They can Again be Clothed with Earthly Bodies

Plutarch, *De Defectu Oraculorum* 415C

But with some of these souls it comes to pass that they do not maintain control over themselves, but yield to temptation and are again clothed with mortal bodies and have a dim and darkened life, like mist or vapour.

(The Loeb edition supplies a note on Hesiod's calculation that a demigod lives 9,720 years, and a discussion of how to interpret one "generation"; resistance to the Stoic theory of conflagration [415C–416B].)

2.4. It is Impossible to Imagine the Cosmos Without the Daimons

Plutarch, *De Defectu Oraculorum* 416E–F

Now if the air that is between the earth and the moon were to be removed and withdrawn, the unity and consociation of the universe would be destroyed, since there would be an empty and unconnected space in the middle; and in just the same way those who refuse to leave us the race of demigods make the relations of gods and men remote and alien by doing away with the "interpretative and ministering nature" as Plato has called it; or else they force us to a disorderly confusion of all things, in which we bring the god into men's emotions and activities, drawing him down to our needs, as the women of Thessaly are said to draw down the moon.

2.5. Just as with Human Beings, so too Among the Demigods there are Different Degrees of Excellence

Plutarch, *De Defectu Oraculorum* 417B

For as among men, so also among the demigods, there are different degrees of excellence, and in some there is a weak and dim remainder of the emotional and irrational, a survival, as it were, while in others this is excessive and hard to stifle. Of these things there are, in many places, sacrifices, ceremonies, and legends which preserve and jealously guard vestiges and tokens embodied here and there in their fabric.

2.6. The Gloomy Practices on Festival Days are Meant to Ward Off the Evil Spirits

Plutarch, *De Defectu Oraculorum* 417C, D, E

As for festivals and sacrifices, which may be compared with ill-omened and gloomy days, in which occur the eating of raw flesh, rending of victims, fasting, and beating of breasts, and again in many places scurrilous language at the shrines, frenzy and shoutings of throngs in excitement with tumultuous tossings of heads in the air. I should say that these acts are not performed for any god, but are soothing and appeasing rites for the averting of evil spirits [*daimonon*].

2.7. A Possessed Man: Demons Effect the Signs of Madness such as Shrieking, Running and Nakedness

Plutarch, *Lives, Marcellus*, 20.5f.[7]

Just as they were ready to arrest him [Nicias], an assembly of the citizens was held, and here Nicias, right in the midst of some advice that he was giving to the people, suddenly threw himself upon the ground, and after a little while, amid the silence and consternation which naturally prevailed, lifted his head, turned it about, and spoke in a low and trembling voice, little by little raising and sharpening its tones. And when he saw the whole audience struck dumb with horror, he tore off his mantle, rent his tunic, and leaping up half naked, ran towards the exit from the theatre, crying out that he was pursued by the Mothers.[8] No man venturing to lay hands upon him or even to come in his way, out of superstitious fear, but all avoiding him, he ran out to the gate of the city, freely using all the cries and gestures that would become a man possessed and crazed.

---

7 Plutarch, *Marcellus, Lives*, vol. 5 (trans. Bernadotte Perrin; London: Heinemann, 1917), 20.5f.

8 This is a reference to mystery cults to two great female deities, Magna Mater and Cybele.

Apuleius of Madaura (123–190 CE [?])

Apuleius, a poet and philosopher, was named chief priest of the province of Carthage in 161 CE. But only six years previously, he had run into difficulties when he was charged with having used magic to induce a wealthy widow to marry him. He had defended himself admirably before the court and was found innocent of the charges. The following passage is taken from Apuleius' *Apologia* on the matter.

2.8. All Divination and Miracles of Magicians are Controlled by Daimons

Apuleius of Madaura, *Apologia* 43[9]
I believe Plato when he asserts that there are certain divine powers holding a position and possessing a character mid-way between gods and men, and that all divination and the miracles of magicians are controlled by them.

Celsus: Origen's Contra Celsum (177–180 CE)

2.9. It is Sorcerers Who Deal With Daimons, Blow away Diseases and Invoke the Souls of the Heroes Only for Base Gain

Celsus: Origen, *Contra Celsum* 1.68[10]
[Celsus] puts them [the Jesus miracles] on a level with the "works of sorcerers who profess to do wonderful miracles, and the accomplishments of those who are taught by the Egyptians, who for a few obols make known their sacred lore in the middle of the market place and drive daemons out of men and blow away diseases and invoke the souls of heroes . . . "

Note

One way to denounce the exorcist caustically is to call him a "sorcerer." The foreigners, the Egyptians, are the conventional scapegoats for the knowledge of black magic, and if Romans are involved, it is only due to the instructions of these suspicious healers from

---

9 Apuleius of Madaura, *Apologia, The Apologia and Florida of Apuleius of Madaura* (trans. H. E. Butler; Oxford: Clarendon Press, 1909), 78.

10 *Origen: Contra Celsum* (trans. with an introduction and notes by Henry Chadwick; Cambridge: Cambridge University Press, 1953, repr. 1965), 62–63.

the East. A second way is to attack the integrity of the person with the accusation that sacred matters are made profane for base gain. Finally the grouping of activities is important to notice. Driving out a daimon is placed in the same list as "blowing away" a disease and communicating with the heroes' souls – i.e. sacred divination, perhaps with dark tones of necromancy. The association of disease and daimon possession is inescapable.

Lucian of Samosata (120–190 CE [?])

Lucian of Samosata is chiefly known for his satirical dialogues lampooning all aspects of life, especially religious "superstitions." It is worthy of note that Lucian's home was in the East, and he can be expected to know something of the culture particular to Syria and Palestine.

In Lucian's *The Lover of Lies* Ion scolds the story teller [narrator] for his incredulity over the miraculous and gives testimony about a "Syrian" who exorcizes daimons.

2.10. It is Ridiculous to Doubt Everything. What about those who Free the Daimon-Possessed from their Terrors?

Lucian, *The Lover of Lies* 16[11]

"You act ridiculously," said Ion, "to doubt everything. For my part, I should like to ask you what you say to those who free possessed men from their terrors by exorcising the spirits so manifestly. I need not discuss this: everyone knows about the Syrian from Palestine, the adept in it, how many he takes in hand who fall down in the light of the moon and roll their eyes and fill their mouths with foam; nevertheless, he restores them to health and sends them away normal in mind, delivering them from their straits for a large fee. When he stands beside them as they lie there and asks: 'Whence came you into his body?' the patient himself is silent, but the spirit answers in Greek or in the language of whatever foreign country he comes from, telling how and whence he entered into the man; whereupon, by adjuring the spirit and if he does not obey, threatening him, he drives him out. Indeed, I actually saw one coming out, black and smoky in colour."

Note

Lucian's satirical portayal attests to the popularity of exorcists in his society. When we look to see how such a power is to be

---

11 Lucian, *The Lover of Lies*, *Lucian*, vol. 3 (trans. A. M. Harmon; London: Heinemann, 1921), 16.

understood, Lucian shows his hand when he says that the exorcist wants money. Meanwhile for his character Ion the exorcist's act of casting out a daimon is a liberation of the demoniacs from "their terrors." Here Lucian represents the beliefs of the "gullible," with tongue in cheek.

Diogenes Laertius (circa 250 CE)

We know nothing about this scholar and must even deduce his dates from his writings. His presentation of the lives and teachings of famous philosophers begins with Thales and ends with Epicurus, suggesting that he had not lived to see the rise of Neoplatonism. Therefore, a date of early to mid-second century CE seems fair for him. In Book 8 of *The Lives of Eminent Philosophers* he treats Pythagoras, representing ideas that antiquity ascribed to him.

2.11.1. Impure Souls May Not Approach the Pure but are Bound by the Furies

Diogenes Laertius, *Pythagoras, Lives of Eminent Philosophers* 8.31[12]
Hermes is the steward of souls, and for that reason is called Hermes the Escorter, Hermes the Keeper of the Gate, and Hermes of the Underworld, since it is he who brings in the souls from their bodies both by land and sea; and the pure are taken into the uppermost region, but the impure [*akathartous*] are not permitted to approach the pure or each other, but are bound by the Furies in bonds unbreakable.

2.11.2. The Whole Air is Full of Souls Called Genii (*Daimones*) or Heroes Who Send People Dreams and Signs of Future Diseases

Diogenes Laertius, *Pythagoras, Lives of Philosophers* 8.32
The whole air is full of souls which are called genii [*daimones*] or heroes; these are they who send men dreams and signs of future disease and health, and not to men alone, but to sheep also and cattle as well; and it is to them that purifications and lustrations, all divination, omens and the like, have reference.

---

12 All quotations are taken from Diogenes Laertius, *Pythagoras, The Lives of Eminent Philosophers*, vol. 2 (trans. R. D. Hicks; London: Heinemann, 1925).

Papyrus Berolinensis

2.12. Daimons are Capable of Freezing Waters so that they Can Run Over them

Papyrus Berolinensis 1.20[13]

He [the daimon] will quickly freeze rivers and seas and in such a way that you can run over them firmly.

Note

The obvious difference between this miracle and Jesus' walking on water (Mark 6:45–52) is that the daimon must make the water firm before he can cross it. The power that the daimon has is his ability to freeze large expanses of water, not his power to cross water in its ordinary liquid state.

Exorcism stories from non-Jewish sources of Greco-Roman antiquity

This section presents exorcism stories that belong to the ordinary world of Greco-Roman antiquity. The stories are grouped according to similarities in topic or content rather than by authorship. They are presented in movements with subheadings to help emphasize the particular features of each story. I shall only allude to similar Jesus miracles here. The collection of Jesus exorcisms will be presented in the last section of Chapter 5.

Parents Petition the Exorcism of Their Child

Apollonius of Tyana (circa 80–98 CE)

Apollonius of Tyana was an itinerant holy man, teacher and healer who was active especially in the Flavian period, 69–98 CE. We rely on his biography, *The Life of Apollonius of Tyana*, written by the third-century Neo-Pythagorean philosopher Philostratus, for the details of his life and activities. It has been argued that Philostratus fabricated these stories to contest the Christians. This argument deserves a

---

13 Papyrus Berolinensis 1.20. See R. Reitzenstein, *Hellenistische Wundererzählungen* (1st ed. 1906; repr. Darmstadt; Wissenschaftliche Buchgesellschaft, 1963), 125.

lengthy treatment for which there is no room here; however, the most obvious response is that there are too many embarrassing features about Apollonius' miracles for Neo-Pythagoreans to suggest that they were invented by the Neo-Pythagoreans.[14] But let us notice here that if they did copy the Jesus exorcisms, it is a clear signal that they did not recognize anything about the Jesus miracles that supported a cosmology as odd as apocalypticism.

A mother petitions for the exorcism of a soldier's ghost enamored of her son

2.13. Philostratus (b. 170 CE), *Life of Apollonius of Tyana* 3.38[15]

This discussion [Apollonius' response to his Indian hosts about the relation of the sea to the earth (chapter 37)] was interrupted by the appearance among the sages of the messenger bringing in certain Indians who were in want of succour. And he brought forward a poor woman who interceded in behalf of her child, who was, she said, a boy of sixteen years of age, but had been for two years possessed by a devil [*daimon*]. Now the character of the devil was that of a mocker and a liar. Here one of the sages asked, why she said this, and she replied: "This child of mine is extremely good-looking, and therefore the devil is amorous of him and will not allow him to retain his reason, nor will he permit him to go to school, or to learn archery, nor even to remain at home, but drives him out into desert places. And the boy does not even retain his own voice, but speaks in a deep hollow tone, as men do; and he looks at you with other eyes rather than with his own. As for myself I weep over all this, and I tear my cheeks, and I rebuke my son so far as I well may; but he does not know me. And I made up my mind to repair hither, indeed I planned to do so a year ago; only the demon discovered himself, using my child as a mask, and what he told me was this, that he was the ghost of a man, who fell long ago in battle, but that at death he was passionately attached to his wife. Now he had been dead for only three days when his wife insulted their union by marrying another man, and the consequence was that he had come to detest the love of women, and had transferred himself wholly into this boy. But he promised, if I would only not denounce him to yourselves, to endow the child with many noble blessings. As for myself, I was influenced by these promises; but he has put me off and off for such a long time now, that he has got sole

---

14 See the excellent contemporary treatment of Philostratus' *Life of Apollonius* in Jaap-Jan Flintermann's *Power, Paideia and Pythagoreanism: Greek Identity, Conceptions of the Relationship between Philosophers and Monarchs and Political Ideas in Philostratus' Life of Apollonius* (Amsterdam: J. C. Gieben, 1995).

15 All quotations are taken from Philostratus, *The Life of Apollonius of Tyana*, vol. 1 (trans. F. C. Conybeare; London: Heinemann, 1912), 3.38.

control of my household, yet has no honest or true intentions." Here the sage asked afresh, if the boy was at hand; and she said not, for, although she had done all she could to get him to come with her, the demon had threatened her with steep places and precipices and declared that he would kill her son, "in case," she added, "I haled him hither for trial." "Take courage," said the sage, "for he will not slay him when he has read this." And so saying he drew a letter out of his bosom and gave it to the woman; and the letter, it appears, was addressed to the ghost [*to eidolon*] and contained threats of an alarming kind.

Note

First, the term "daimon" is being used here for a spirit who does evil, thus supporting Plutarch's view that daimons can be either good or evil. Second, the daimon robs the person of his reason, and drives him away from family to a desert place. Third, the daimon reveals that he is really the ghost of a dead soldier who is angry and embittered since his wife was eager to find another man to marry. So here the daimon does not belong to some special creation apart from the human but represents the idea of the dead becoming spirits to do damage to the living.

Appollonius deals with the daimon as he would with an outrageous human who threatens another. A letter of threat is sent to warn off the ghost.

(Compare Mark 9:14–29 (Matt. 17:14–21; Luke 9:37–43) and Mark 7: 24–30 (Matt. 15:21–28.)

The Exorcism of Daimons who Cause their Victims to Harm Themselves

Apollonius of Tyana

A ghost hides and leads a young man into excessive behavior

2.14. He No Longer Showed Himself Licentious, nor Did He Stare Madly About, but He Had Returned to His Own Self, as Thoroughly as if He had been Treated by Drugs

Philostratus, *Life of Apollonius of Tyana* 4.20

Now while he was discussing the question of libations, there chanced to be present in his audience a young dandy who bore so evil a reputation for licentiousness, that his conduct had long been the subject of coarse street-corner songs. His home was Corcyra, and he traced his pedigree to Alcinous the Phaeacian who entertained Odysseus. Apollonius then was talking about libations, and was urging them not to drink out of a particular cup, but to reserve it for the gods, without ever touching it or drinking out of it. But when he also urged them to have handles on the cup, and to pour the libation over the handle, because that is the part of the cup at which men are least likely to drink, the youth burst out into loud and coarse laughter, and quite drowned his voice. Then Apollonius looked up at him and said: "It is not yourself that perpetrates this insult, but the demon [*ho daimon*] who drives you on without your knowing it." And in fact the youth was, without knowing it, possessed by a devil [*daimonion*]; for he would laugh at things that no one else laughed at, and then he would fall to weeping for no reason at all, and he would talk and sing to himself. Now most people thought that it was the boisterous humour of youth which led him into such excesses; but he was really the mouthpiece of a devil [*to daimonion*], though it only seemed a drunken frolic in which on that occasion he was indulging. Now when Apollonius gazed on him, the ghost [*to eidolon*] in him began to utter cries of fear and rage, such as one hears from people who are being branded or racked; and the ghost swore that he would leave the young man alone and never take possession of any men again. But Apollonius addressed him with anger, as a master might a shifty, rascally, and shameless slave and so on, and he ordered him to quit the young man and show by a visible sign that he had done so. "I will throw down yonder statue," said the devil, and pointed to one of the images which were in the king's portico, for there it was that the scene took place. But when the statue began by moving gently, and then fell down, it would defy anyone to describe the hubbub which arose thereat and the way they clapped their hands with wonder. But the young man rubbed his eyes as if he had just woke up, and he looked towards the rays of the sun, and assumed a modest aspect, as all had their attention concentrated on him; for he no longer showed himself licentious, nor did he stare madly about, but he had returned to his own self, as thoroughly as if he had been treated with drugs; and he gave up his dainty dress and summery garments and the rest of his sybaritic way of life, and he fell in love with the austerity of philosophers, and donned their cloak, and stripping off his old self modelled his life in future upon that of Apollonius.

Note

The young man causes consternation among those who know him by his excessive emotions. Here the narrator knows the portrait of daimons as given to great passionate outbursts and also violence. The visual sign that the daimon has gone shows the crowd that the man is well. As for the young man, he gives evidence that he is free of the daimon by his embrace of the life of philosophy. In this exorcism, Apollonius displays his heroism in rescuing this young man from disastrous slavery to this daimon.

(Compare Mark 5:1–20.)

Apollonius of Tyana dispels an "empusa" (a hobgoblin)

2.15. Apollonius Realized What it Was, and Himself Heaped Abuse on the Hobgoblin and Instructed His Party to Do the Same, Saying that This Was the Right Remedy for Such a Visitation. And the Phantasm Fled Away Shrieking Even as Ghosts Do

Philostratus, *Life of Apollonius of Tyana* 2.4

Having passed the Caucasus our travellers (Apollonius and his party) say they saw men four cubits high, and that they were already black, and that when they passed over the river Indus they saw others five cubits high. But on their way to this river our wayfarers found the following incidents worthy of notice. For they were travelling by bright moonlight, when the figure of an empusa or hobgoblin appeared to them, that changed from one form into another, and sometimes it vanished into nothing. And Apollonius realised what it was, and himself heaped abuse on the hobgoblin and instructed his party to do the same, saying that this was the right remedy for such a visitation. And the phantasm fled away shrieking even as ghosts do.

Apollonius of Tyana exorcizes an empusa who was disguised as a beautiful woman

2.16. This is the Best-Known Story of Apollonius; for Many People are Aware of It and Know that the Incident Occurred in the Centre of Hellas

Philostratus: *Life of Apollonius of Tyana* 4.25

Now there was in Corinth at that time a man named Demetrius who studied philosophy and had embraced in his system all the masculine vigour of the Cynics. Of him Favorinus in several of his own works subsequently made the most generous mention, and his attitude towards Apollonius was exactly that which they say Antisthenes took up towards the system of Socrates; for he followed him and was anxious to be his disciple, and was devoted to his doctrines, and converted to the side of Apollonius the more esteemed of his own pupils. Among the latter was Menippus a Lycian of twenty-five years of age, well endowed with good judgement, and of a physique so beautifully proportioned that in mien he resembled a fine and gentlemanly athlete. Now this Menippus was supposed by most people to be loved by a foreign woman, who was good-looking and extremely dainty, and said that she was rich; although she was really, as it turned out, none of these things, but was only so in semblance. For as he was walking all alone along the road towards Cenchreae, he met with an apparition, and it was a woman who clasped his hand and declared that she had been long in love with him, and that she was a Phoenician woman and lived in a suburb of Corinth, and she mentioned the name of the particular suburb, and said: "When you reach the place this evening, you will hear my voice as I sing to you, and you shall have wine such as you never before drank, and there will be no rival to disturb you; and we two beautiful beings will live together." The youth consented to this, for although he was in general a strenuous philosopher, he was nevertheless susceptible to the tender passion; and he visited her in the evening, and for the future constantly sought her company as his darling, for he did not yet realise that she was a mere apparition.

Then, Apollonius looked over Menippus as a sculptor might do, and sketched an outline of the youth and examined him, and having observed his foibles, he said: "You are a fine youth and are hunted by fine women, but in this case you are cherishing a serpent, and a serpent cherishes you." And when Menippus expressed his surprise, he added: "For this lady is of a kind you cannot marry. Why should you? Do you think that she loves you?" "Indeed I do," said the youth, "since she behaves to me as if she loves me." "And would you then marry her?" said Apollonius. "Why, yes, for it would be delightful to marry a woman who loves you." Thereupon Apollonius asked when the wedding was to be. "Perhaps to-morrow," said the other, "for it brooks no delay." Apollonius therefore waited for the occasion of the wedding breakfast, and then, presenting himself before the guests who had just arrived, he said: "Where is the dainty lady at whose instance ye are come?" "Here she is," replied Menippus, and at the same moment he rose slightly from his seat, blushing. "And to which of you belong the silver and gold and all the rest of the decorations of the banqueting hall?" "To the lady," replied the youth, "for this is all I have of my own," pointing to the philosopher's cloak which he wore.

And Apollonius said: "Have you heard of the gardens of Tantalus, how they exist and yet do not exist?" "Yes," they answered, "in the poems of Homer, for we certainly never went down to Hades." "As such," replied Apollonius, "you must regard this adornment, for it is not reality but the semblance of reality. And that you may realise the truth of what I say, this fine bride is one of the vampires, that is to say of those beings whom the many regard as lamias and hobgoblins. These beings fall in love, and they are devoted to the delights of Aphrodite, but especially to the flesh of human beings, and they decoy with such delights those whom they mean to devour in their feasts." And the lady said: "Cease your ill-omened talk and begone"; and she pretended to be disgusted at what she heard, and no doubt she was inclined to rail at philosophers and say that they always talked nonsense. When, however, the goblets of gold and the show of silver were proved as light as air and all fluttered away out of their sight, while the winebearers and the cooks and all the retinue of servants vanished before the rebukes of Apollonius, the phantom pretended to weep, and prayed him not to torture her nor to compel her to confess what she really was. But Apollonius insisted and would not let her off, and then she admitted that she was a vampire, and was fattening up Menippus with pleasures before devouring his body, for it was her habit to feed upon young and beautiful bodies, because their blood is pure and strong. I have related at length, because it was necessary to do so, *this is the best-known story of Apollonius*;[16] for many people are aware of it and know that the incident occurred in the centre of Hellas; but they have only heard in a general and vague manner that he once caught and overcame a *lamia* in Corinth, but they have never learned what she was about, nor that he did it to save Menippus, but I owe my own account to Damis and to the work which he wrote.

Note

Damis is supposed to have been a disciple of Apollonius, but scholars conclude that there is little evidence for his actual historical existence. Nevertheless, the stories seem to have been passed along for centuries!

THE NATURE AND IDENTITY
OF DAIMONS/DEMONS IN THE
NON-APOCALYPTIC JEWISH WRITINGS
OF THE IMPERIAL PERIOD

Since Jewish observance usually bases itself on an interpretation of scripture, this section will open with two texts from the Septuagint that deal with the demons: Gen. 6:1–4 and Tobit 6:1–8:9. Then certain texts will be presented from Jewish sources of the Greco-Roman period that treat the nature and role of daimons/demons, including extracts from Philo, Josephus and the Mishnah. Following this will be two accounts of demon expulsion, one from the Genesis Apocryphon and the other from Josephus.

16 My italic.

Scripture

The sons of God unite with human women who give birth to the giants

2.17. The Sons of God Went in to the Daughters of Humans, who Bore Children to Them. These were the Heroes that were of Old, Warriors of Renown

Gen. 6:1–4

1. When people began to multiply on the face of the ground, and daughters were born to them, 2. the sons of God saw that they were fair; and they took wives for themselves of all they chose. 3. Then the Lord said, "My spirit shall not abide in mortals forever, for they are flesh; their days shall be one hundred twenty years." 4. The Nephilim were on the earth in those days – and also afterward – when the sons of God went in to the daughters of humans, who bore children to them. These were the heroes that were of old, warriors of renown.

Note

The half-breeds mentioned in these scriptures are not daimons/ demons, but the story's mention of "sons of God" in the monotheistic context of Hellenistic Judaism opened the door to the idea that certain creatures exist between the human and the one God. We shall see that this text will form a foundation for apocalyptic texts to be presented in the first section of Chapter 5.

Tobit exorcizes the demon who has killed the seven former husbands of his new wife

2.18.1. An Angel Raphael Instructs Tobias that Smoked Fish Heart and Liver will Exorcize a Demon

Tobit 6:1–9

1. The young man [Tobias] went out and the angel went with him; 2. and the dog came out with him and went along with them. So they both journeyed along, and when the first night overtook them they camped by the Tigris river. 3. Then the young man went down to wash his feet in the Tigris river. Suddenly a large fish leaped up from the water and tried to swallow the young man's foot, and he cried out. 4. But the angel said to the young man, "Catch hold of the fish and hang on to it!" So the young man grasped the fish and drew it up on the land. 5. Then the angel said to him, "Cut open the fish and take out its gall, heart, and liver. Keep them with you, but throw away the intestines. For its gall, heart, and liver are useful as medicine." 6. So after cutting open the fish the young man gath-

ered together the gall, heart, and liver; then he roasted and ate some of the fish, and kept some to be salted. The two continued on their way together until they were near Media. *7.* Then the young man questioned the angel and said to him, "Brother Azariah, what medicinal value is there in the fish's heart and liver, and in the gall?" *8.* He replied, "As for the fish's heart and liver, you must burn them to make a smoke in the presence of a man or woman afflicted by a demon or evil spirit, and every affliction will flee away and never remain with that person any longer. *9.* And as for the gall, anoint a person's eyes where white films have appeared on them; blow upon them, upon the white films, and the eyes will be healed."

2.18.2. Raphael Instructs Tobias How to Exorcize the Demon who Killed His Betrothed's Seven Husbands

Tobit 6:10–18

10. When he entered Media and already was approaching Ecbatana, *11.* Raphael [the angel] said to the young man, "Brother Tobias." "Here I am," he answered. Then Raphael said to him, "We must stay this night in the home of Raguel. He is your relative, and he has a daughter named Sarah. *12.* He has no male heir and no daughter except Sarah only, and you, as next of kin to her, have before all other men a hereditary claim on her. Also it is right for you to inherit her father's possessions. Moreover, the girl is sensible, brave, and very beautiful, and her father is a good man." *13.* He continued, "You have every right to take her in marriage. So listen to me, brother; tonight I will speak to her father about the girl, so that we may take her to be your bride. When we return from Rages we will celebrate her marriage. For I know that Raguel can by no means keep her from you or promise her to another man without incurring the penalty of death according to the decree of the book of Moses. . . .

14. Then Tobias said in answer to Raphael, "Brother Azariah, I have heard that she already has been married to seven husbands and that they died in the bridal chamber. On the night when they went in to her, they would die. I have heard people saying that it was a demon that killed them. *15.* It does not harm her, but it kills anyone who desires to approach her. So now, since I am the only son my father has, I am afraid that I may die and bring my father's and mother's life down to their grave, grieving for me – and they have no other son to bury them."

16. But Raphael said to him, "Do you not remember your father's orders when he commanded you to take a wife from your father's house? Now listen to me, brother, and say no more about this demon. Take her. I know that this very night she will be given to you in marriage. *17.* When you enter the bridal chamber, take some of the fish's liver and heart, and put them on the embers of the incense. An odor will be given off; *18.* the demon will smell it and flee, and will never be seen near her any more. Now when you are about to go to bed with her, both of you must first stand up and pray, imploring the Lord of heaven that mercy and safety may be granted to you.

Do not be afraid, for she was set apart for you before the world was made. You will save her, and she will go with you. I presume that you will have children by her, and they will be as brothers to you. Now say no more!" When Tobias heard the words of Raphael and learned that she was his kinswoman, related through his father's lineage, he loved her very much, and his heart was drawn to her.

[The marriage is proposed, and the contract is written out and sealed and a dinner is prepared [Tobit 7:9–15].

2.18.3. Tobias Obediently Follows Raphael's Instructions

Tobit 7:15–8:9

15. Raguel called his wife Edna and said to her, "Sister, get the other room ready, and take her there." 16. So she went and made the bed in the room as he had told her, and brought Sarah there. She wept for her daughter. Then, wiping away the tears, she said to her, "Take courage, my daughter; the Lord of heaven grant you joy in place of your sorrow. Take courage, my daughter." Then she went out.
8:1. When they had finished eating and drinking they wanted to retire; so they took the young man and brought him into the bedroom. 2. Then Tobias remembered the words of Raphael and he took the fish's liver and heart out of the bag where he had them and put them on the embers of the incense. 3. The odor of the fish so repelled the demon that he fled to the remotest parts of Egypt. But Raphael followed him, and at once bound him there hand and foot.

4. When the parents had gone out and shut the door of the room, Tobias got out of bed and said to Sarah, "Sister, get up, and let us pray and implore our Lord that he grant us mercy and safety." 5. So she got up, and they bagan to pray and implore that they might be kept safe. Tobias began by saying,
"Blessed are you, O God of our ancestors,
and blessed is your name in all generations forever.
Let the heavens and the whole creation bless you forever.
6. You made Adam, and for him you made his wife Eve as a helper and support.
From the two of them the human race has sprung.
You said, 'It is not good that the man should be alone;
let us make a helper for him like himself.'
7. I now am taking this kinswoman of mine, not because of lust, but with sincerity. Grant that she and I may find mercy and that we may grow old together."
8. And they both said, "Amen, Amen." 9. Then they went to sleep for the night.

Note

When we compare the evidence of the ideas about demons in this account with the sort of concepts we find in Plutarch and in the exorcism stories of Apollonius, one noticeable difference is in the clear and separate category given to the angels. In Plutarch's treatment, good and evil are both called daimons, as we have seen. In this account, the angels seem to belong to a special group and their names plainly identify them as messengers. In fact the angel Raphael could be an embodiment of the good daimons in Plutarch. He serves God, acting as a messenger, a unifier and a prophet in oracles. In this story the good "daimon" Raphael acts as an oracle to the obedient Tobit against the bad "daimon." A second important difference is the explicit demand for prayer. It is not the technique alone that will ensure the expulsion of the demon, but the technique accompanied by a sincere appeal to "the merciful God."

Philo (30 BCE – 45 CE)

The perspective of Philo is not as easily represented since there are developments of his own thought concerning daimons throughout his scholarly career, as shown by Frederick Brenk.[17] His summary of these three stages states:[18]

> Philo's daimonology can be divided into three different parts, probably corresponding to the date of his writings and the development of his thought. In the first he would envisage the angels as *daimones-psychai* filling up the air, and essentially incorporeal human souls.[19] The second mode of thought seems to be a transition in which the angels are spoken of as *daimones-psychai*, but also are *logoi*.[20] Finally in the third part or period, the angels are simply *logoi*, i.e. good thoughts, or inspirations – a rather bold leap from

17 For his treatment of Philo in particular, see Brenk, "Demonology in the Early Imperial Period," esp. 2098–2107.
18 Brenk, "Demonology in the Early Imperial Period," 2101.
19 This first phase is represented in: " 'On the Creation of the World,' the lives of the patriarchs to the life of Moses, and the works on the ten commandments, ending with 'Rewards and Punishments' " (ibid., 2101).
20 This stage is represented by *On the Giants* 6–24 (Brenk, "Demonology in the Early Imperial Period," 2102).

traditional daimonology in which at best the *daimones* would give good thoughts or inspirations.[21]

Philo's treatment of Gen. 6:1–4, *On the Giants*, belongs to the second mode of thought according to this chronology. It is of special interest, of course, because it addresses the very text by which the idea of daimons as a separate hybrid species seeks the credibility of scriptural support. But for Philo, this myth is to be seen in a symbolic way, the heavenly souls descending into a bodily life of fleshly concerns. In no way will he understand the offspring of this "union" in a literal way. Rather, the text is a lever for him to correct all those who are afraid of such imaginary creatures. Notice that Philo's interpretation does not necessitate a commentary on Genesis 1 and 2 to explain the subsequent creation of hybrid creatures after humankind. Philo claims that the air produces souls as naturally as all the other elements give birth to creatures appropriate to their environment. These souls may remain in heaven, where they are consecrated, or may descend into humanity, but do not mutate into a hybrid species, foreign to both angels and humans.

2.19.1. Some Souls Descend into Bodies and Some Become Consecrated for the Service of God. These Earthly Souls can become Immersed in Superficial Concerns or Soar to Heaven through Philosophy

Philo, *On the Giants* 12–15[22]
Now some of the souls have descended into bodies, but others have never deigned to be brought into union with any of the parts of the earth. They are consecrated and devoted to the service of the Father and Creator whose wont it is to employ them as ministers and helpers, to have charge and care of mortal man. But the others descending into the body as though

---

21 For example, *On Dreams* 1.134 and 141–142. "[These texts] contain a number of motifs: the fall of souls into bodies through corporeal attraction – with imagery similar to that of Plato's 'Phaidros' and 'Symposion,' the mediating function of the *daimones* from Plato's 'Symposion' (Plato's middle period, and elements more from Plato's later period – the natural place of different beings, and the incorporation of *logoi* into the *kosmos*. Built into the Old Testament framework of Jacob's ladder, *nous* is at the top and matter (earth) at the bottom of the *kosmos* (1.134–135)" (Brenk, "Demonology in the Early Imperial Period," 2103).

22 All quotations are taken from Philo, *On the Giants*, *Philo*, vol. 2 (trans. F. H. Colson and G. H. Whitaker; London: Heinemann, 1929).

into a stream have sometimes been caught in the swirl of its rushing torrent and swallowed up thereby, at other times have been able to stem the current, have risen to the surface and then soared upwards back to the place from whence they came. These last, then, are the souls of those who have given themselves to genuine philosophy, who from first to last study to die to the life in the body, that a higher existence immortal and incorporeal, in the presence of Him who is Himself immortal and uncreate, may be their portion. But the souls which have sunk beneath the stream, are the souls of the others who have held no count of wisdom. They have abandoned themselves to the unstable things of chance, none of which has aught to do with our noblest part, the soul or mind, but all are related to that dead thing which was our birth-fellow, the body, or to objects more lifeless still, glory, wealth, and offices, and honours, and all other illusions which like images or pictures are created through the deceit of false opinion by those who have never gazed upon true beauty.

2.19.2. It is a Superstitious Idea to Imagine that Bad Daimons are a Special Species Distinct from Good Daimons. The Difference between Them is in Unfaithfulness to a Previous Divine Consecration, Not a Difference in Species

Philo, *On the Giants* 16

So if you realize that souls and demons [*daimonas*] and angels are but different names for the same one underlying object, you will cast from you that most grievous burden, the fear of demons or superstition. The common usage of men is to give the name of demon [*daimonas*] to bad and good demons alike, and the name of soul [*psychas*] to good and bad souls. And so, too, you also will not go wrong if you reckon as angels, not only those who are worthy of the name, who are as ambassadors backwards and forwards between men and God and are rendered sacred and inviolate by reason of that glorious and blameless ministry, but also those who are unholy and unworthy of the title.

Note

The contribution that both Josephus and Philo bring to our efforts to reconstruct ideas available to people living in Greco-Roman antiquity is that spirits are to be expected just as surely as one knows of the existence of air or wind. Second, these creatures are intelligent and make choices, rather than being by nature only capable of good or only capable of evil. Third, the soul within a person longs for spiritual life and one must beware of sinking into the mire of the physical.

Josephus 70–90 CE

Everett Ferguson's *Demonology of the Early Christian World* notes that Josephus shows his concurrence with the general views of the Greco-Roman world with regard to his use of "daimon."[23] He employs it in reference to "the Deity" or divine power,[24] for destiny including the force that brings misfortune,[25] and for an evil demon.[26] Ferguson astutely notes that when Josephus stipulates a good force he will add the adjective "good" to "daimon."[27]

The so-called demons are spirits of wicked men

2.20. The Root of the Plant Baaras is Used to Expel Demons

Josephus, *Jewish War* 7.181–182, 185[28]
Flame-coloured and towards evening emitting a brilliant light, it [the plant Baaras] eludes the grasp of persons who approach with the intention of plucking it, as it shrinks up and can only be made to stand still by pouring upon it certain secretions of the human body. Yet even then to touch it is fatal, unless one succeeds in carrying off the root itself, suspended from the hand. . . . With all these attendant risks, it possesses one virtue for which it is prized; for the so-called demons – in other words, the spirits of wicked men which enter the living and kill them unless aid is forthcoming – are promptly expelled by this root, if merely applied to the patients.

King Solomon's gift of exorcism

2.21. And God Granted him [Solomon] Knowledge of the Art Used Against Demons (*Daimonion*) for the Benefit and Healing of People

Josephus, *Jewish Antiquities* 8.44–45[29]
There was no form of nature with which he [King Solomon] was not acquainted or which he passed over without examining, but he studied them all philosophically and revealed the most complete knowledge of their

---

23 I am indebted to Ferguson for the sources from Josephus in the review of his various uses of "daimon" in this paragraph. See his p. 85.
24 Josephus, *The Jewish War* 1.69 ("Let heaven cease to mock").
25 Ibid., 1.233.
26 Ibid., 1.613.
27 Josephus, *Jewish Antiquities* 16.20.
28 Josephus, *The Jewish War, Josephus*, vol. 3 (trans. H. St. J. Thackeray; London: Heinemann, 1928), 7.181–182, 185.
29 Josephus, *Jewish Antiquities, Josephus*, vol. 5 (trans. H. St. J. Thackeray and Ralph Marcus; London: Heinemann, 1934), 8.44–45.

several properties. And God granted him knowledge of the art used against demons [*daimonion*] for the benefit and healing of men. He also composed incantations by which illnesses are relieved, and left behind forms of exorcisms with which those possessed by demons drive them out, never to return.

Note: Three concepts about the nature and identity of daimons/demons

1. Successful exorcism is joined to erudition. Josephus claims that Solomon had probed the understanding of the phenomenon of possession "philosophically." God grants "knowledge of the art." The association of exorcism with specialized study backs up Plutarch's scholarly discussion of the nature of daimons within the larger cosmology. This underlines the fact that one may not assume that possession and exorcism were universally regarded as superstitious and low-class by men of letters in antiquity.
2. Josephus explains exorcism as a type of "healing." This means that when exorcisms occur in the Christian material, they cannot be assumed to imply the beginning of Satan's downfall or of an imminent Endtime.
3. Successful exorcisms require the knowledge of efficacious "forms" so that the daimons/demons do not return. The notion that Solomon left this legacy provides an honorable context for the exorcism stories attached to important Jewish figures. Thus, any hint of "magic" in a pejorative sense is dispelled.

Mishnah (codified 190 CE) and the Nature and Identity of Evil Spirits

The completion of the codification of the Mishnah has been dated about 190 CE and therefore postdates New Testament material. Even though the codification was to assist emerging rabbinic orientations, much of the Mishnah is recognized to have existed well in advance of the second century!

There are three passages in the Mishnah that assume the existence of demons: Pirke Aboth (5.6); Shabbath (2.5); and Erubin (4.1).

2.22. The Evil Spirits were Created on the Eve of the Sabbath

Pirke Aboth 5.6[30]

Ten things were created on the eve of the Sabbath between the suns at nightfall: the mouth of the earth, the mouth of the well, the mouth of the she-ass, the rainbow, and the manna and the rod and the Shamir, the letters and the writing and the Tables [of stone]. Some say also: The evil spirits and the sepulchre of Moses and the ram of Abraham our father. Some say also: The tongs made with tongs.

2.23. Because Evil Spirits are Attracted to a Light, the Sabbath Lamp may be Extinguished if One Fears an Evil Spirit is Near

Shabbath 2.5[31]

If a man put out the lamp [on the night of the Sabbath] from fear of the gentiles or of thieves or of an evil spirit, or to suffer one that was sick to sleep, he is not culpable; [but if he did it with a mind] to spare the lamp or to spare the oil or to spare the wick, he is culpable. But R. Jose declares him exempt in every case excepting that of the wick, since he thereby forms charcoal.[32]

2.24. Evil Spirits have Power to Transport a Person from One Place to Another

Erubin 4.1[33]

If a man was taken out [beyond the Sabbath limit] by gentiles or an evil spirit, he may only move within four cubits. If they brought him back again it is as though he had never gone out. If they brought him to another town, or set him in a cattle-pen or a cattle-fold, Rabban Gamaliel and R. Eleazar b. Azariah say: He may traverse their whole [area]; but R. Joshua and R. Akiba say: He may only move within four cubits. It happened when they came from Brundisium and when their ship was sailing in the sea that Rabban Gamaliel and R. Eleazar b. Azariah walked the whole length of the ship, but R. Joshua and R. Akiba did not stir beyond four cubits, since they were minded to apply to themselves the more stringent ruling.

---

30 Herbert Danby, *The Mishnah* (London; Oxford University Press, 1933, repr, 1964), 456.

31 Ibid., 102.

32 The note in Danby explains that the person is therefore "working" by making a product, like charcoal (ibid., 102, n. 5).

33 Ibid., 126.

Note

These three texts, then, signal some common traditions about the nature and character of the demons such as we have seen in the non-Jewish texts. Pirke Aboth 5.6 shows that some Jewish communities do regard evil spirits as a hybrid species rather than the singular pure beings, the "angels" or "souls" of Philo. Sabbath and Erubin suggest that living with demons is as possible a danger as living subject to gentiles. When we find Torah prescriptions that deal with observance in the face of gentile or demon interference, we have a sign that the community expects both gentiles and demons to feature in ordinary life.

What we do not find is any evidence that the community sees these demons as the lackeys of any great identifiable demon Lord such as Beelzebul or Belial. Nor is there a reference to the coming End when these demons will be punished by God's avenging angels. In other words the apocalyptic themes and expectations do not seem to be present in the treatment of demonic interference with ordinary Jewish life. Rather, the sense of the demon as a creature of the liminal space between the divine and the human, and capable of bringing grief to humans, is what we find, as we do in the speech of Plutarch's Cleombrotis. So, in this way, the Mishnah reflects the more general ideas of daimons/demons in the Greco-Roman world rather than echoing the organization of demonic and angelic armies and the organization of time that we find so prominently in apocalyptic documents.

Evil spirit/demon stories from Jewish sources in Greco-Roman antiquity

Qumran documents: the Genesis Apocryphon[34]

The title of this scroll is a modern scholarly attempt to describe its contents as "a little Genesis." J. C. Trevor notes its relation to Jubilees in character and content. Here the legends of the Patriarch's are given high color and vivid portrayal. The text has been dated within the period 50 BCE–70 CE. It is column 20, a retelling of Gen. 12:10–20, which holds a reference to the expulsion of a demon

---

34 See the complete treatment of the document in Joseph A. Fitzmyer, *The Genesis Apocryphon of Qumran Cave 1: A Commentary* (Biblica et Orientalia 18A; 2nd (ed.) revised; Rome: Biblical Institute Press, 1971).

by Abram. It is through this story that we shall infer concepts about the nature and identity of demons held by the community from which the document came.

[2.25. Genesis 12:10–20

10. Now there was a famine in the land. So Abram went down to Egypt to reside there as an alien, for the famine was severe in the land. *11.* When he was about to enter Egypt, he said to his wife Sarai, "I know well that you are a woman beautiful in appearance; *12.* and when the Egyptians see you, they will say, 'This is his wife'; then they will kill me, but they will let you live. *13.* Say you are my sister, that it may go well with me because of you, and that my life may be spared on your account." *14.* When Abram entered Egypt the Egyptians saw that the woman was very beautiful. *15.* When the officials of Pharaoh saw her, they praised her to Pharaoh. And the woman was taken into Pharaoh's house. *16.* And for her sake he dealt well with Abram; and he had sheep, oxen, male donkeys, male and female slaves, female donkeys, and camels.

17. But the Lord afflicted Pharaoh and his house with great plagues because of Sarai, Abram's wife. *18.* So Pharaoh called Abram, and said, "What is this you have done to me? Why did you not tell me that she was your wife? *19.* Why did you say, 'She is my sister,' so that I took her for my wife? Now then, here is your wife, take her, and be gone." *20.* And Pharaoh gave men orders concerning him; and they set him on the way, with his wife and all that he had.]

2.26.1. Having Lied to Pharaoh that Sarah is his Sister, Abram Calls on God to Prevent Pharaoh from Having Relations with her

Genesis Apocryphon 20:8–16[35]

[vv. 2–7: the beauty of Sarah is praised by the Pharaoh's servants]
v. 8 When the king heard the words of Hirqanos and the words of his two companions – for the three of them spoke as one man – he coveted her very much. He sent off (v. 9) in haste (and) had her brought (to him). When he beheld her, he marvelled at all her beauty and took her to himself as a wife. He sought to kill me [Abram], but Sarai said (v. 10) to the king, "He is my brother," so that I might be benefitted by her. And I,

---

35 "Square bracket [] in the translation indicate lacunae in the Aramaic text. Material so enclosed is subject to various degrees of conjecture; see the notes for comments.

Parentheses () enclose matter added for the sake of the sense of the English translation. . . . Italics indicate a literal Aramaic translation of the Hebrew text of Genesis," Fitzmyer, *Genesis Apocryphon*, 49, n. 1.

Abram, was spared because of her. I was not killed but I wept (v. 11) bitterly – I, Abram, and Lot, my nephew, with me – on the night when Sarai was taken away from me by force. (v. 12) That night I prayed, I entreated, and I asked for mercy; in (my) sorrow I said, as my tears ran down (my cheeks), "Blessed (are) you, O God Most High, my Lord, for all (v. 13) ages! For you are Lord and Master over all, and have power to mete out justice to all the kings of the earth. Now (v. 14) I lodge my complaint with you my Lord, against the Pharaoh Zoan, the king of Egypt, because my wife has been taken away from me by force. Mete out justice to him for me and show forth your great hand (v. 15) against him and against all his house. May he not be able to defile my wife tonight – that it may be known about you, my Lord, that you are the Lord of all the kings of (v. 16) the earth." And I wept and talked to no one.

2.26.2. The Lord Sends a "Pestilential Spirit" to Afflict Pharaoh and All the Men of his Household for the Next Two Years

Genesis Apocryphon 20:6–18
(But) that night God Most High sent him a pestilential spirit to *afflict him* and all the men of *his household*, an evil spirit (v. 17) that kept afflicting him and all the men of his household. He was not able to approach her, nor did he have intercourse with her, though he was with her (?) (v. 18) for two years. At the end of two years the plagues and afflictions became more severe and more intense for him and all the men of his household.

2.26.3. When Pharaoh Calls on All the Wise Men, Physicians, Magicians to Cure him, and the Spirit Afflicts them too, he Turns to Abram as he has been Led to Do by a Dream

Genesis Apocryphon 20:19–22
So he sent (v. 19) for all the [wise men] of Egypt, all the magicians and all the physicians of Egypt, (to see) if they could cure him of this plague, and the men (v. 20) of his household. But none of the physicians, the magicians, nor any of the wise men were able to rise up and cure him, for the spirit afflicted all of them (too), (v. 21) and they fled. Then Hirqanos came to me and begged me to come and pray over (v. 22) the king and lay my hands upon him that he might be cured, for [he had seen me] in a dream.

2.26.4. When Lot Explains that Abram Cannot Pray for Pharaoh while Abram's Wife is Still with Him, Pharaoh Upbraids Abram for His Lie and Gives Her to Abram

Genesis Apocryphon 20:23–28:

But Lot said to him, "Abram, my uncle, cannot pray for (v. 23) the king, while his wife Sarai is with him. Now go, tell the king that he should send his wife away from him, (back) to her own husband. Then he (Abram) will pray for him that he might be cured." v. 24. When Hirqanos heard Lot's words, he went (and) said to the king, "All these plagues and afflictions with which my lord, the king, is beset and afflicted (are) due to Sarai, the wife of Abram. Let Sarai be returned to her husband, Abram, (v. 26) and this plague will depart from you, as well as the spirit of purulence." So he (the Pharaoh) summoned me to him and said to me, "What have you done to me for [Sar]ai's sake, in telling me, 'She is my sister,' when she was (really) your wife? And I took her to be my wife. Here is your wife; take her away; go, depart from (v. 28) all the provinces of Egypt. But now pray for me and for my household that this evil spirit may be commanded (to depart) from us."

2.26.5. Abram Lays Hands on Pharaoh's Head and the Evil Spirit is Commanded to Depart

Genesis Apocryphon 20:29–34

So I prayed for that [   ] . . . , (v. 29) and I laid my hands upon his [he]ad. The plague was removed from him and the evil [spirit] was commanded (to depart) [from him], and he was cured. And the king rose (and) [made] known (v. 30) to me [   ]; and the king swore an oath to me that [he had] not [touched her?]. And then [they brought] (v. 31) Sarai to [me]. The king gave her [mu]ch [silver and go]ld; many garments of fine linen and purple [. . . and he laid them] (v. 32) before her, and Hagar too. H[e hand]ed her over to me, and appointed men to escort me [out of Egypt . . .]. (v. 33) So I, *Abram*, went (forth) *with very many flocks* and *with silver and gold* too, and I *went up from {Egy}pt*. [Lot], my brother's son, (was) *with* me, and *Lot too* (had) acquired many flocks; he had taken for himself a wife from the daughters [of Egypt].

Note

In this story, the evil spirit is not presented as a being who is rebellious to God but rather, one obedient to his commands. It is not a ghost but a separate spiritual being meant to serve God. In this way the ideas cohere with those of Plutarch, who sees daimons as capable of good or evil. In this case the evil spirit fulfills the role of meting out justice on God's behalf. While the evil spirit brings trouble to Pharaoh and his servants, his service is a help to Abram. Thus the "evil" description is really relative to the situation and the people involved.

Notice that just as the demon is sent by God, so too he is commanded to leave by God. Thus, although Abram is said to lay hands on Pharaoh, it is clear that the narrator does not want it understood that Abram exerts direct authority over the demon.[36] His laying on of hands becomes part of his sincere prayer to God so that the demon is ordered to depart.

Josephus

King Saul is exorcized from his demons by David

2.27. And Against that Trouble Caused by the Evil Spirits, Whensoever They Assailed Him, He had No Other Physician than David, Who, by Singing His Songs and Playing Upon the Harp, Restored Saul to Himself

Josephus: *Antiquities of the Jews* 6.166–169[37]

So after these exhortations [to the youth David], Samuel went his way, and the Deity abandoned Saul and passed over to David, who when the divine spirit had removed to him, began to prophesy. But as for Saul, he was beset by strange disorders and evil spirits [*ta daimonia*] which caused him such suffocation and strangling that the physicians could devise no other remedy save to order search to be made for one with power to charm away spirits and to play upon the harp, and, whensoever the evil spirits should assail and torment Saul, to have him stand over the king and strike the strings and chant his songs. Saul did not neglect this advice, but ordered search to be made for such a man. And when one of those present said that he had seen in the city of Bethlehem a son of Jesse, a mere boy in years, but of pleasing and fair appearance and in other ways worthy of regard, who was, moreover, skilled in playing on the harp and in the

---

36 Fitzmyer's commentary, *Genesis Apocryphon* (pp. 140–141), provides a discussion of the laying on of hands in exorcisms. We must note here, however, that such an action in this story is followed by the statement that the spirit "was commanded to depart." This use of the passive, as we know, means that it is God who commanded the demon to leave. That is to say, in this version, the laying on of hands becomes part of Abram's sincere prayer for Pharaoh, and not the authoritative act of other exorcists in taking authority over the demon in a personal way.

37 *Josephus*, vol. 5 (trans. Thackeray and Marcus), 6.1.166–169.

singing of songs, and an excellent soldier, Saul sent to Jesse and ordered him to take David from the flocks and send him to him; he wished, he said, to see the young man, having heard of his comeliness and valour. So Jesse sent his son, also giving him presents to carry to Saul. When he came, Saul was delighted with him, made him his armour-bearer and held him in the highest honour, for his illness was charmed away by him; and against that trouble caused by the evil spirits, whensoever they assailed him, he had no other physician than David, who, by singing his songs and playing upon the harp, restored Saul to himself. He accordingly sent to Jesse, the lad's father, desiring him to leave David with him, since the sight of the boy and his presence gave him pleasure. Jesse would not gainsay Saul, but permitted him to keep David.

Note

Here, Josephus represents the story of David bringing peace of mind as a kind of constant exorcism by his powerful "charm." The method is just to sing songs and play the harp – no incantations or spells. The singing and playing is sufficient to cause the demons to leave.

Josephus is speaking to pagans who are obviously prepared to understand a story such as this, and Josephus presumes that this explanation of David's singing and playing will be seen as credible and a very good explanation for Saul's feeling better. Evil spirits bring great disturbance to mind and spirit. The text calls David a physician. Exorcism of this type, if it brings wholeness to the patient's health, is the job of a doctor. So Josephus calls exorcism a healing. For the Romans, these songs would have the power of the well-known *carmen*.

Eleazar the Pharisee (70–90 CE) draws on Solomon's method for exorcisms

2.28. We have been Induced to Speak of These Things, in order that All May Know the Greatness of Solomon's Nature and How God Favored Him

Josephus *Antiquities* 8.46–49
And this kind of cure [Solomon's forms of exorcisms] is of very great power among us to this day, for I have seen a certain Eleazar, a countryman of mine [Josephus], in the presence of Vespasian, his sons, tribunes and a number of other soldiers, free men possessed by demons, and this was the manner of the cure: he put to the nose of the possessed man a ring which had under its seal one of the roots prescribed by Solomon, and

then, as the man smelled it, drew out the demon through his nostrils, and, when the man at once fell down, adjured the demon never to come back into him, speaking Solomon's name and reciting the incantations which he had composed. Then, wishing to convince the bystanders and prove to them that he had this power, Eleazar placed a cup or foot-basin full of water a little way off and commanded the demon, as it went out of the man, to overturn it and make known to the spectators that he had left the man. And when this was done, the understanding and wisdom of Solomon were clearly revealed, on account of which we have been induced to speak of these things, in order that all men may know the greatness of his [Solomon's] nature and how God favoured him, and that no one under the sun may be ignorant of the king's surpassing virtue of every kind.

Note

Notice that Eleazar gets the demon to behave so that he can prove to his audience how efficacious his power is. This is what we see also in Apollonius' exorcism of the young dandy. Both Philostratus and Josephus show that a listening audience appreciates some proof that demons are indeed present, and are subject to the hero.

5

DAIMONS/DEMONS IN APOCALYPTIC AND CHRISTIAN SOURCES

THE NATURE AND IDENTITY OF DAIMONS/DEMONS IN APOCALYPTIC SOURCES

The oddity of apocalyptic expectations within the larger Greco-Roman world must be acknowledged immediately. Here in an explicit, dramatic and terrible way, the imminent Endtime influences the significance of every act. Although there are no exorcisms within the apocalyptic material, there is a distinctive understanding of the identity and nature of demons. The existence of the demons is based on a "foundational legend," namely, The Watchers. It is within this greater, overarching story with its prophecies of ultimate judgment and punishment that demons are given their role. Only when we see that a Christian narrator has taken pains to include some of these distinctive features in a Jesus exorcism story may we conclude that the meaning of the exorcism as well as its implications for the role of Jesus is meant to be situated against the unusual cosmological expectation of apocalypticism.

In this section, a selection of texts drawn from 1 Enoch and Jubilees is presented. These texts seem to represent the most common ideas of demons to be found in Jewish apocalypses. Since both texts rely on the Watchers' Tale from Gen. 6:1–4, that text will be presented first.

Jewish scriptures: the Watchers' Tale

2.29. The Sons of God Went in to the Daughters of Humans, Who Bore Children to Them. These were the Heroes that were of Old, Warriors of Renown

Gen. 6:1–4

1. When people began to multiply on the face of the ground, and daughters were born to them, *2.* the sons of God saw that they were fair; and they took wives for themselves of all they chose. *3.* Then the Lord said, "My spirit shall not abide in mortals forever, for they are flesh; their days shall be one hundred twenty years." *4.* The Nephilim were on the earth in those days – and also afterward – when the sons of God went in to the daughters of humans, who bore children to them. These were the heroes that were of old, warriors of renown.

Note

The half-breeds mentioned in these scriptures are not daimons/demons, but the story's mention of "sons of God" in the monotheistic context of Hellenistic Judaism opened the door to the idea that certain creatures exist between the human and the one God. We shall see that this text forms a foundation for apocalyptic texts.

1 Enoch

1 Enoch may be accepted as representative of common ideas about demons in apocalyptic/eschatological thought because it was one of the most widely circulated works of the Intertestamental period. Dated between the second century BCE and the first century CE, it exerted its influence on Jubilees, the Testaments of the Twelve Patriarchs, the Assumption of Moses, 2 Baruch and 4 Ezra.[1]

---

1 I am completely indebted to the scholarship of E. Isaac for this introduction to 1 Enoch: E. Isaac, "1 (Ethiopic Apocalypse of) Enoch," in *The Old Testament Pseudepigrapha* (ed. James H. Charlesworth; 2 vols; Garden City, NY: Doubleday & Co., 1983), vol. 1, pp. 5–89. For this treatment of influences, see his p. 8.

2.30.1. The Angels Swear an Oath to Beget Children through the Women on Earth

1 Enoch 6:1–5

In those days, when the children of man had multiplied, it happened that there were born unto them handsome and beautiful daughters. And the angels, the children of heaven, saw them and desired them; and they said to one another, "Come let us choose wives for ourselves from among the daughters of man and beget us children." And Semyaz, being their leader, said unto them, "I fear that perhaps you will not consent that this deed should be done, and I alone will become (responsible) for this great sin." But they all responded to him, "Let us all swear an oath and bind everyone among us by a curse not to abandon this suggestion but to do the deed." Then they all swore together and bound one another by (the curse).

2.30.2. The Angels Teach the Women Magical Medicine and Beget Gluttonous, Cannibalistic Giants

1 Enoch 7:1–6

And they took wives unto themselves, and everyone (respectively) chose one woman for himself, and they began to go unto them. And they taught them magical medicine, incantations, the cutting of roots, and taught them (about) plants. And the women became pregnant and gave birth to great giants whose heights were three hundred cubits. These giants consumed the produce of all the people until the people detested feeding them. So the giants turned against (the people) in order to eat them. And they began to sin against birds, wild beasts, reptiles, and fish. And their flesh was devoured the one by the other, and they drank blood. And then the earth brought an accusation against the oppressors.

2.30.3. The Angels Teach Humankind the Making of Weapons; Jewelry; Cosmetic Application and Alchemy, as well as Incantations, Astrology, Divination, and the Deception of Human Beings

1 Enoch 8: 1–4

And Azaz'el taught the people (the art of) making swords and knives, and shields, and breastplates; and he showed to their chosen ones bracelets, decorations, (shadowing of the eye) with antimony, ornamentation, the beautifying of the eyelids, all kinds of precious stones, and all coloring tinctures and alchemy. And there were many wicked ones and they committed adultery and erred, and all their conduct became corrupt. Amasras taught incantation and the cutting of roots; and Armaros the resolving of incantations; and Baraqiyal astrology, and Kokarer'el (the knowledge of) the signs, and Tam'el taught the seeing of the stars, and Asder'el taught the course of the moon as well as the deception of man. And (the people) cried and their voice reached unto heaven.

[1 Enoch 9: Michael, Surafel and Gabriel bring the distastrous situation to the throne of the Most High.]

2.30.4. The Punishment of the Fallen Angels

1 Enoch 10:1–7

And then spoke the Most High, the Great and Holy One! And he sent Asuryal to the son of Lamech, (saying), "Tell him in my name, 'Hide yourself!' and reveal to him the end of what is coming; for the earth and everything will be destroyed. And the Deluge is about to come upon all the earth; and all that is in it will be destroyed. And now instruct him in order that he may flee, and his seed will be preserved for all generations." And secondly the Lord said to Raphael, "Bind Azaz'el hand and foot (and) throw him into the darkness!" And he made a hole in the desert which was in Duda'el and cast him there; he threw on top of him rugged and sharp rocks. And he covered his face in order that he may not see light; and in order that he may be sent into the fire on the great day of judgment. And give life to the earth which the angels have corrupted.
[The Watchers beg Enoch to intercede for them, and to write down their prayers for forgiveness (1 Enoch 13). As Enoch does so he falls asleep and has a vision in which the Lord gives him a message to the Watchers. First he condemns their actions, and then gives them their role on earth.]

2.30.5. Enoch's Vision: the Earthly Giants will Corrupt until the Endtime

1 Enoch 15:6–12

Indeed you, formerly you were spiritual, (having) eternal life, and immortal in all the generations of the world. That is why (formerly) I did not make wives for you, for the dwelling of spiritual beings of heaven is heaven.

But now the giants who are born from the (union of) the spirits and the flesh shall be called evil spirits upon the earth, because their dwelling shall be upon the earth and inside the earth. Evil spirits have come out of their bodies. ... They will become evil upon the earth and shall be called evil spirits. The dwelling of spiritual beings of heaven is heaven; but the dwelling of the spirits of the earth, which are born upon the earth, is in the earth. The spirits of the giants oppress each other, they will corrupt, fall, be excited, and fall upon the earth, and cause sorrow. They eat no food, nor become thirsty, nor find obstacles. And these spirits shall rise up against the children of the people and against the women, because they have proceeded forth (from them).

2.30.6. The Punishment of the Fallen Angels

1 Enoch 54:1–6

Then I looked and turned to another face of the earth and saw there a valley, deep and burning with fire. And they were bringing kings and potentates and were throwing them into this deep valley. And my eyes saw there their chains while they were making them into iron fetters of immense weight. And I asked the angel of peace, who was going with me, saying, "For whom are these imprisonment chains being prepared?" And he said unto me, "These are being prepared for the armies of Azaz'el, in order that they may take them and cast them into the abyss of complete condemnation, and as the Lord of the Spirits has commanded it, they shall cover their jaws with rocky stones. Then Michael, Raphael, Gabriel, and Phanuel themselves shall seize them on that great day of judgment and cast them into the furnace (of fire) that is burning that day, so that the Lord of the Spirits may take vengeance on them on account of their oppressive deeds which (they performed) as messengers of Satan, leading astray those who dwell upon the earth.

2.30.7. Noah Reports God's Promise of the Evil Angels' Punishment

1 Enoch 67:1, 4–7

In those days, the word of God came unto me [Noah], and said unto me . . . "They [the good angels] shall imprison those angels who revealed oppression in that burning valley which my grandfather Enoch had formerly shown me in the West among the mountains of gold, silver, iron, bronze and tin. I also saw that valley in which there took place a great turbulence and the stirring of waters. Now, when all this took place, there was produced from that bronze and fire a smell of sulfur (which) blended with those waters. This valley of the perversive angels shall (continue to) burn punitively underneath that ground; in respect to its troughs, they shall be filled with rivers of water by which those angels who perverted those who dwell upon the earth shall be punished."

Notes

DISTINGUISHING CONCEPTS PARTICULAR TO THIS TEXT

There are several characteristics that distinguish this Jewish tradition from those more commonly found in Greco-Roman references to daimons:

1   The creation of these spirits has a "historicizing" myth.

2 Demons are given place in holy writings by expanding a scripture text. In this case, Gen. 6:1–4 is refashioned to include the
demons.

3 There is a clear distinction between good and evil angels because
of the division of the heavenly host. We find no similar cosmic
myth in the rest of the Greco-Roman collections, where
daimons either good or evil seem to fill a natural space between
the divine and the human. In 1 Enoch, however, the evil spirits
are separated from the good through a "historical" sin.

4 The daimons have a nature separate from that of humans, and
no transmutation appears to be possible. That is, dead heroes
do not seem to be able to join this spiritual assembly, nor do
these spirits become demoted to human hero status for their
transgressions.

5 Unlike Xenocrates' theory that the daimon must eventually die
if it is not divine, 1 Enoch gives us the impression that the
evil spirits have an eternal life. In fact this element of immortality means that an eternal suffering will be borne by the
wicked spirits.

6 There will be an Endtime judgment with specific punishments
for the evil angels.

7 The punishments invoke a realistic, physical kind of suffering.
The good angels will make chains to bind them (1 Enoch
54:4–5) and then throw them into a depression in the earth,
such as a pit or a valley (1 Enoch 54:5; 67:4), and in a desert
or rocky place (1 Enoch 10:4). The pit is on fire and filled with
the smell of sulfur (1 Enoch 67:6). Such ideas occur nowhere
else in Greco-Roman religious traditions.

ROLES OF THE DEMONS

Similarities to common concepts about their role in Greco-Roman writings

They cause bloodshed and horrible acts of violence on earth.

Distinguishing features of their role in 1 Enoch

1 They communicate "rejected mysteries" to humans (1 Enoch
16:3).

2 They try to communicate the sins of humankind to the judgment seat of God (1 Enoch 15:12).

3   They are "messengers of Satan" who lead the people astray
    (1 Enoch 54:6).

The book of Jubilees

Although this second-century BCE work was influenced by 1 Enoch,
it does not have the apocalyptic features characteristic of that work.
O. S. Wintermute lists these important omissions:

> 1) bizarre imagery, 2) limited esoteric appeal, and 3) preoc-
> cupation with the type of eschatology characteristic of
> apocalyptic writings. The beasts, the horns, the heavenly
> scenes, the thrones, the rivers of fire, the otherworldly
> figures with brightly shining bodies, and the many other
> terrifying objects that populate the world of Daniel, Enoch,
> and other apocalyptic writings are not found in Jubilees.[2]

And he concludes,

> Granted the presence of angels, demons, and an occasional
> prodigy (23:25), the world described in the revelation to
> Moses is very much like the historical world in which the
> author of Jubilees lived.[3]

Furthermore, Jubilees does not presume a special select community awaiting the Endtime, but is addressed to all of Israel in the
ordinary context of their lives. The lessons derived from the retelling
of the Genesis stories are meant to reinforce the importance of Torah
observance. Thus, Jubilees gives evidence of the mixture and integration of traditions derived from apocalyptic worldviews but
utilized within the context of a non-apocalyptic and Torah oriented
community. Second, this document illustrates that such integration
and synthesizing was already operative as early as the second
century BCE.

---

2 For the treatment of Jubilees I am completely indebted to O. S. Wintermute,
   "Jubilees," in *The Old Testament Pseudepigrapha*, vol. 2, pp. 35–142. Here the
   reference is to p. 37.
3 Ibid., 37.

2.31.1. The Angels Beget Children with the Women of Earth and Beget Giants, after which Every Sort of Sin Including Cannibalism is Committed on Earth

Jubilees 5:1–2

And when the children of men began to multiply on the surface of the earth and daughters were born to them, that the angels of the Lord saw in a certain year of that jubilee that they were good to look at. And they took wives for themselves from all of those whom they chose. And they bore children for them; and they were the giants. And injustice increased upon the earth, and all flesh corrupted its way; man and cattle and beasts and birds and everything which walks on the earth. And they all corrupted their way and their ordinances, and they began to eat one another. And injustice grew upon the earth and every imagination of the thoughts of all mankind was thus continually evil.

2.31.2. The Lord has the Wicked Angels Bound in the Depths of the Earth and the Progeny Kill Each Other, While the Parents are Punished

Jubilees 5:6–7

And against his angels whom he had sent to the earth he was very angry. He commanded that they be uprooted from all their dominion. And he told us to bind them in the depths of the earth, and behold, they are bound in the midst of them, and they are isolated. And against their children a word went forth from before his presence so that he might smite them with the sword and remove them from under heaven. And he said, "My spirit will not dwell upon man forever; for they are flesh, and their days will be one hundred and ten years." And he sent his sword among them so that each one might kill his fellow and they began to kill one another until they all fell on the sword and they were wiped out from the earth. And their parents also watched. And subsequently they were bound in the depths of the earth forever, until the day of judgment in order for judgment to be executed upon all of those who corrupted their ways and their deeds before the Lord. And he wiped out every one from their places and not one of them remained whom he did not judge according to all his wickedness.

2.31.3. The Flood is the Fault of the Watchers

Jubilees 7:21–25

For on account of these three the Flood came upon the earth. For (it was) because of the fornication which the Watchers, apart from the mandate of their authority, fornicated with the daughters of men and took for themselves wives from all whom they chose and made a beginning of impurity. And they begot sons, the Naphidim, and all of them were dissimilar. And each one ate his fellow. The giants killed the Naphil, and the Naphil killed the Elyo, and the Elyo mankind, and man his neighbor. And everyone sold himself in order that he might do injustice and pour out much blood, and the earth was full of injustice. And afterward, they sinned against beasts, and birds and everything which moves or walks upon the earth. And they poured out much blood upon the earth. And all the thoughts and desires of men were always contemplating vanity and evil. And the Lord blotted out everything from the face of the earth on account of the evil of their deeds. And on account of the blood which they poured out in the midst of the land, he blotted out everything.

2.31.4. Noah's Prayer Against the Demons who Tempt his Sons

Jubilees 10:1–6
In the third week of that jubilee the polluted demons began to lead astray the children of Noah's sons and to lead them to folly and to destroy them. And the sons of Noah came to Noah, their father, and they told him about the demons who were leading astray and blinding and killing his grandchildren. And he prayed before the Lord his God and he said, "God of the spirits which are in all flesh, who has acted mercifully with me and saved me and my sons from the water of the Flood and did not let me perish as you did the children of perdition, because

Great was your grace upon me,
and great was your mercy upon my soul.
Let your grace be lifted up upon my sons,
and do not let the evil spirits rule over them,
lest they destroy them from the earth.

But bless me and my sons. And let us grow and increase and fill the earth. And you know that which your Watchers, the fathers of these spirits, did in my days and also these spirits who are alive. Shut them up and take them to the place of judgment. And do not let them cause corruption among the sons of your servant, O my God, because they are cruel and were created to destroy. And let them not rule over the spirits of the living because you alone know their judgment, and do not let them have power over the children of the righteous henceforth and forever."

2.31.5. The Lord Orders the Demons to the Pit, but Grants Mastema's Request that One-Tenth of Them Be Left to Follow Satan's Bidding

Jubilees 10:7–14
And the Lord our God spoke to us so that we might bind all of them. And the chief of the spirits, Mastema, came and he said, "O Lord, Creator, leave some of them before me, and let them obey my voice. And let them

do everything which I tell them, because if some of them are not left for me, I will not be able to exercise the authority of my will among the children of men because they are (intended) to corrupt and lead astray before my judgment because the evil of the sons of men is great." And he said, "Let a tenth of them remain before him, but let nine parts go down into the place of judgment."

And he told one of us to teach Noah all of their healing because he knew that they would not walk uprightly and would not strive right-eously. And we acted in accord with all of his words. All of the evil ones, who were cruel, we bound in the place of judgment, but a tenth of them we let remain so that they might be subject to Satan on earth. And the healing of all their illnesses together with their seductions we told Noah so that he might heal by means of herbs of the earth. And Noah wrote everything in a book just as we taught him according to every kind of healing. And the evil spirits were restrained from following the sons of Noah. And he gave everything which he wrote to Shem, his oldest son, because he loved him much more than all of his sons.

2.31.6. The Remaining Evil Spirits Turn Everyone to Sin

Jubilees 11:3–6
And 'Ur, the son of Kesed, built the city of 'Ur of the Chaldees and he named it after his name and his father's name. And they made for them-selves molten images, and everyone worshiped the icon which they made for themselves as a molten image. And they began making graven images and polluted likenesses. And cruel spirits assisted them and led them astray so that they might commit sin and pollution. And the prince, Mastema, acted forcefully to do all of this. And he sent other spirits to those who were set under his hand to practice all error and sin and all transgression, to destroy, to cause to perish and to pour out blood upon the earth. Therefore he called the name of Seroh, "Serug," because everyone had turned back to commit all sin and transgression.

2.31.7. The Sabbaths and Jubilees will Purify Israel from All Evil

Jubilees 50:4–5
On account of this I ordained for you the weeks of years, and the years, and the jubilees (as) forty-nine jubilees from the days of Adam until this day and one week and two years. And they are still forty further years to learn the commands of the Lord until they cross over the shore of the land of Canaan, crossing over the Jordan to its western side. And jubilees will pass until Israel is purified from all the sin of fornication, and defilement, and uncleanness, and sin and error. And they will dwell in confidence in all the land. And then it will not have any Satan or any evil (one). And the land will be purified from that time and forever.

Notes

DISTINGUISHING CONCEPTS PARTICULAR TO THIS TEXT

1   The sabbaths and jubilees help to purify the world constantly of the evil brought to it by the presence of the demons.
2   Nine-tenths of all the demons are already suffering eternal torments in the pit for their sins.
3   God has allowed one-tenth of the demons to remain on earth at the request of Prince Mastema (Satan), who asks for some demons to enact his commands.
4   There is a time-limit for the demons on earth. There is an Endtime approaching when the demons will face judgment and eternal punishment.

CONCLUSION

When we compare the treatment of demons in Jubilees with that in 1 Enoch it becomes clear that this later document is much more attentive to the issue of humankind's responsibility for sin than it is to detailing the culpability of the evil spirits. Surely Jubilees is dependent on 1 Enoch for the Watchers myth and the scenes of God's promises of punishments. The place of punishments also repeats the notion of a depression in the earth, but Jubilees has the idea that the place of judgment will be in a judgment chamber located inside the earth. Eliminated also are the scenes of the evil angels entering into their conspiratorial oath of secrecy about their fornication (1 Enoch 6:4–5). We do not see the elaborate list of special Hebrew names that identify specific good and evil angels, or notice any concern over the number of the host of heaven. We do not find the precise and detailed explanation of evil education given to humankind. Rather Jubilees adopts the generalized complaint that the demons lead the people astray and pollute them. It is significant that when sins are itemized, as they are in Jubilees 11:1–6, they are attributed directly to the human agents, in this case, the sons of Noah. Only after this itemized list does the author mention the "assistance" of the demons:

> And cruel spirits assisted them and led them astray so that they might commit sin and pollution.
>
> (Jubilees 11:4)

Thus the writer of Jubilees is not ready to grant that the demons bear the total responsibility for the sinful conduct of the community. They "assist."

This community is interested in the observing of sabbaths and jubilees as a purification of the land. The attention is on Torah and it is faithfulness to the Law, then, that keeps the demons away from the community.

We can see that the expectation of Judgment on the earth shows that it carries a sense of linear time, as do apocalypses. But we are given the sense that the demons' control belongs to a time long past. It is the responsibility of the person and the community to protect the earth through Torah observance.

Distinguishing Features of Apocalyptic/Eschatological Demonology

Trevor Ling's examination of apocalpytic/eschatological literature of the Intertestamental period in his monograph *The Significance of Satan*[4] arrives at the conclusion that two features distinguish apocalyptic/eschatological demonology.

First, the apocalyptic demonology is distinguished by the direction in which it was developing at this time, that is, toward the conception of a single source of all evil. The movement of thought away from the explanation of evil in terms of innumerable capricious spirits operating at random toward an explanation in terms of a hierarchy or unified body of evil reaches its climax in the New Testament. But it is in apocalyptic literature that this important movement of thought is first to be observed clearly.

The second is the explanation of the birth of demons by reference to the myth in Gen. 6:1–4, where the Watchers have intercourse with the women of the earth.[5] Notice that in Justin Martyr's *Dialogue with Trypho* (79) Trypho is offended at any notion that the angels would rebel against God:

---

4 Trevor Ling, *The Significance of Satan* (London: SPCK, 1961).

5 Such a conclusion required an accommodating commentary on Genesis 1 and 2 which is found, not in apocalyptic documents but in the Mishnah, Pirke Aboth 5:6: "Ten things were created on the eve of the Sabbath between the suns at nightfall: the mouth of the earth, the mouth of the well, the mouth of the she-ass, the rainbow, and the manna and the rod and the Shamir, the letters and the writing and the Tables [of stone]. Some say also: The evil

> On this, [Justin Martyr is quoting Isa. 29:13, 14 to justify
> a theory of the displacement of the Jews with Gentiles as
> God's chosen people] Trypho, who was somewhat angry,
> but respected the Scriptures, as was manifest from his coun-
> tenance, said to me, "The utterances of God are holy, but
> your expositions are mere contrivances, as is plain from
> what has been explained by you; namely, even blasphemies,
> for you assert that angels sinned and revolted against God."

Trypho's opposition to the apocalyptic myths concerning warring angels alerts us to the fact that not all Jews would have fully supported the expectations or worldview of apocalyptic communities. In the light of this difference, the two features elucidated by Trevor Ling in apocalyptic material seem to provide the distinguishing features, controls for the identification of material arising from the apocalyptic perspective. Since exorcisms already exist in the Greco-Roman world in general, well ahead of Christianity, it is that worldview which represents the general, or the norm. Only when a Christian story bears signs of the narrator and audience's appeal to an apocalyptic expectation or worldview may that "norm" be replaced by the more particular and odd worldview of apocalyptic expectation. Thus, according to Trevor Ling's analysis, one would expect some mention of one of the Lords notable to the apocalyptic view of the demon army, for example Satan, Belial Aza'el or Beelzebul. Second, one would expect some indication of a final judgment and vengeance to be visited on the demons.

The further difficulty, however, is that illustrated by Jubilees. In that document, the influence of 1 Enoch is seen in the myth of the Watchers, in the presentation of the good and evil angels, in the organization of the armies of angels, in the names of the Lords and in the expectation of a final justice to occur on the earth. But as we have seen, Jubilees is more interested in the observance of Torah than in an apocalyptic/eschatological judgment day. A document such as Jubilees reminds the scholar that even if we should find evidence of the two supposedly distinguishing features of apocalyptic material, we may not conclude definitively that the community sees the world and time through this same

---

spirits and the sepulchre of Moses and the ram of Abraham our father. Some say also: The tongs made with tongs" (Herbert Danby, "Aboth," *The Mishnah* [London: Oxford University Press, 1933], 5.6).

lens. Nevertheless, with this cautionary note, the two features isolated by Trevor Ling give us an important control for identifying a community at least familiar with apocalyptic material who find some of its explanations helpful and significant, whether or not they accept the entirety of its worldview and expectations.

There are no exorcisms in apocalyptic writings

There are no exorcism stories in apocalyptic material. This absence is surely due to the genre. However, one does not find allusions to apocalyptic expectations in the expulsion of demons by Moses or Rabbi Eliezer, as related by Josephus. For him, the exorcism is for the "healing of humankind." One has to ask, then, how prevalent such apocalyptic ideas were, and how preoccupying they actually were in the face of the everyday problems and responsibilities of daily life.

THE EXORCISMS OF JESUS

Jesus exorcizes a man in the synagogue in Capernaum

2.32. They Were All Amazed and they Kept on Asking One Another, "What is This? A New Teaching – With Authority! He Commands Even the Unclean Spirits, and They Obey him

Mark 1:21–28

21. They went to Capernaum; and when the sabbath came, he entered the synagogue and taught. 22. They were astounded at his teaching, for he taught them as one having authority, and not as the scribes. 23. Just then there was in their synagogue a man with an unclean spirit, 24. and he cried out, "What have you to do with us, Jesus of Nazareth? Have you come to destroy us? I know who you are, the Holy One of God." 25. But Jesus rebuked him, saying, "Be silent, and come out of him!" 26. And the unclean spirit, convulsing him and crying with a loud voice, came out of him. 27. They were all amazed, and they kept on asking one another, "What is this? A new teaching – with authority! He commands even the unclean spirits, and they obey him." 28. At once his fame began to spread throughout the surrounding region of Galilee.

Note

A number of features suggest that the narrator is familiar with Jewish religious texts/tradition. First, the demon's cry to Jesus in v. 24, "What have you to do with us?," or literally, "What between you and me?," is too odd to be claimed for ordinary Greco-Roman parlance. Furthermore, it shows itself to be frequent in the LXX: Josh. 22:24; Judg. 11:12; 2 Sam. 16:10; 19:23; 1 Kgs. 17:18; 2 Kgs. 3:13; 2 Chr. 35:21; Jer. 2:18 and Hos. 14:9. Second, the demon's title for Jesus, "Holy One of God," echoes the title given to Elisha in 2 Kgs. 4:9 and to Aaron in (LXX) Ps. 106 [105]:16.

Robert Gundry claims that "primitive tradition is reflected in the characteristically Jewish expectation that the messianic age will bring destruction to the demonic world."[6] Here he refers to 1 Enoch 55:4. It is true that when the demon represents himself as part of a much larger group ("Have you come to destroy us?" [v. 24]) the idea is not usual in Greco-Roman texts, as we have already observed. Moreover, the idea of the "legion" or army as applied to demons is especially strong in 1 Enoch, as Gundry has noted. We should note, however, that while apocalyptic expectations do promise the destruction of the demonic world, demons themselves cannot be destroyed, since they are spirits. It is Xenocrates who reminds us that demons must be mortal if they are not gods.

Nevertheless, it is indisputable that the cry of the demons to Jesus is unusual in comparison to other heroes' exorcism stories. The cosmic authority of Jesus on earth is clearly attested. His power to effect a destruction of the demons illustrates the Christian community's keen sense of the Endtime that hovers on the breath of the age.

Jesus exorcizes the man with the legion of demons: the Markan version

2.33. He Shouted at the Top of His Voice, "What Have You to Do with Me, Jesus, Son of the Most High God? I Adjure You by God, Do Not Torment Me"

Mark 5:1–20 (Matt. 8:28–34//Luke 8:26–39)
1. They came to the other side of the sea, to the country of the Gerasenes. *2.* And when he had stepped out of the boat, immediately a man out of the tombs with an unclean spirit met him. *3.* He lived among the tombs;

---

6 Robert H. Gundry, *Mark: A Commentary on His Apology for the Cross* (Grand Rapids, Michigan: Eerdmans, 1993), 75.

and no one could restrain him any more, even with a chain; *4.* for he had often been restrained with shackles and chains, but the chains he wrenched apart, and the shackles he broke in pieces; no one had the strength to subdue him. *5.* Night and day among the tombs and on the mountains he was always howling and bruising himself with stones. *6.* When he saw Jesus from a distance, he ran and bowed down before him; *7.* and he shouted at the top of his voice, "What have you to do with me, Jesus, Son of the Most High God? I adjure you by God, do not torment me." *8.* For he had said to him, "Come out of the man, you unclean spirit!" *9.* Then Jesus asked him, "What is your name?" He replied, "My name is Legion; for we are many." *10.* He begged him earnestly not to send them out of the country. *11.* Now there on the hillside a great herd of swine was feeding; *12.* and the unclean spirits begged him, "Send us into the swine; let us enter them." *13.* So he gave them permission. And the unclean spirits came out and entered the swine; and the herd, numbering about two thousand, rushed down the steep bank into the sea, and were drowned in the sea.

14. The swineherds ran off and told it in the city and in the country. Then people came to see what it was that had happened. *15.* They came to Jesus and saw the demoniac sitting there, clothed and in his right mind, the very man who had had the legion; and they were afraid. *16.* Those who had seen what had happened to the demoniac and to the swine reported it. *17.* Then they began to beg Jesus to leave their neighborhood. *18.* As he was getting into the boat the man who had been possessed by demons begged him that he might be with him. *19.* But Jesus refused, and said to him, "Go home to your friends, and tell them how much the Lord has done for you, and what mercy he has shown you." *20.* And he went away and began to proclaim in the Decapolis how much Jesus had done for him, and everyone was amazed.

Note

In this exorcism, the emphasis is on the powerful authority of Jesus, rather than on any apocalyptic message. The bulk of the description of the condition of the demoniac (vv. 1–5) draws attention to the frightening character of his uncontrollable behavior (vv. 3–4), and then to the pitiable condition of his state, lonely, desperate and self-destructive at the hands of the demon (v. 5). The fact that Jesus' mere arrival is sufficient to begin the exorcism is a testimony to Jesus' empowerment, for the demon recognizes Jesus' genuine authority. The multiple mention of the tombs (vv. 2, 3, 5) would lead the listener to suppose that the demon might be a spirit of the dead. With the extended exorcism now involving multiple demons, the Legion, this impression might be all the more secure.

The spirits of the dead who love the pigs might well refer to Romans who have died there in the Decapolis, and now threaten the living, as they did when they were alive. In other words, there is a good excuse to recognize political satire inserted into the earlier and simpler exorcism story.

The message of the exorcism encourages confidence in the listener about Jesus, rather than teaching the listener to be alert for the imminent Judgment.

Jesus exorcizes two demoniacs from Gerasa: the Matthean version of Mark 5:1–20

2.34. Suddenly They Shouted, "What Have You to Do with Us, Son of God? Have You Come Here to Torment Us Before the Time?"

Matthew 8:28–34
28. When he came to the other side, to the country of the Gadarenes, two demoniacs coming out of the tombs met him. They were so fierce that no one could pass that way. 29. Suddenly they shouted, "What have you to do with us, Son of God? Have you come here to torment us before the time?" 30. Now a large herd of swine was feeding at some distance from them. 31. The demons begged him, "If you cast us out, send us into the herd of swine." 32. And he said to them, "Go!" So they came out and entered the swine; and suddenly, the whole herd rushed down the steep bank into the sea and perished in the water. 33. The swineherds ran off, and on going into the town, they told the whole story about what had happened to the demoniacs. 34. Then the whole town came out to meet Jesus; and when they saw him, they begged him to leave their neighborhood.

Note

Matthew has inserted an apocalyptic Endtime reference into the account by changing the demon's cry to Jesus. Instead of "What have you to do with me, Jesus, Son of the Most High God?" (Mark 5:7), the demon cries out, "What have you to do with us, Son of God? Have you come here to torment us before the time?" (Matt. 8:29). As we have seen, non-apocalyptic material has no concept of a time when demons are destroyed. By using such a reference, Matthew situates Mark's story in the apocalyptic traditions he received from both Q and other Markan material.

Jesus exorcizes the daughter of the Syrophoenician woman

2.35. But She Answered Him, "Sir, Even the Dogs Under the Table Eat the Children's Crumbs." Then He Said to Her, "For Saying That, You May Go – the Demon Has Left Your Daughter

Mark 7: 24–30 (Matt. 15:21–28)

24. From there he set out and went away to the region of Tyre. He entered a house and did not want anyone to know he was there. Yet he could not escape notice, *25.* but a woman whose little daughter had an unclean spirit immediately heard about him and she came and bowed down at his feet. *26.* Now the woman was a Gentile, of Syrophoenician origin. She begged him to cast the demon out of her daughter. *27.* He said to her, "Let the children be fed first, for it is not fair to take the children's food and throw it to the dogs." *28.* But she answered him, "Sir, even the dogs under the table eat the children's crumbs." *29.* Then he said to her, "For saying that, you may go – the demon has left your daughter." *30.* So she went home, found the child lying on the bed, and the demon gone.

Jesus exorcizes and heals a man's possessed son

2.36. "You Spirit that Keeps this Boy from Speaking and Hearing, I Command You, Come Out of Him, and Never Enter Him Again!" After Crying Out and Convulsing him Terribly, It Came Out, and the Boy Was Like a Corpse

Mark 9:14–29 (Matt. 17:14–21; Luke 9:37–43)

14. When they came to the disciples, they saw a great crowd around them, and some scribes arguing with them. *15.* When the whole crowd saw him, they were immediately overcome with awe, and they ran forward to greet him. *16.* He asked them, "What are you arguing about with them?" *17.* Someone from the crowd answered him, "Teacher, I brought you my son; he has a spirit that makes him unable to speak; *18.* and whenever it seizes him, it dashes him down; and he foams and grinds his teeth and becomes rigid; and I asked your disciples to cast it out, but they could not do so." *19.* He answered them, "You faithless generation, how much longer must I be among you? How much longer must I put up with you? Bring him to me." *20.* And they brought the boy to him. When the spirit saw him, immediately it convulsed the boy, and he fell on the ground and rolled about, foaming at the mouth. *21.* Jesus asked the father, "How long has this been happening to him?" And he said, "From childhood. *22.* It has often cast him into the fire and into the water, to destroy him; but if you are able to do anything have pity on us and help us." *23.* Jesus said to him, "If you are able! – All things can be done for the one who believes."

24. Immediately the father of the child cried out, "I believe; help my unbelief!" *25.* When Jesus saw that a crowd came running together, he rebuked the unclean spirit, saying to it, "You spirit that keeps this boy from speaking and hearing, I command you, come out of him, and never enter him again!" *26.* After crying out and convulsing him terribly, it came out, and the boy was like a corpse, so that most of them said, "He is dead." *27.* But Jesus took him by the hand and lifted him up, and he was able to stand. *28.* When he had entered the house, his disciples asked him privately, "Why could we not cast it out?" *29.* He said to them, "This kind can come out only through prayer."

Jesus heals a woman from her eighteen-year infirmity on the Sabbath

2.37. "Woman, You Are Set Free From Your Ailment." When He Laid His Hands on Her, Immediately She Stood Up Straight and Began Praising God

Luke 13:10–17
10. Now he was teaching in one of the synagogues on the sabbath. *11.* And just then there appeared a woman with a spirit that had crippled her for eighteen years. She was bent over and was quite unable to stand up straight. *12.* When Jesus saw her, he called her over and said to her, "Woman you are set free from your ailment." *13.* When he laid his hands on her, immediately she stood up straight and began praising God. *14.* But the leader of the synagogue, indignant because Jesus had cured on the sabbath, kept saying to the crowd, "There are six days on which work ought to be done; come on those days and be cured, and not on the sabbath day." *15.* But the Lord answered him and said, "You hypocrites! Does not each of you on the sabbath untie his ox or his donkey from the manger, and lead it away to give it water? *16.* And ought not this woman, a daughter of Abraham whom Satan bound for eighteen long years, be set free from this bondage on the sabbath day?" *17.* When he said this, all his opponents were put to shame; and the entire crowd was rejoicing at all the wonderful things that he was doing.

Jesus exorcizes a demon causing a man to be mute

2.38. But Some of Them Said, "He Casts Out Demons by Beelzebul, the Ruler of the Demons"

Luke 11:14–26 (Matt. 12:22–32; cf. Mark 3:20–30)
14. Now he was casting out a demon that was mute; when the demon had gone out, the one who had been mute spoke, and the crowds were amazed. *15.* But some of them said, "He casts out demons by Beelzebul, the ruler of the demons." *16.* Others, to test him, kept demanding from him a sign

from heaven. *17*. But he knew what they were thinking and said to them, "Every kingdom divided against itself becomes a desert, and house falls on house. *18*. If Satan also is divided against himself, how will his kingdom stand? – for you say that I cast out the demons by Beelzebul. *19*. Now if I cast out the demons by Beelzebul, by whom do your exorcists cast them out? Therefore, they will be your judges. *20*. But if it is by the finger of God that I cast out demons, then the kingdom of God has come to you. *21*. When a strong man, fully armed, guards his castle, his property is safe. *22*. But when one stronger than he attacks him and overpowers him, he takes away his armor in which he trusted and divides his plunder. *23*. Whoever is not with me is against me, and whoever does not gather with me scatters.

24. When the unclean spirit has gone out of a person, it wanders through waterless regions looking for a resting place, but not finding any, it says, 'I will return to my house from which I came.' *25*. When it comes, it finds it swept and put in order. *26*. Then it goes and brings seven other spirits more evil than itself, and they enter and live there; and the last state of that person is worse than the first."

Note

The association of an exorcism with this controversy story occurs only in Q (Luke 11:11–26//Matt. 12:22–30,43–45). In Mark, the cluster exists as a controversy story alone. Both the charges against Jesus and his defense demand that the listener know the identity of Beelzebul and Satan. This requires familiarity with Jewish apocalyptic traditions, where these figures and their roles are defined. Moreover, the theme of a kingdom and house falling to the coming Kingdom of God makes it clear that for the Christians who created the cluster, Jesus' exorcisms are an expression of Satan's imminent End.

EXORCISMS IN THE ACTS OF THE APOSTLES

The issue of how Jesus' exorcisms would have been understood in various Christian traditions may receive light from the various accounts of exorcisms presented in the Acts of the Apostles.

The disastrous results of a failed exorcism by the sons of the Jewish high priest Sceva

2.39. The Evil Spirit Said to Them, "Jesus I Know, and Paul I Know; but Who are You?"

Acts 19:11–20

11. God did extraordinary miracles through Paul, *12.* so that when the handkerchiefs or aprons that had touched his skin were brought to the sick their disease left them, and the evil spirits came out of them. *13.* Then some itinerant Jewish exorcists tried to use the name of the Lord Jesus over those who had evil spirits, saying, "I adjure you by the Jesus whom Paul proclaims." *14.* Seven sons of a Jewish high priest named Sceva were doing this. *15.* But the evil spirit said to them in reply, "Jesus I know, and Paul I know; but who are you?" *16.* Then the man with the evil spirit leaped on them, mastered them all, and so overpowered them that they fled out of the house naked and wounded. *17.* When this became known to the residents of Ephesus, both Jews and Greeks, everyone was awestruck; and the name of the Lord Jesus was praised. *18.* Also many of those who became believers confessed and disclosed their practices. *19.* A number of those who practiced magic collected their books and burned them publicly; when the value of these books was calculated, it was found to come to fifty thousand silver coins. *20.* So the word of the Lord grew mightily and prevailed.

Note

This story is meant to show the superiority of Paul's heavenly authorization to that of the Jewish religious leaders. The demons demonstrate their superhuman power and violent disposition, which serves to emphasize the magnitude of Paul's exorcisms in Jesus' name. Notice that nakedness is associated with demonic possession, as implied also in Mark 5:1–20, where the one sign that the Gerasene demoniac is healed is his being clothed (v.15).

Paul exorcizes a spirit of divination in Jesus' name

2.40. But Paul, Very Much Annoyed, Turned and Said to the Spirit, "I Order You in the Name of Jesus Christ to Come Out of Her." And It Came Out that Very Hour

Acts 16:16–24

16. One day, as we were going to the place of prayer, we met a slave girl who had a spirit of divination and brought her owners a great deal of money by fortune-telling. *17.* While she followed Paul and us, she would cry out, "These men are slaves of the Most High God, who proclaim to you a way of salvation." *18.* She kept doing this for many days. But Paul, very much annoyed, turned and said to the spirit, "I order you in the name of Jesus Christ to come out of her." And it came out that very hour. *19.* But when her owners saw that their hope of making money was gone, they seized Paul and Silas and dragged them into the marketplace before the authorities. *20.* When they had brought them before the magistrates, they said, "These men are disturbing our city; they are Jews *21.* and are advocating customs that are not lawful for us as Romans to adopt or observe." *22.* The crowd joined in attacking them, and the magistrates had them stripped of their clothing and ordered them to be beaten with rods. *23.* After they had given them a severe flogging, they threw them into prison and ordered the jailer to keep them securely. *24.* Following these instructions, he put them in the innermost cell and fastened their feet in the stocks.

Note

In this Christian exorcism story, the idea that spirits are responsible for oracles is a basic assumption. The spirit of divination is encouraged to possess the girl so that her owners can use her. But when the spirit calls out the truth about Paul, he interferes with Paul's method of spreading the good news. In this case, an annoyed Paul uses the power of Jesus to order the spirit to leave the girl. Now here there is no idea that the spirit itself is evil, or that the story serves the bigger picture of an imminent Endtime. So this story is not caught up in the proclamation of such realities. Rather it is one of the intriguing and wonderful stories in which the author of Acts delights to demonstrate his heroes' true authorization from heaven as Jesus' ministers.

Part III

GODS AND HEROES
WHO CONTROL NATURE

6

GODS AND HEROES WHO CONTROL WIND AND SEA

INTRODUCTION

When a miracle story claims that a god or a hero controls nature, what set of meanings for it was available to the ordinary person in Greco-Roman antiquity? These selected texts center on four major nature miracles of the Jesus tradition: a. the stilling of the storm, b. the walking on the water, c. the changing of water into wine and d. the multiplication of food. In this part, each of the four nature miracles will be treated in turn, first with the gods and then with the heroes who were commonly associated with such a feat.

With respect to the control of sea storms, the gods of the Greco-Roman pantheon most commonly mentioned are Poseidon/ Neptune, who reigns over the sea, and also Aphrodite/Venus, probably by virtue of the fact that she was supposed to have been born from the seafoam. Outside the Olympian pantheon, five other deities or groups of deities were prayed to for the cessation of storms: (1) the Dioscuri, brothers who once sailed with the Argonauts and later became divine; (2) the Samothrace deities, sea-rescue gods who had their own mystery cult; (3) Isis, that major deity from Egypt whose devotion around the Mediterranean also included mystery initiations, (4) Serapis, a deity from hellenized Egypt, a god of the underworld but merciful in saving his devotees from death at sea; and (5) the Jewish deity, who as creator of the cosmos in its entirety was sole authority over all its movements.

The seven heroes connected with calming the sea belong to four main types: (1) the hero of the ancient Greek myth, Orpheus, famous for his charming voice; (2) the Pythagoreans (Pythagoras, who is known and respected by the living elements of nature; and Empedocles, Pythagoras' student, who is famous for his powers over the natural elements); (3) the holy men (Apollonius of Tyana, who

131

would later be claimed as a Neo-Pythagorean, whose blessedness seems to protect him from harm and Jesus of Nazareth, whose great authority the wind and the sea obey); and (4) military leaders (Julius Caesar, whose devotees claim for him a destiny that will not allow any sea storm to claim his life; and Augustus Caesar, whose great Pax is said to have stilled the storms of the world).

The gods who are described as traveling across the water are only two: (1) Poseidon, who is lord of the sea, and is described as being pulled through the waters by the sea beasts; and (2) the Jewish God, who is creator of heaven and earth and is described as walking across the sea.

The ten heroes who are able to cross the sea "dryshod," so to speak, are of four main types: (1) heroes from the Pythagorean legends (Abaris and Pythagoras, who can fly over the sea on an arrow); (2) heroes from Jewish scriptures (Moses, Joshua, Elijah, Elisha, all of whom divide water to walk across on the bottom); (3) the holy hero Jesus, who walks on top of the sea; and (4) military leaders (Xerxes, whose bridge of boats allows him to imitate the god Poseidon; Alexander, whose grandeur causes the sea to allow him passage; and Caligula, whose bridge of boats is said to frighten Neptune).

We shall see that the changing of water into wine is a miracle that is connected with one god, Dionysus. And it has one hero, namely, Jesus of Nazareth.

The multiplication of food is a miracle that belongs to the God of the Jews. And the four heroes who are credited with such a miracle are all prophets of that same God: Moses, Elijah, Elisha and Jesus. It is clear that the Jesus miracle is in dialogue with Jewish tradition, and it is in that context that the meaning of the miracle is to be found.

STILLING A STORM

The gods who control the wind and the sea

Olympian deities

Aphrodite

In this text, Athenaeus reports a story told by Polycharnus of Naucratis, about a sea-storm rescue by Aphrodite due to the prayers of her devotee Herostratus of Naucratis (circa 688 BCE), who had bought a statue of the goddess and brought it with him on board ship for the journey.

3.1. They All Took Refuge at the Statue of Aphrodite, Begging her to Save Them. . . . Then the Sun Shone Forth and they could See their Anchorage, and so Arrived in Naucratis

Athenaeus, *Deipnosophistae* 15.576a–b[1]

As he [Herostratus of Naucratis] approached Egypt a storm suddenly broke out upon him and it was impossible to see where in the world they were; so they all took refuge at the statue of Aphrodite, begging her to save them. The goddess, being friendly to the Naucratites, suddenly caused everything that lay beside her to be covered with fresh green myrtle, filling the ship with a most plesant odour, when the men sailing in her were by this time despairing of their safety . . . then the sun shone forth and they could see their anchorage, and so arrived in Naucratis.

Poseidon

3.2. Poseidon, Savior of Ships and Help of Sailors[2]

Homeric Hymns, To Poseidon

> I begin to sing about Poseidon, the great god, mover of the earth
> and fruitless sea, god of the deep who is also lord of Helicon
> and wide Aegae. A two-fold office the gods allotted you,
> O Shaker of the Earth, to be a tamer of horses
> and a saviour of ships!
> Hail Poseidon, Holder of the Earth, dark-haired lord!
> O blessed one, be kindly in heart
> and help those who voyage in ships!

3.3. Neptune, Angered that the Winds Create a Sea Storm at Juno's Orders, Upbraids them, and Banishes them from the Area

Virgil, *Aeneid* 1.133–134, 137–139, 142–143[3]

Do ye now dare, O winds, without command of mine, to mingle earth and sky, and raise confusion thus? . . . Speed your flight and bear this word to your king [Aeolus]: Not to him, but to me were given by lot the lordship of the sea. . . . Thus he speaks, and swifter than his word he calms the swollen seas, puts to flight the gathered clouds, and brings back the sun.

1 Athenaeus, *Deipnosophistae*, vol. 7 (trans. C. B. Gulick; London: Heinemann, 1941), 15.676a–b.

2 Hesiod, *To Poseidon, Homeric Hymns* (trans. Hugh G. Evelyn-White; London: Heinemann, 1914), p. 449.

3 Virgil, *The Aeneid, Virgil*, vol. 1 (trans. H. Rushton Fairclough; London: Heinemann, 1927).

Non-Olympian deities

The Dioscuri

The Dioscuri are sometimes confused with the Samothrace deities, understandably, since they too are the patrons of sailors.

3.4. The Dioscuri, Deliverers of Shipmen from Stormy Seas

Homeric Hymns, To the Dioscuri[4]

> Bright-eyed Muses, tell of the Tyndaridae, the sons of Zeus,
> glorious children of neat-ankled Leda,
> Castor the tamer of horses, and blameless Polydeuces.
> When Leda had lain with the dark-clouded Son of Cronos,
> she bare them beneath the peak of the great hill Taÿgetus,
> – children who are the deliverers of men on earth and of swift-going ships
> when stormy gales rage over the ruthless sea.
> Then the shipmen call upon the sons of great Zeus
> with vows of white lambs, going to the forepart of the prow;
> but the strong wind and the waves of the sea lay the ship under water,
> until suddenly these two are seen darting through the air on tawny wings.
> Forthwith they allay the blasts of the cruel winds and
> still the waves upon the surface of the white sea:
> fair signs are they and deliverance from toil.
> And when the shipmen see them they are glad
> and have rest from their pain and labour.
> Hail Tyndaridae, riders upon swift horses!
> Now I will remember you and another song also.

3.5. A Hymn to the Dioscuri, who Calm Sea Storms

Theocritus (300–260 BCE), *Hymn to the Dioscuri* 22.14–22[5]

> Night comes, and with it a great storm from the sky,
> and the broad sea rattles and plashes
> with the battery of the blast and of the irresistible hail.
> But for all that, ye, even ye, do draw both ship
> and despairing shipmen from out the hell;
> the winds abate, the sea puts on a shining calm,
> the clouds run asunder this way and that way;
> till out come the Bears peeping,
> and betwixt the Asses lo! that Manger so dim,
> which betokens all fair for voyaging on the sea.

---

4 Hesiod, *To the Dioscuri*, ibid., pp. 461–463.
5 Theocritus, *The Hymn to the Dioscuri*, *The Greek Bucolic Poets* (trans. J. M. Edmonds; London: Heinemann, 1912), 14–22.

Non-Homeric Greek deities

The Samothrace deities

The Samothrace deities are also called "the Great Gods." They are known for their protection in sea storms. The number and sex of these gods is unknown. There were mystery rites associated with their worship.

3.6. The Samothrace Deities Save a Ship Because of the Prayers of Orpheus, a Voyager Who Had Been Initiated into Their Mysteries

Diodorus Siculus, *The Library of History* 4.43.1–2[6]

But there came on a great storm and the chieftains had given up hope of being saved, when Orpheus, they say, who was the only one on shipboard who had ever been initiated in the mysteries of the deities of Samothrace, offered to these deities the prayers for their salvation. And immediately the wind died down and two stars fell over the heads of the Dioscori [Castor and Polydeuces], and the whole company was amazed at the marvel which had taken place and concluded that they had been rescued from their perils by an act of Providence of the gods. For this reason . . . sailors when caught in storms always direct their prayers to the deities of Samothrace and attribute the appearance of the two stars [the Gemini, thought to have a calming effect on the sea] to the epiphany of the Dioscori.

Foreign deities

Isis

This Egyptian goddess became prominent in Hellenistic and Greco-Roman antiquity.[7] Her myth featured a search for her murdered and dismembered husband/brother Osiris, which forced her to travel over the seas. Thus, she was mistress of the seas. As one of the great gods of the East, Isis was attractive for her multivalent and deeply tender aspects, her welcome to the humblest devotees and her power over Fate.

6 Diodorus Siculus, *The Library of History*, vol. 2 (trans. C. H. Oldfather; London: Heinemann, 1935), 4.43.1–2.
7 For a review of her worship, see R. E. Witt, *Isis in the Greco-Roman World* (London: Thames and Hudson, 1971); Vincent Tran Tam Tinh, *Le Culte d'Isis à Pompéi* (Paris: Editions E. de Boccard, 1964).

Our texts are drawn from two sources. The first is Isidorus, a devotee from the middle of the first century BCE, while the second is Apuleius, a devotee from the second century CE.

3.7. I Conquer Fate

Isidorus (circa 50 BCE), *Hymn One, The Four Hymns of Isidorus*[8]
I conquer Fate; Fate is obedient to me.

3.8. I Am the Mistress of Rivers and Winds and Sea[9]

Isidorus, *Hymn One, The Four Hymns of Isidorus* 1.39, 43, 49, 50[9]
I am Mistress of rivers, and winds and sea. . . . I calm and swell the sea[10] . . . I am the Mistress of sailing. . . . I render navigable things unnavigable when it might be to my glory.

3.9. "O Many-Named Isis, Saving Those Who Sail on the Great Sea in Winter, when Men May be Destroyed and Their Ships Wrecked and Sunk"

Isidorus, *Hymn One, The Four Hymns of Isidorus* 1.1–2, 25–34
  O wealth-giver, Queen of the gods . . .
  Omnipotent Agathe Tyche [Good Fortune], greatly renowned Isis . . .
  Mighty One, I shall not cease to sing of your great power,
  Deathless Saviour, many-named Isis,
  saving from war, cities and all their citizens:
  Men, their wives, possessions and children.
  As many as are bound fast in prison, in the power of death,
  As many as are in pain through long, anguished sleepless nights,
  All who are wanderers in a foreign land,
  And as many sail on the Great Sea [Mediterranean] in winter
  When men may be destroyed and their ships wrecked and sunk.
  All (these) are saved if they pray that You be present to help.

---

8 Vera F. Venderlip, "The Memphis Document," *The Four Hymns of Isidorus* (Toronto: Hakkert, 1971), text, p. 95.

9 Ibid., plate 15 and published text; my translation. See commentary on her pp. 55–56. See also the classic treatment of Isis in R. E. Witt, *Isis in the Greco-Roman World* (Ithaca, NY: Cornell University Press, 1971).

10 Isis' power over the sea allowed an association with the figure of Tyche/Fortune/Chance. Many times her iconography includes her hand upon a helm – the sign of the Greek goddess of Chance, Tyche – and a cornucopia in her arms – the sign of the Roman version, Fortuna.

3.10. At Isis' Will, the Wholesome Winds of the Seas are Disposed

Apuleius, *Metamorphoses* 11.5[11]

Behold, Lucius, moved by your prayers I [Isis] have come, I the mother of the universe, mistress of all the elements, and first offspring of the ages; mightiest of deities, queen of the dead, and foremost of heavenly beings my one person manifests the aspect of all gods and goddesses. With my nod I rule the starry heights of heaven, the health-giving breezes of the sea, and the plaintive silences of the underworld.

Serapis

Since Serapis is the consort of Isis, his cult accompanied hers throughout the Mediterranean world. Yet her popularity seems to have been much greater than his. Nevertheless, Serapis had many devotees. Two inscriptions from the second century CE acknowledge his power to rescue his devotees from sea storms. The first is a testimony from Aelius Aristides, the second a tribute from a young soldier writing to his father.

3.11. Serapis Allows People Caught in a Sea Storm to See Port Suddenly

Aelius Aristides, *Regarding Serapis* 45.33[12]

O universal light for all mankind, you who were recently manifested to us when, at the time that the vast sea rose from all sides and rushed upon us and nothing was visible except the destruction which was approaching and had well-nigh arrived, you stretched out your hand, revealed the hidden heavens, and granted us to behold the earth and to make port, so much beyond our expectation that we were unconvinced even when we set foot on shore.

3.12. A Soldier Thanks Serapis for Saving him from Peril in the Sea

Letter from a soldier (second century CE), *BGU* 2.423[13]

I thank the Lord Serapis that, when I was in peril in the sea, he saved me completely . . .

---

11 Apuleius, *Metamorphoses*, vol. 2 (trans. J. Arthur Hanson; Cambridge, MA: Harvard University Press, 1989), 11.5.
12 Aelius Aristides, *Regarding Serapis, Aelius Aristides: The Complete Works* (trans. C. A. Behr; 2 vols; Leiden: E. J. Brill, 1981), 45.33.
13 Adolf Deissmann, *Light from the Ancient East* (trans. L. R. M. Strachan; London: Hodder and Stoughton, 1927), 180; *BGU* 2.423.

The Jewish deity

There are five sources for texts available in the Greco-Roman period in which the God of the Jews is shown stilling a storm. The first source is the *Jewish scripture/Septuagint*, where the Psalms and particularly the Jonah story describe the Jewish God's power to still storms instantly. The second source is found in the *Testament of Naphtali*, a part of a larger pseudepigraphical work, *the Testaments of the Twelve Patriarchs*, dated about the second century BCE.[14] The prayerbook of Qumran, *Hodayot*, is the third source, and can be fairly dated from the later second century to the mid-first century BCE.[15]

The other two sources belong to rabbinic traditions, one from the *Babylonian Talmud*, the other from the *Jerusalem Talmud*.[16] Paul Fiebig's research leads him to situate the former in the Tannaitic period (pre-200 CE), while the latter belongs to the Amoritic generation (early third century CE).[17]

JEWISH SCRIPTURE/SEPTUAGINT

3.13. The Jewish God Rules the Raging Sea and Stills its Waves

Ps. 89:8–9
> 8. O Lord God of Hosts,
> who is as mighty as you,

---

14 See James H. Charlesworth, ed., *The Old Testament Pseudepigrapha* (2 vols; Garden City, NY: Doubleday, 1983), vol. 1, pp. 810–814.

15 For these references I am indebted to the research of John Paul Heil, *Jesus Walking on the Sea* (Analecta Biblica 87; Rome: Pontifical Biblical Institute, 1981), 19–21, 25–30. Heil sees such common elements between these documents and the Jesus sea miracles that he suggests some knowledge of them by the Christian narrator. Of course, the problem is that the sea-storm theme and imagery are too common for any such conclusion to hold. Moreover, Heil is not able to find any material in the Jewish collection where a hero walks on the sea. Thus, although his monograph treats the walking on the water, the only texts he can find are those dealing with the cessation of storms.

16 For these references I am indebted to the research of Paul Fiebig, *Jüdische Wundergeschichten des neutestamentlichen Zeitalters* (Tübingen: J. C. B. Mohr, 1911), 12, and *Rabbinische Wundergeschichten* (Berlin: Walter de Gruyter, 1933), 23–24.

17 Fiebig, *Jüdische Wundergeschichten des neutestamentlichen Zeitalters*, 12, and *Rabbinische Wundergeschichten*, 23–24.

O Lord?
Your faithfulness surrounds you,
9. You rule the raging sea; when its waves rise,
you still them.

3.14. Ps. 107:23–30

23. Some went down to the sea in ships,
doing business on the mighty waters;
24. they saw the deeds of the Lord,
his wondrous works in the deep.
25. For he commanded and raised the stormy wind,
which lifted up the waves of the sea.
26. They mounted up to heaven,
they went down to the depths;
their courage melted away in their calamity;
27. they reeled and staggered like drunkards,
and were at their wits' end.
28. Then they cried to the Lord in their trouble,
and he brought them out from their distress;
29. he made the storm be still,
and the waves of the sea were hushed.
30. They were glad because they had quiet,
and he brought them to their desired haven.

3.15. The Lord Stills a Storm When the Prophet Jonah is Cast Overboard into the Sea

[Jonah refuses to preach repentance to the people of Nineveh as the Lord has commanded him. So he tries to take a boat to Tarshish, which is in the opposite direction.]
Jonah 1:4–17
4. But the Lord hurled a great wind upon the sea, and such a mighty storm came upon the sea that the ship threatened to break up. 5. Then the mariners were afraid, and each cried to his god. They threw the cargo into the sea, to lighten it for them. But Jonah, meanwhile, had gone down into the hold of the ship and had lain down, and was fast asleep. 6. The captain came and said to him, "What are you doing sound asleep? Get up, call on your god! Perhaps the god will spare us a thought so that we do not perish."
7. The sailors said to one another, "Come, let us cast lots, so that we may know on whose account this calamity has come upon us." So they cast lots, and the lot fell on Jonah. 8. Then they said to him, "Tell us why this calamity has come upon us. What is your occupation? Where do you come from? What is your country? And of what people are you?" 9. "I am a Hebrew," he replied. "I worship the Lord, the God of heaven, who made the sea and the dry land." 10. Then the men were even more afraid, and

said to him, "What is this that you have done!" For the men knew that he was fleeing from the presence of the Lord, because he had told them so.

11. Then they said to him, "What shall we do to you, that the sea may quiet down for us?" For the sea was growing more and more tempestuous. *12.* He said to them, "Pick me up and throw me into the sea; then the sea will quiet down for you; for I know it is because of me that this great storm has come upon you." *13.* Nevertheless the men rowed hard to bring the ship back to land, but they could not, for the sea grew more and more stormy against them. *14.* Then they cried out to the Lord, "Please, O Lord, we pray, do not let us perish on account of this man's life. Do not make us guilty of innocent blood; for you, O Lord, have done as it pleased you." *15.* So they picked Jonah up and threw him into the sea; and the sea ceased from its raging. *16.* Then the men feared the Lord even more, and they offered a sacrifice to the Lord and made vows.

17. But the Lord provided a large fish to swallow up Jonah; and Jonah was in the belly of the fish three days and three nights.

TESTAMENT OF NAPHTALI (CIRCA 150 CE)

In this text, the son of Jacob describes a dream he has had. The symbolism of the storm is easily understood with reference to the well-founded anxiety that persecution would destroy the nation. In the dream, Levi's prayers win the Lord's intervention and a safe resolution of the danger.

3.16. Levi Prayed to the Lord on our Behalf and the Storm Ceased

Testament of Naphtali 6:1–10[18]

1. And again after seven days I saw our father Jacob standing at the sea of Jamnia and we, his sons, with him. *2.* And behold, a ship came sailing by without sailors and pilot, and the ship was inscribed "Jacob." *3.* And our father said to us, "Let us climb into our ship!" *4.* As we entered, there came a violent storm, and a tempest of strong wind. And our father, who was holding the helm, was taken from us. *5.* And overtaken by the storm we were driven over the sea. And the ship was filled with water, beaten here and there by the waves, so that it was also shattered. *6.* And Joseph fled upon a little boat. And we also were divided upon ten planks. And Levi

18 Charlesworth, Testament of Naphtali, *Testament of the Twelve Patriarchs, The Old Testament Pseudepigrapha*, vol. 1, 6.1–10. Translation by John P. Heil, *Jesus Walking on the Sea: Meaning and Gospel Functions of Matt 14:22–33, Mark 6:45–52 and John 6:15b–21* (Analecta Biblica 87; Rome: Biblical Institute Press, 1981), 19.

and Juda were together. 7. We were all scattered then to the ends of the earth. 8. But Levi, girt about with sackcloth, prayed for us all to the Lord. 9. And as the storm ceased, the ship came upon the land as in peace. 10. And behold, our father came, and we all rejoiced with one accord.

HODAYOT: THE QUMRAN BOOK OF HYMNS

3.17. O My God, I Was Like a Sailor You Saved from Stormy Seas

1QH 6:22–26a[19]

And I was like a sailor on a ship in the storming of the seas, their waves and all their breakers raged against me, a whirlwind so that there was no pause to revive the soul and there was no path to straighten a way on the surface of the waters and the abyss roared at my anguish and I approached the gates of death. And I was as one who comes into a fortified city and strengthened by a high wall unto deliverance. And I rejoiced in your truth, O my God, for you set a foundation on rock.

BABA MEZIA, BABYLONIAN TALMUD (TANNAITIC PERIOD, PRE-200 CE)

Rabbi Gamaliel has chastised Rabbi Eliezer ben Hyrcanus and subsequently takes a sea voyage.

3.18. Rabbi Gamaliel Justifies His Behavior to God and the Storm Stops

Baba Mezia 59b–f, Babylonian Talmud[20]

C. And also Rabban Gamaliel was coming by ship. A big wave arose to drown him.

D. He said, "It appears to me that this is on account only of Rabban Eliezer ben Hyrcanus."

E. He stood upon his feet and said, "Lord of the world, it is perfectly obvious to you that it was not for my own honor that I have acted, nor for the honor of the house of my father have I acted, but it was for the honor owing to you, specifically, so that dissension should not become rife in Israel."

F. The sea subsided.

---

19 Heil, *Jesus Walking on the Sea*, 27–28.
20 Jacob Neusner (trans.), "Bava Mesia, Chapters 3–4," *The Babylonian Talmud: An American Translation* (Atlanta, GA: Scholars Press, 1990), vol. 21B, p. 156.

3.19. A Jewish Boy Saves a Gentile Ship from Sea Storms by His Prayers. Berachoth, Jerusalem Talmud (Amoraic Period, post-200 CE)

Berachoth 9, Jerusalem Talmud[21]

Rabbi Tanhuma said: It happened that a pagan ship made a voyage on the Great Sea [the Mediterranean] and on it was one Jewish child. While at sea a great storm on the sea arose against them, and then each one stood and began to raise his hands and call out to his god. But the child did nothing. Seeing that he did nothing they said to the Jewish boy, "My son, stand up! Call on your god! For we have heard that he answers you, if you cry out to him and he is strong." Thereupon the child stood up and with his whole heart he cried out [to God] and the sea was silent.

Note

This story seems inspired by Jonah 1:4–16 without the negative elements of Jonah's stubbornness and his intended avoidance of God and the Ninevites. Here, however, we do find the idea of one Jewish person on board being more powerful than all the crew because only the God of Israel, the one true God, can still the storm, and the prayers of a faithful Jewish child are sufficient to call down that divine rescue.

Heroes who control the wind and the sea

Homeric/Greek heroes

Orpheus

Orpheus joined Jason's expedition as the man who sings to keep the rowing in unison.[22] Orpheus' singing was so superhuman in its quality that he was able to stop a quarrel between two Argonauts because

---

21 Paul Fiebig's translation, *Rabbinische Wundergeschichten*, 23–24 (my English translation).

22 Pindar, *Pythian Odes*, "Of Apollo's blood the harper came and father of the lyric voices, Orpheus the admired" (trans. Richard Lattimore, *The Odes of Pindar* [Chicago and London: Phoenix Books and University of Chicago Press, 1947], 64).

they were enthralled at the sound of his voice. But Orpheus is most famous for his rescue of the Argonauts from the Sirens. As the sailors heard their call, they became enchanted, but Orpheus filled their ears with the sound of his music so that their ship would not be dashed against the rocks. While this story is recounted by Apollonius Rhodius, a scholar from the Hellenistic period, his purpose was to capture the ancient story which belongs to pre-philosophical times.

3.20. Orpheus Uses His Voice to Save His Comrades from Shipwreck at the Temptation of the Sirens' Call

Apollonius Rhodius (third century BCE), *Argonautica* 4.903–911[23]
> And they were already about to cast from the ship the hawsers to shore,
> had not Thracian Orpheus, son of Oeagrus, stringing in his hands
> his Bistonian lyre, rung forth the hasty snatch of a rippling melody
> so that their ears might be filled with the sound of his twanging;
> and the lyre overcame the maidens' voice.
> And the west wind and the sounding wave rushing astern bore the ship on.

3.21. Orpheus is Beguiling the Sea by his Singing

Philostratus (circa 200 CE), *Imagines* 2.15.1[24]
> The Argo is already cutting its way through the midst of the surging Euxine
> and Orpheus is beguiling the sea by his singing, moreover the Euxine listens and is calm under the spell of his song.

Pythagorean philosophers

Pythagoras (circa 531 BCE)

By the time of the Neo-Pythagorean movement of the second and third centuries, the myths and legends of their founder, Pythagoras, had taken on a superhuman character. Whether these legends and stories are historical or not, however, their existence shows us ideas about the powers of a superhuman man that were extant and relatively familiar to some degree around the Greco-Roman Mediterranean.

23 Apollonius Rhodius, *Argonautica* (trans. R. C. Seaton; London: Heinemann, 1912), 4.903–911.
24 Philostratus, *Imagines* (trans. Arthur Fairbanks; London: Heinemann, 1931), 2.15.1.

Pythagoras is credited with the first probings of the new cosmology. For him, such a step was a movement into the world of sacred laws and secrets of the universe. Thus the life of philosophy according to the myth of Pythagoras was almost monastic in its discipline, asceticism, moral rectitude and community sense, all in the name of worthiness for communication with the divine laws of cosmic order.

Since Pythagoras was privy to nature and its laws, it is only expected that stories would include his communication with the rational elements of nature, and theirs with him.

Such stories emphasize in various ways the special status of Pythagoras, and the authority his knowledge gave him over the very natural elements whose secrets had been revealed to him.

3.22. Pythagoras Calmed Rivers and Seas So that His Disciples Might More Easily Pass over Them

Iamblichus (250–325 CE), *Life of Pythagoras* 28[25]
Many other more admirable and divine particulars are likewise unanimously and uniformly related of the man, such as infallible predictions of earthquakes, rapid expulsions of pestilences, and hurricanes, instantaneous cessations of hail, and tranquillizations of the waves of rivers and seas, in order that his disciples might the more easily pass over them.

Empedocles

Empedocles was both a statesman and a Pythagorean philosopher, both a poet and a miracle worker. Diogenes Laertius (first half of the third century CE) preserves a poem in which Empedocles promises his students the power to perform the wonders that he can do. In the later work of Iamblichus, his *Life of Pythagoras*, Empedocles is mentioned as one of those who could control the elements just as Pythagoras had done.

3.23. "You Will be Able to Arrest the Violence of the Unwearied Winds"

Diogenes Laertius, *Empedocles*, *Lives of Eminent Philosophers* 8.59[26]
Thou shalt arrest the violence of the unwearied winds that arise and sweep the earth, laying waste the cornfields with their blasts; and again, if thou

---

25 Iamblichus, *Life of Pythagoras*, in *The Pythagorean Sourcebook* (ed. and trans. K. S. Guthrie; Grand Rapids: Phanes, 1987), pp. 57–120, esp. p. 91.

26 Diogenes Laertius, *Empedocles*, *The Lives of Eminent Philosophers*, vol. 2 (trans. R. D. Hicks; London: Heinemann, 1925). For a more complete discussion of

so will, thou shall call back winds in requital. Thou shalt make after the dark rain a seasonable drought for men, and again after the summer drought thou shalt cause tree-nourishing streams to pour from the sky. Thou shalt bring back from Hades a dead man's strength.

3.24. Empedocles was surnamed "The Wind-Stiller"

Iamblichus (250–325 CE), *Life of Pythagoras* 135–136[27]
The power of effecting miracles of this kind [predictions of earthquakes, expulsion of diseases and hurricanes, instantaneous cessations of hail and tranquilizations of seas and rivers] was achieved by Empedocles of Agrigentum, Epimenes the Cretan and Abaris the Hyperborean, and these they performed in many places. Their deeds were so manifest that Empedocles was surnamed "the Wind-Stiller," Epimenes an "expiator" and Abaris an "air-walker."

Holy men

Apollonius of Tyana (60–100 CE)

Apollonius was renowned as a sage, healer and exorcist. Various traditions about him were gathered by the Neo-Pythagoreans and presented in Philostratus' *Life of Apollonius of Tyana* about the year 200 CE. The book was written at the request of the emperor Julian's mother, Julia Domna, who had great devotion to the philosopher/holy man. She wanted to refute charges that Apollonius had been nothing more than a wizard.

In Philostratus' work, Apollonius is presented as a Pythagorean, and there is much more emphasis on his life as a philosopher than as a miracle worker. This may be a strategic move on the part of Philostratus to diminish the aspects of Apollonius' tradition that would encourage a charge of wizardry.

In the passage quoted Apollonius had just visited the tomb of Ajax in Troy and was about to sail to Aeolia in a small ship. However, when the people saw him they all tried to crowd aboard his vessel because they saw him as "Master of the Tempest." Here, Philostratus does not see anything like wizardry in the acclamation of the people. Philostratus does not explain how the people would

the passage see M. R. Wright, *Empedocles: The Extant Fragments* (New Haven and London: Yale University Press, 1981), 261–263.
27 Iamblichus, *Life of Pythagoras*, in *The Pythagorean Sourcebook*, pp. 57–120 esp. p. 91.

understand Apollonius' mastery of nature. It may be that since he has portrayed Apollonius as a Pythagorean, he hopes that the reader will see a union with Nature most appropriate for one who follows Pythagoras.

3.25. Apollonius, Master of the Tempest and Perils of All Sorts

Philostratus, *Life of Apollonius of Tyana* 4.13.5–13[28]
It was already autumn and the sea was not to be trusted. They [the people sailing for Aeolia] all then regarded Apollonius as one who was master of the tempest and of fire and of perils of all sorts, and so wished to go on board with him, and begged him to allow them to share the voyage with him. But as the company was many times too great for the ship, spying a larger ship – for there were many in the neighbourhood of the tomb of Ajax, – he said, "Let us go on board this, for it is a good thing to get home safely with as many as may be."

Jesus of Nazareth

Jesus stills a storm

3.26. He Woke up and Rebuked the Wind, and Said to the Sea, "Peace! Be Still!" Then the Wind Ceased, and there was a Dead Calm

Mark 4:35–41 (Matt. 8:23–27//Luke 8:22–25)
35. On that day, when evening had come, he said to them, "Let us go across to the other side." 36. And leaving the crowd behind, they took him with them in the boat, just as he was. Other boats were with him. 37. A great windstorm arose, and the waves beat into the boat, so that the boat was already being swamped. 38. But he was in the stern, asleep on the cushion; and they woke him up and said to him, "Teacher, do you not care that we are perishing?" 39. He woke up and rebuked the wind, and said to the sea, "Peace! Be still!" Then the wind ceased, and there was a dead calm. 40. He said to them, "Why are you still afraid? Have you still no faith?" 41. And they were filled with great awe and said to one another, "Who then is this, that even the wind and the sea obey him?"

28 Philostratus, *The Life of Apollonius of Tyana*, vol. 1 (trans. F. C. Conybeare; London: Heinemann, 1912), 4.13.5–13.

Military leaders/kings/emperors

Julius Caesar (100–44 BCE)

This entry is important because it illustrates how very much a hero wanted to claim that Nature recognized his destiny and had to bow to his empowerment from heaven. Although only the account from Dio Cassius is presented, there are several accounts of Julius Caesar's challenge to the sea.[29] The political propaganda to be spread with this tale sheds light on its importance for any hero,[30] and shows the deliberation with which Caesar's followers would have promulgated the event.[31] Stefan Weinstock observes that it was crucial for Caesar to outdo Pompey's reputation as a man of extraordinary good fortune.[32]

DIO CASSIUS (WROTE 194–229 CE)

3.27. Caesar Felt Firm Confidence in His Safety: "Be of Good Cheer: You Carry Caesar"

Dio Cassius, *Roman History* 46.1–4[33]

Now Antony, to whom had been assigned the duty of conveying across those who remained at Brundisium, continued to tarry, and no message even came about them because of the winter and because of Bibulus [Caesar's foe], Caesar suspected that they had adopted a neutral attitude and were watching the course of events, as often happens in civil strife. Wishing, therefore, to sail to Italy in person and unattended, he embarked on a small boat in disguise, saying that he had been sent by Caesar; and he forced the captain to sail, although there was a wind. When, however, they had got away from the land, and the gale swept violently down upon them and the waves buffeted them terribly, so that the captain did not longer dare even under compulsion to sail further, but undertook to return even without his passenger's consent, *then Caesar revealed himself, as if by this act he could stop the storm,*[34] and said, "Be of good cheer: you carry

---

29 The frequency with which this story was repeated by the historians is ample evidence of the power of its claims: Lucan, *The Civil War* 5.476–699; Plutarch, *Lives: Julius Caesar* 38.2–6; *Moralia: The Fortune of the Romans* 6; Appian, *Roman History* 8.56–57; 21.148; Suetonius, *Divus Julius* 58.2; Florus, *Roman History* 2.13.35–38.

30 See n.29 above.

31 See the discussion by Iiro Kajanto, "Fortuna," *ANRW* II 17.1 (1981) 537.

32 Stefan Weinstock, *Divus Julius* (Oxford: Clarendon Press, 1971), 124.

33 Dio Cassius, *Roman History*, vol. 4 (trans. Earnest Cary; London: Heinemann, 1916), 46.1–4 (my italic).

34 My italic.

Caesar." Such spirit and such hope had he, either naturally or as the result of some oracle, that he felt firm confidence in his safety even contrary to the appearance of things. Nevertheless, he did not get across, but after struggling for a long time in vain sailed back.

Augustus Caesar (65 BCE – 14 CE)

This reference from Philo is especially significant for our investigation of Jesus' miracle of stilling the storm. Philo is trying to shame the new emperor Gaius (Caligula) with his great-grandfather Augustus' example. In describing the effects of Augustus' rule, Philo, a Jew, chooses two metaphors ordinarily associated with God, namely, calming a sea storm and healing a world-wide pestilence. Philo is referring to the great Roman Pax, of course, but his choice of these images shows us that the idea of a hero stilling a storm is already alive in the Greco-Roman world. Clearly whoever holds such powers must have received them from heaven, for the good of the earth.

3.28. This is the Caesar who Calmed the Torrential Storms on Every Side

Philo, *The Embassy to Gaius* 144–145[35]

The whole human race exhausted by mutual slaughter was on the verge of utter destruction, had it not been for one man and leader Augustus whom men fitly call "the averter of evil." This is the Caesar who calmed the torrential storms on every side, who healed the pestilences common to Greeks and barbarians, pestilences which descending from the south and the east coursed to the west and north sowing the seeds of calamity over the places and waters which lay between.

WALKING/TRAVELING ON THE SEA

The gods who walk on water

In the Greco-Roman world, the one god who is associated with traveling over the sea is Poseidon/Neptune. As we see from the Homeric description, this king of the sea is drawn across the water by the sea beasts. However, the god who walks across the sea as well as trampling it with sea horses is the Jewish God.

---

35 Philo, *The Embassy to Gaius*, *Philo*, vol. 10 (trans. F. H. Colson and J. W. Earp; London: Heinemann, 1962), 144–145.

The Olympian diety who travels across the sea

Poseidon/Neptune

3.29. Poseidon Travels through the Sea in a Horse-Drawn Chariot

Homer, *Iliad* 13.27–29[36]
Then gambolled the sea-beasts beneath him [Poseidon] on every side from out the deeps, for well they knew their lord, and in gladness the sea parted before him.

The foreign diety who travels across the water

The Jewish God

3.30. The Lord like a Warrior Tramples Down the Sea with His Horses

Hab. 3:12–15
12. In fury you trod the earth,
in anger you trampled nations.
13. You came forth to save your people,
to save your anointed.
You crushed the head of the wicked house,
laying it bare from foundation to roof.
14. You pierced with his own arrows
the head of his warriors,
who came like a whirlwind to scatter us,
gloating as if ready to devour the poor
who were in hiding.
15. You trampled the sea with your horses,
churning the mighty waters.

3.31. He Alone Stretched Out the Heavens and Trampled the Waves of the Sea

Job 9:6–11
6. [The Lord] shakes the earth out of its place,
and its pillars tremble;

---

36 Homer, *Iliad*, vol. 2 (trans. A. T. Murray; London: Heinemann, 1925), 13.27–29.

7. who commands the sun, and it does not rise;
who seals up the stars;
8. who alone stretched out the heavens,
and trampled the waves of the Sea;
9. who made the Bear and Orion,
the Pleiades and the chambers of the south.
10. who does great things beyond understanding,
and marvelous things without number,
11. Look, he passes by me, and I do not see him;
he moves on, but I do not perceive him.

3.32. In the Exodus, it is the Lord who Makes a Path through the Waters so that the People can Follow Him

Ps. 77:19–20

19.Your way was through the sea,
your path through the great waters;
yet your footprints were unseen.
20. You led your people like a flock
by the hand of Moses and Aaron.

3.33. The Lord Makes a Way in the Sea, a Path in the Mighty Waters

Isa. 43:16–17

16. Thus says the Lord,
who makes a way in the sea,
a path in the mighty waters,
17. who brings out chariot and horse,
army and warrior;
they lie down, they cannot rise,
they are extinguished,
quenched like a wick.

3.34 Isa. 51:9–10

9. Awake, awake, put on strength,
O arm of the Lord;
Awake, as in days of old,
the generations of long ago.
Was it not you who cut Rahab in pieces,
who pierced the dragon?
10. Was it not you who dried up the sea,
the waters of the great deep;
who made the depths of the sea a way
for the redeemed to cross over?

150

Heroes who walk/travel across the sea

There are no Homeric heroes who are said to walk across the sea. In the traditions of the Pythagoreans, Abaris, the holy man of the Hyperboreans, is said to travel over land and sea on a magic arrow given to him by Apollo. The idea of a body of water acknowledging a human hero is found in the story of Pythagoras' being greeted by a stream. Jewish tradition holds no story of a hero walking on the sea, which is possibly because it is seen as a prerogative of the Most High. The one sea miracle repeated among Jewish heroes is that of dividing water. This is done by Moses and afterward leaders such as Joshua, Elijah and Elisha to show the people that they are authorized by heaven.

Heroes from Pythagorean legend

Abaris

Herodotus is reluctant to tell the legend of Abaris because it seems so very fanciful to him.

3.35. Abaris Carried the Arrow over the Whole World

Herodotus, *Histories* 4.32, 36[37]
Concerning the Hyperborean people neither the Scythians nor any other dwellers in these lands tell us anything, except perchance the Issedones. . . . I do not tell the story of that Abaris, alleged to be a Hyperborean, who carried the arrow [given by Apollo] over the whole world, fasting the while.

Pythagoras (circa 531 CE)

3.36. The River Caucase Responds to Pythagoras' Greeting as He Crosses It

Porphyry (232–305 CE), *Life of Pythagoras* 27[38]
It is said that once, while crossing the river Caucase together with many of his friends, he [Pythagoras] greeted it [the river]. And the river responded in a voice so audible and distinct that everyone heard, "Greetings to you, Pythagoras."

---

37 Herodotus, *Histories*, vol. 2 (trans. A. D. Godley; London: Heinemann, 1938), 4.32, 36.
38 Porphyry, *Life of Pythagoras* 29, in Guthrie *The Pythagorean Sourcebook*, 129.

Note

This story has some relevance for the stilling of the storm as well, since the hero speaks to the natural elements and receives a response. Some scholars presume that if Jesus speaks to the wind and the sea, there must be a demon within the element. Stories like this one illustrate the Greco-Roman sensitivity to the elements as living and intelligent entities.

Foreign heroes: heroes from Jewish scriptures

Moses

3.37.1. As the Egyptian Army Pursues the Israelites, the Lord Instructs Moses to Raise His Staff and Divide the Sea

Exod. 14:15–18, 21–22

15. Then the Lord said to Moses, "Why do you cry out to me? Tell the Israelites to go forward. *16.* But you lift up your staff, and stretch out your hand over the sea and divide it, that the Israelites may go into the sea on dry ground. *17.* Then I will harden the hearts of the Egyptians so that they will go in after them; and so I will gain glory for myself over Pharaoh and all his army, his chariots, and his chariot drivers. *18.* And the Egyptians shall know that I am the Lord, when I have gained glory for myself over Pharaoh, his chariots, and his chariot drivers." . . .

21. Then Moses stretched out his hand over the sea. The Lord drove the sea back by a strong east wind all night, and turned the sea into dry land; and the waters were divided. *22.* The Israelites went into the sea on dry ground, the waters forming a wall for them on their right and on their left.

3.37.2. The Egyptians Try to Follow after Them, but God Orders Moses to Stretch His Hand Over the Waters and the Waters Close on the Egyptian Army

Exod. 14:23–29

23. The Egyptians pursued, and went into the sea after them, all of Pharaoh's horses, chariots, and chariot drivers. *24.* At the morning watch the Lord in the pillar of fire and cloud looked down upon the Egyptian army, and threw the Egyptian army into panic. *25.* He clogged their chariot wheels so that they turned with difficulty. The Egyptians said, "Let us flee from the Israelites, for the Lord is fighting for them against Egypt."

26. Then the Lord said to Moses, "Stretch out your hand over the sea, so that the water may come back upon the Egyptians, upon their chariots and chariot drivers." *27.* So Moses stretched out his hand over the sea, and at dawn the sea returned to its normal depth. As the Egyptians fled before it, the Lord tossed the Egyptians into the sea. *28.* The waters returned and covered the chariots and the chariot drivers, the entire army of Pharaoh that had followed them into the sea; not one of them remained. *29.* But the Israelites walked on dry ground through the sea, the waters forming a wall for them on their right and on their left.

JOSEPHUS (CIRCA 75 CE)

3.38. Moses' Miracle is as Believable as Alexander's When the Pamphylian Sea Retired and Coiled before Him and Alexander was Granted the Conquest of Persia

Josephus, *Jewish Antiquities* 2.347–348[39]

Nor let anyone marvel at the astonishing nature of the narrative or doubt that it was given to men of old, innocent of crime, to find a road of salvation through the sea itself, whether by the will of God or maybe by accident, seeing that the hosts of Alexander king of Macedon, men but born the other day, beheld the Pamphylian Sea retire before them and when there was none, offer a passage through itself, what time it pleased God to overthrow the Persian empire; and on that all are agreed who have recorded Alexander's exploits.

Note

It is intriguing that Josephus is well aware that Alexander's legends are sacred to his listeners and can be used as proofs of miracles made possible to those whom the gods favor.

Joshua

3.39. The Lord Said to Joshua, "This Day I Will Begin to Exalt You in the Sight of All Israel so that the People will Know that I Am With You as I Was With Moses"

Joshua 3:1, 7–11, 15–16

1. Early in the morning Joshua rose and set out from Shittim with all the Israelites, and they came to the Jordan. They camped there before crossing over.

---

39 Josephus, *Jewish Antiquities, Josephus*, vol. 4 (trans. H. St. J. Thackeray; London: Heinemann, 1930), 2.347–348.

... 7. The Lord said to Joshua, "This day I will begin to exalt you in the sight of all Israel, so that they may know that I will be with you as I was with Moses. 8. You are the one who shall command the priests who bear the ark of the covenant, 'When you come to the edge of the waters of the Jordan, you shall stand still in the Jordan.'" 9. Joshua then said to the Israelites, "Draw near and hear the words of the Lord your God." 10. Joshua said, "By this you shall know that among you is the living God who without fail will drive out from before you the Canaanites, Hittites, Hivites, Perizzites, Girgashites, Amorites, and Jebusites: 11. the ark of the covenant of the Lord of all the earth is going to pass before you into the Jordan.

... 15. Now the Jordan overflows all its banks throughout the time of harvest. So when those who bore the ark had come to the Jordan, and the feet of the priests bearing the ark were dipped in the edge of the water, 16. the waters flowing from above stood still, rising up in a single heap far off at Adam, the city that is beside Zarethan, while those flowing toward the sea of the Arabah, the Dead Sea, were wholly cut off. Then the people crossed over opposite Jericho.

Elijah

3.40. Elijah Parts the Jordan with his Mantle

2 Kgs. 2:6–8

6. Then Elijah said to him. "Stay here; for the Lord has sent me to the Jordan." But he said, "As the Lord lives, and as you yourself live, I will not leave you." So the two of them went on. 7. Fifty men of the company of prophets also went, and stood at some distance from them, as they both were standing by the Jordan. 8. Then Elijah took his mantle and rolled it up, and struck the water; the water was parted to the one side and to the other, until the two of them crossed on dry ground.

Elisha

3.41.1. Elisha Receives a Double Portion of Elijah's Spirit

2 Kgs. 2:9–12

9. When they had crossed, Elijah said to Elisha, "Tell me what I may do for you, before I am taken from you." Elisha said, "Please let me inherit a double share of your spirit." 10. He responded, "You have asked a hard thing; yet, if you see me as I am being taken from you, it will be granted you; if not, it will not." 11. As they continued walking and talking, a chariot of fire and horses of fire separated the two of them, and Elijah ascended in a whirlwind into heaven. 12. Elisha kept watching and crying out, "Father, father! The chariots of Israel and its horsemen!" But when he could no longer see him, he grasped his own clothes and tore them in two pieces.

3.41.2. Elisha Picks up Elijah's Mantle and Separates the Jordan with It in the Presence of the Fifty Prophets

2 Kgs. 2:13–15

13. He picked up the mantle of Elijah that had fallen from him, and went back and stood on the bank of the Jordan. *14.* He took the mantle of Elijah that had fallen from him, and struck the water, saying, "Where is the Lord, the God of Elijah?" When he had struck the water, the water was parted to the one side and to the other, and Elisha went over.

15. When the company of prophets who were at Jericho saw him at a distance, they declared, "The spirit of Elijah rests on Elisha." They came to meet him and bowed to the ground before him.

Foreign hero: the holy man Jesus of Nazareth

Jesus walks on the sea

3.42. When he Saw that they were Straining at the Oars Against an Adverse Wind, He Came Towards Them Early in the Morning, Walking on the Sea

Mark 6:45–52 (//Matt. 14:22–32; cf. John 6:15–21)

45. Immediately he made his disciples get into the boat and go on ahead to the other side, to Bethsaida, while he dismissed the crowd. *46.* After saying farewell to them, he went up on the mountain to pray.

47. When evening came, the boat was out on the sea, and he was alone on the land. *48.* When he saw that they were straining at the oars against an adverse wind, he came towards them early in the morning, walking on the sea. He intended to pass them by. *49.* But when they saw him walking on the sea, they thought it was a ghost and cried out; *50.* for they all saw him and were terrified. But immediately he spoke to them and said, "Take heart, it is I; do not be afraid." *51.* Then he got into the boat with them and the wind ceased. And they were utterly astounded, *52.* for they did not understand about the loaves, but their hearts were hardened.

Military leaders/kings/emperors

Xerxes, king of Persia (486–465 BCE)

In his *Third Discourse on Kingship*, Dio Chrysostom presents an interrogator asking Socrates about Xerxes' feat of making a bridge across the Hellespont. If only deities are able to cross water without getting wet, then did Xerxes' successful venture make him the equal of a god? Here, we see a question of interpretation. If the gods allow someone to achieve the end product of what a god can do, in this case, travel over a vast expanse of water, then isn't that a sign of divinity of some kind?

3.43. If Xerxes Traveled Across the Sea Dryshod, Like Poseidon, Is He Divine?

Dio Chrysostom, *Third Discourse on Kingship* 30–31[40]

"Socrates," said he [an interrogator], "you know perfectly well that of all men under the sun that man [Xerxes] is most powerful and in might no whit inferior to the gods themselves who is able to accomplish the seemingly impossible – if it should be his will, to have men walk dryshod over the sea, to sail over the mountains, to drain rivers dry by drinking – or have you not heard that Xerxes, the king of the Persians, made of the dry land a sea by cutting through the loftiest of the mountains and separating Athos from the mainland, and that he led his infantry through the sea, riding upon a chariot just like Poseidon in Homer's description?

Alexander the Great (356–323 BCE)

The idea of waters acting in a subservient way to a man destined for greatness occurs in the legends of Alexander. There are three ancient authors whose versions will be presented here. Callisthenes travelled with Alexander and Strabo is a geographer from the beginning of the first century, while Arrian wrote a biography of Alexander in the second century CE that is largely dependent on the biographies of Alexander's associates.

The different versions of the same story suggest that the ideas discussed here belong to the Greco-Roman world in a general way. The variety of interpretations shows us how fondness for a hero can cast a special light on an event.

CALLISTHENES (CIRCA 327 BCE)[41]

Callisthenes' biography of Alexander must be pieced together from fragments quoted by other authors. The reference to his statement about Alexander is found in the discussion of a twelfth-century

---

40 Dio Chrysostom, *Third Discourse on Kingship*, vol. 1 (trans. J. W. Cohoon and H. L. Crosby; London: Heinemann, 1932), 30–31.

41 Callisthenes' biography should be distinguished from the "Alexander Romance" attributed to a Pseudo-Callisthenes. For a discussion of that collection of ancient traditions see E. A. W. Budge, *The Alexander Book in Ethiopia* (London: Oxford University Press, 1933), esp. xv–xxix. For a discussion of

rhetorician, Eustathius, who was commenting on the *Iliad*. The text under discussion is Homer's description of Poseidon riding over the waves: "Then gambolled the sea beasts beneath him [Poseidon] on every side from out of the deep, for well they knew their Lord, and in gladness the sea parted before him." (Iliad, 29)

3.44. The Waves Know their Lord and Recede Before him

Eustathius, *On the Iliad* 29[42]
Even though he [Callisthenes] does not make the sea part before him [Alexander] in delight, as in making way before Poseidon, nevertheless [he] says that it withdrew from before his march as though recognizing him, and *that it too did not fail to know its lord* so that in arching itself and bowing it may seem to do obeisance [proskuneīn].[43]

The Roman emperor Gaius "Caligula" Caesar (12–41 CE)

The short reign of Gaius (37–41 CE) was marked by various excesses in the use and abuse of power.[44] He is the first of the Roman emperors to demand worship of his person as a god. Suetonius describes his expectations.

3.45. Gaius Desires to be Recognized as a God

Suetonius, *Gaius Caligula, Lives of the Caesars* 4.22.2–3[45]
On being reminded that he had risen above the elevation both of princes and kings, he began from that time on to lay claim to divine majesty . . .

---

the life and work of the historical Callisthenes, see L. Pearson, *The Lost Histories of Alexander* (London: Blackwell, 1960), 22–49.

42 Eustathius, *Iliad* 29, in Felix Jacoby, *Die Fragmente der griechischen Historiker* (2 vols; Leiden: Brill, 1962), vol. 2, B.650. Translation by Pearson, *The Lost Histories*, 36–37; my italic.

43 The verb translated at "to do obeisance" is *proskunein*. This is the bow on the floor in which the body is arched and curled under in subservience. Alexander had received this type of bow from the Persians, but when he suggested it to his own Greek commanders, there was protest, in particular from Callisthenes. For the Greeks, such a bow was reserved for the gods. Callisthenes certainly suggests the divinity of Alexander when he claims that the waves seemed to recognize his status and honour him.

44 Suetonius, *Gaius Caligula, Lives of the Caesars*; Dio Cassius, *Roman History* 7.59; Josephus, *Jewish Antiquities* 19.1–17. See also A. Barrett, *Caligula: The Corruption of Power* (London: B. T. Batsford, 1989).

45 All quotations are taken from Suetonius, *The Lives of the Caesars*, vol. 1 (trans. J. C. Rolfe; London: Heinemann, 1914).

Making a temple of Castor and Pollux its vestibule, he often took his place between the divine brethren and exhibited himself there to be worshipped by those who presented themselves; and some hailed him as Jupiter Latiaris. He also set up a special temple to his own godhead, with priests and with victims of the choicest kind. In this temple was a life-sized statue of the emperor in gold, which was dressed each day in clothing such as he wore himself.

The emperor Gaius rides across the Bay of Baiae

About the year 39 CE, while Gaius was at the Imperial Palace on the Bay of Baiae, he ordered that a bridge of merchant vessels be lashed together to span the distance between Baiae and the mole at Puteoli, three and a half Roman miles. Suetonius calls it "a novel and unheard of kind of pageant."[46]

The ships were anchored in double file and earth was deposited on the decks. Gaius ordered that the road imitate the method of the Appian Way. Gaius saw himself outdoing Xerxes' feat of the bridge across the Hellespont. Moreover, he boasted that Neptune allowed the bridge because he was afraid of Gaius' power. In the emperor's mind, whether the bridge was human made or not, the fact that he could ride across the waves of the sea made him equal to Neptune, since it duplicated the act that defined his sovereignty over the sea.

SUETONIUS (CIRCA 120 CE)

3.46.1. Gaius Rides Back and Forth Across the Water, like a Conqueror of the World

Suetonius, *Gaius Caligula, Lives of the Caesars* 4.19.2
Over this bridge he rode back and forth for two successive days, the first day on a caparisoned horse, himself resplendent in a crown of oak leaves, a buckler, a sword, and a cloak of cloth of gold; on the second, in a dress of a charioteer in a car drawn by a pair of famous horses, carrying before him a boy named Dareus, one of the hostages from Parthia, and attended by the entire Praetorian guard and a company of his friends in Gallic chariots.

46 Ibid., 4.19.1.

3.46.2. Suetonius' Grandfather Said that Tiberius' Astrologer Joked that Young Gaius had No More Chance of Becoming Emperor than of Riding Over the Gulf of Baiae with Horses

Suetonius, *Gaius Caligula, Lives of the Caesars* 4.19.3

I know that many have supposed that Gaius devised this kind of bridge in rivalry of Xerxes, who excited no little admiration by bridging the much narrower Hellespont; others, that it was to inspire fear in Germany and Britain, on which he had designs, by the fame of some stupendous work. But when I was a boy, I used to hear my grandfather say that the reason for the work, as revealed by the emperor's confidential courtiers, was that Thrasyllus the astrologer had declared to Tiberius, when he was worried about his successor and inclined toward his natural grandson [Tiberius Gemellus], that Gaius had no more chance of becoming emperor than of riding over the gulf of Baiae with horses.

Note

This remembrance of Suetonius shows us that in the administration of Tiberius, which was the time of Jesus himself, the image of a man riding over the waves was already used as a metaphor for what is impossible for a human being.

JOSEPHUS (37–95 CE?)

3.47. He Considered It His Privilege as Lord of the Sea to Require the Same Service of the Sea as He Received from the Land

Josephus, *Jewish Antiquities* 19.1.6[47]

He considered it his privilege as lord of the sea to require the same service of the sea as he received from the land. So the thirty furlongs from headland to headland were connected with pontoons, which cut off the whole bay, and over this bridge he drove in his chariot. That way of travelling, said he, befitted his godhead.

Note: The Jewish heroes and Jesus' walking on the sea

These stories of Moses, Joshua, Elijah and Elisha are retellings of the same miracle: a body of water, be it the Red Sea (Moses) or the Jordan (Joshua, Elijah, Elisha) is divided in two, and someone

---

47 Josephus, *Jewish Antiquities, Josephus*, vol. 9 (trans. L. H. Feldman; London: Heinemann, 1965), 19.16.

walks across on the dry sea/river bed. The performance of this miracle signals that a hero is a heavenly designated leader.

This repetition of the image so that in each case the waters will part, will separate, will divide, is not given to Jesus. If the intent of his walking on the sea was to call up such figures and their miracles, the Christian author needs to indicate that some body of water divided in two. The Jesus miracle does not even include a verb that suggests division or separation, but rather walking *on* the sea. Walking on the sea is not an image associated with the powers of Moses or any other ancient Jewish hero, but as the prerogative of the Jewish God.

Sea-walking heroes in literature: satire and dream interpretations

The two categories of satire and dream interpretation are extremely valuable for our reconstruction of authorial intent in a Jesus miracle story because they supply testimonies about the society and culture from which the first Christian communities would spring. Satire cannot be successful if it "bombs an empty trench." The foibles it mocks must be true enough for the ridicule to make an impact.

Dream imagery, on the other hand, works more subtly. It does not matter whether the stated associations between the dream images and meanings are correct, but only that this society thought that they were. Artemidorus' collection of dream interpretations from around the Mediterranean gives us evidence of the easy connections between images and life.

This information contributes to our reconstruction of the intended significance of Jesus' miracle stories. It is one more aid in our reconstruction of associations that were conventional to a society, the majority of whose members left little evidence of their symbol system.

Lucian of Samosata (120–180 CE)

Lucian of Samosata is famous for his satirical essays, many of which earned him rebukes for their impious character. This is proof enough that he was close to the very nerves of his own society.[48] Lucian features men walking on water in two of his wonderfully funny

---

48 C. P. Jones, *Culture and Society in Lucian* (London and Cambridge, MA: Harvard University Press, 1986), esp. 14. For a discussion of Lucian's life and literary contribution see also Barry Baldwin, *Studies in Lucian* (Toronto: Hakkert,

spoofs, *A True Story* and *The Lover of Lies*. In both cases the characters are freaks, as we shall see. Before addressing the texts, however, it is pertinent to say a word about Lucian and the Christians.

3.48. I Saw Men Running Across the Sea on Feet Made of Cork

Lucian, *A True Story* 2.4[49]
(In this account, Lucian spoofs the journey of Odysseus. The protagonist and fifty comrades decide to sail to the furthest point west in the world. Their voyage takes them across the western sea, where they meet every sort of unbelievable person and creature. The text that follows occurs just after the crew have spent five days on an island made of cheese. After shoving off and sailing through milky seas for two full days, they finally enter the blue briny water of the sea once more. They see a group of men running on top of the sea.)

On the eighth day . . . we came in sight of many men running over the sea, like us in every way, both in shape and in size, except only their feet, which were of cork: that is why they were called Corkfeet, if I am not mistaken. We were amazed to see that they did not go under, but stayed on top of the waves and went about fearlessly. Some of them came up to us and greeted us in the Greek language; they said that they were on their way to Cork, their native city. For some distance they travelled with us, running alongside, and then they turned off and went their way, wishing us luck on our voyage.

3.49.1. What Was I to Do When I Saw the Hyperborean Fly Through the Air, Walk on Water and Go Through Fire Slowly on Foot?

Lucian, *The Lover of Lies* 13[50]
(In this dialogue, Tychiades has recently visited the home of Eucrates, where a conversation about the supernatural took place among a group of philosophers. Now Tychiades regales his own friend Philocles with the details of the discussion. The texts below

---

1973); Graham Anderson, *Studies in Lucian's Comic Fiction* (Leiden: Brill, 1976); R. Bracht Branham, *Unruly Eloquence: Lucian and the Comedy of Traditions* (London: Cambridge, MA: Harvard University Press, 1989).

49 Lucian, *A True Story*, *Lucian*, vol. 1 (trans. A. M. Harmon; London: Heinemann, 1913), 1–4.
50 Lucian, *The Lover of Lies*, *Lucian*, vol. 3 (trans. A. M. Harmon; London: Heinemann, 1921), 3.13.

are part of the story of Cleodemus, the Peripatetic, who is trying to convince Tychiades that he should believe in a magician who is a Hyperborean and who could cast spells on snakes and toads.[51])

I myself was formerly more incredulous than you in regard to such things [magic spells on snakes and toads], for I thought it in no way possible that they could happen; but when first I saw the foreign stranger fly – he came from the land of the Hyperboreans, he said[52] –, I believed and was conquered after long resistance. What was I to do when I saw him soar through the air in broad daylight and walk on water and go through fire slowly on foot?

3.49.2. "Did Cleodemus himself See the Hyperborean Flying or Crossing the Water?", Tychiades Asks

Lucian, *The Lover of Lies* 13–14[53]

"Certainly," said he [Cleodemus], "with brogues on his feet such as people of that country commonly wear. As for the trivial feats, what is the use of telling all that he performed, sending Cupids after people, bringing up supernatural beings, calling mouldy corpses to life, making Hecate herself appear in plain sight, and pulling down the moon?"

Note

These texts show us that for Lucian "nature miracles" of any kind are explained by quackery, oddity, or the dishonesty of the reporter. But, at the very same time, he is mocking such feats because within his own society people must be fascinated by them, and because reasonable people are actually persuaded that they can be performed.

Artemidorus Daldianus (circa 90–180 CE)

If Artemidorus' books of dream interpretation were of his own imagination, they would be helpful, of course, but the fact that they represent a collection he made throughout the Mediterranean world makes them invaluable evidence for the associations of images considered conventional in that world.

---

51 This entry is also found in Chapter 8 below because Cleodemus identifies the man as a magician.
52 This is most probably an allusion to the Pythagorean stories about a priest of the Hyperboreans, to whom Apollo gave an arrow that would carry him through the air and over the sea to Delphi.
53 *Lucian*, vol. 3 (trans. Harmon), 13–14.

3.50. "What Does it Mean to Dream that One Walks on the Sea?"

Artemidorus, *The Interpretation of Dreams* 3.16[54]

Walking on the sea is a good sign for a man who wishes to go abroad, especially if he is about to sail. For the dream foretells great safety. It is also good for a slave and for a man who intends to marry. The former will rule his master; the latter will rule his wife. For the sea resembles a master because it is mighty; it resembles a wife because it is moist.[55] It is also good for a man who is involved in a lawsuit. For he will be superior to the judge and will naturally win the trial. For the sea also resembles a judge, since it treats some people well and others badly.

To a young man, it signifies the love of prostitutes. And if a woman has the dream, it means that she will lead a life of prostitution. For the sea resembles a prostitute in that it appears sweet and loving at first, but then, afterwards, treats men most badly. On the other hand, for all those who earn their living from crowds, or statesmen, and popular leaders, it prophesies extraordinary gain together with great fame. For the sea also resembles a crowd because of its instability.

Note

When we eliminate the categories that would not be suitable for the story of Jesus' walking on the sea, namely, those involving women, the slave, and the cases of both young men, the one loving prostitutes and the one about to marry, very interesting associations remain. Beyond the literal meaning of the story, we might also suggest how appropriately it expresses the difference between Jesus' appearance as vulnerable and his true status as divine. Jesus is crucified but resurrected. Jesus turns world power upside down and emerges victorious. Your own examinations of the material will suggest other viable associations based on Artemidorus' collection.

54 Artemidorus, *The Interpretation of Dreams: Oneirocritica* (trans. and commentary by Robert J. White, New Jersey: Noyes Press, 1975), 162.

55 In the ancient world, men were associated with the properties of heat and dryness, their element being fire, while women were associated with the properties of coolness and moistness, their element being water. This association explains also why it is that the young man who dreams that he walks on the sea is thought to be expressing a love for prostitutes.

7

CHANGING WATER INTO WINE AND OTHER NATURE MIRACLES

CHANGING WATER INTO WINE

The god who changes water into wine: Dionysus

Diodorus Siculus (wrote 60–30 BCE)

3.51. The Teans Claim as Proof that Dionysus was Born in their City that Periodic Fountains of Wine Spurt from the Earth

Diodorus Siculus, *The Library of History* 3.66.3[1]

The Teans advance as proof that the god [Dionysus] was born among them the fact that, even to this day, at fixed times in their city a fountain of wine, of unusually sweet fragrance, flows of its own accord from the earth; and as for the peoples of the other cities, they in some cases point out a plot of land which is sacred to Dionysus, in other cases shrines and sacred precincts which have been consecrated to him from ancient times. But, speaking generally, since the god has left behind him in many places over the inhabited world evidences of his personal favour and presence, it is not surprising that in each case the people should think that Dionysus had had a peculiar relationship to both their city and country.

---

1   Diodorus Siculus, *The Library of History*, vol. 2 (trans. C. H. Oldfather; London: Heinemann, 1935), 3.66.

3.52. Water from the Temple in Andros Always Tastes like Wine on January 5

Pliny the Elder, *Natural History* 2.106[2]

It is accredited by the Mucianus who was three times consul that the water flowing from a spring in the temple of Father Liber [Dionysus] on the island of Andros always has the flavour of wine on January 5th: the day is called God's Gift Day.

3.53. On Fixed Seven-Day Festivals of the God, the Springs Flow with Wine

Pliny the Elder, *Natural History* 2.[3]

Disgust at wine, says Eudoxus, comes upon those who have drunk of Lake Clitorius, but Theopompus says that drunkenness is caused by the springs that I have mentioned,[4] and Mucianus that at Andros, from the spring of Father Liber [Dionysus], on fixed seven-day festivals of this god, flows wine, but if its water is carried out of sight of the temple the taste turns to that of water.

The Hero Who Changes Water Into Wine: Jesus of Nazareth

Jesus at the wedding feast of Cana

3.54. The Steward Called the Bridegroom and Said to Him, "Everyone Serves the Good Wine First, and Then the Inferior Wine After the Guests Have Become Drunk. But You Have Kept the Good Wine Until Now"

John 2:1–11

1. On the third day there was a wedding in Cana of Galilee, and the mother of Jesus was there. *2.* Jesus and his disciples had also been invited to the wedding. *3.* When the wine gave out, the mother of Jesus said to him, "They have no wine." *4.* And Jesus said to her, "Woman, what concern is that to you and to me? My hour has not yet come. *5.* His mother said to

---

2 Pliny the Elder, *Natural History*, vol. 1 (trans. H. Rackham; London: Heinemann, 1938), 2.106, 231.

3 Pliny the Elder, *Natural History*, vol. 8 (trans. W. H. S. Jones; London: Heinemann, 1963), 31.16.

4 Pliny the Elder, *Natural History*, vol. 1 (trans. Rackham), 106, 231.

the servants, "Do whatever he tells you." 6. Now standing there were six stone water jars for the Jewish rites of purification, each holding twenty or thirty gallons. 7. Jesus said to them, "Fill the jars with water." And they filled them up to the brim. 8. He said to them, "Now draw some out, and take it to the chief steward." So they took it. 9. When the steward tasted the water that had become wine, and did not know where it came from (though the servants who had drawn the water knew), the steward called the bridegroom 10. and said to him, "Everyone serves the good wine first, and then the inferior wine after the guests have become drunk. But you have kept the good wine until now." 11. Jesus did this, the first of his signs in Cana of Galilee, and revealed his glory; and his disciples believed in him.

MULTIPLYING FOOD

The god who multiplies food for the hungry: the Jewish deity

The miracles worked by the Jewish deity to multiply food for the hungry involve Jewish heroes as well. From Jewish scripture we find Moses, Elijah and Elisha all multiplying food. Then, in Christian scriptures, the hero/god Jesus multiplies bread and fish. All these heroes serve God as revealed by Jewish tradition.

Heroes who multiply food: Jewish heroes

Heroes from Jewish scriptures: Moses, Elijah and Elisha

Moses

Moses makes bitter water in the desert sweet

3.55. Moses Cried Out to the Lord; and the Lord Showed Him a Piece of Wood; He Threw It into the Water, and the Water Became Sweet

Exod. 15:22–27

22. Then Moses ordered Israel to set out from the Red Sea, and they went into the wilderness of Shur. They went three days in the wilderness and found no water. 23. When they came to Marah, they could not drink the water of Marah because it was bitter. That is why it was called Marah [bitterness]. 24. And the people complained against Moses, saying, "What shall we drink?" 25. He cried out to the Lord; and the Lord showed him a piece of wood; he threw it into the water, and the water became sweet.

There the Lord made for them a statute and an ordinance and there he put them to the test. *26.* He said, "If you will listen carefully to the voice of the Lord your God, and do what is right in his sight, and give heed to his commandments and keep all his statutes, I will not bring upon you any of the diseases that I brought upon the Egyptians; for I am the Lord who heals you."

27. Then they came to Elim, where there were twelve springs of water and seventy palm trees; and they camped there by the water.

Moses asks for bread and the Lord gives manna from heaven

3.56.1. The Lord Said to Moses, "I Am Going to Rain Bread from Heaven for You"

Exod. 16.1–5, 13–15

1. Then the whole congregation of the Israelites set out from Elim; and Israel came to the wilderness of Sin, which is between Elim and Sinai, on the fifteenth day of the second month after they had departed from the land of Egypt. *2.* The whole congregation of the Israelites complained against Moses and Aaron in the wilderness. *3.* The Israelites said to them, "If only we had died by the hand of the Lord in the land of Egypt, when we sat by the fleshpots and ate our fill of bread; for you have brought us out into this wilderness to kill this whole assembly with hunger."

4. Then the Lord said to Moses, "I am going to rain bread from heaven for you, and each day the people shall go out and gather enough for that day. In that way, I will test them, whether they will follow my instructions or not. *5.* On the sixth day, when they prepare what they bring in, it will be twice as much as they gather on other days."

. . . *13.* In the evening quails came up and covered the camp; and in the morning there was a layer of dew around the camp. *14.* When the layer of dew lifted, there on the surface of the wilderness was a fine flaky substance, as fine as frost on the ground. *15.* When the Israelites saw it, they said to one another, "What is it?" For they did not know what it was. Moses said to them, "It is the bread that the Lord has given you to eat."

3.56.2. They Gathered as Much as Each of Them Needed

Exod. 16.16–18

16. "This is what the Lord has commanded: 'Gather as much of it as each of you needs, an omer to a person according to the number of persons, all providing for those in their own tents.' " *17.* The Israelites did so, some gathering more, some less. *18.* But when they measured it with an omer, those who gathered much had nothing over, and those who gathered little had no shortage; they gathered as much as each of them needed.

167

Elijah

Elijah gives unfailing oil and wheat to the widow of Zarephath

3.57. The Jar of Meal was Not Emptied, Neither did the Jug of Oil Fail, According to the Word of the Lord that He Spoke by Elijah

1 Kgs. 17:8–16

8. Then the word of the Lord came to him, saying, 9. "Go now to Zarephath, which belongs to Sidon, and live there; for I have commanded a widow there to feed you." 10. So he set out and went to Zarephath. When he came to the gate of the town, a widow was there gathering sticks; he called to her and said, "Bring me a little water in a vessel, so that I may drink." 11. As she was going to bring it, he called to her and said, "Bring me a morsel of bread in your hand." 12. But she said, "As the Lord your God lives, I have nothing baked, only a handful of meal in a jar, and a little oil in a jug; I am now gathering a couple of sticks, so that I may go home and prepare it for myself and my son, that we may eat it, and die." 13. Elijah said to her, "Do not be afraid; go and do as you have said; but first make me a little cake of it and bring it to me, and afterwards make something for yourself and your son. 14. For thus says the Lord the God of Israel: The jar of meal will not be emptied and the jug of oil will not fail until the day that the Lord sends rain on the earth." 15. She went and did as Elijah said, so that she as well as he and her household ate for many days. 16. The jar of meal was not emptied, neither did the jug of oil fail, according to the word of the Lord that he spoke by Elijah.

Elisha

Elisha feeds one hundred people with twenty loaves of barley and some grain

3.58. Elisha said, "Give it to the People and Let Them Eat and Have Some Left"

2 Kgs. 4:42–44

42. A man came from Baal-shalishah, bringing food from the first fruits to the man of God: twenty loaves of barley and fresh ears of grain in his sack. Elisha said, "Give it to the people and let them eat." 43. But his servant said, "How can I set this before a hundred people?" So he repeated, "Give it to the people and let them eat, for thus says the Lord, 'They shall eat and have some left.'" 44. He set it before them, they ate, and had some left, according to the word of the Lord.

The Christians' hero: Jesus of Nazareth

Jesus feeds five thousand people

3.59. Mark 6:30–44 (Matt. 14:13–21//Luke 9:10–17; Matt. 15:32–39; cf. John 6:1–14

30. The apostles gathered around Jesus, and told him all that they had done and taught. *31.* He said to them, "Come away to a deserted place all by yourselves and rest a while." For many were coming and going, and they had no leisure even to eat. *32.* And they went away in the boat to a deserted place by themselves. *33.* Now many saw them going and recognized them, and they hurried there on foot from all the towns and arrived ahead of them. *34.* As he went ashore, he saw a great crowd; and he had compassion for them, because they were like sheep without a shepherd; and he began to teach them many things. *35.* When it grew late, his disciples came to him and said, "This is a deserted place, and the hour is now very late; *36.* send them away so that they may go into the surrounding country and villages and buy something for themselves to eat." *37.* But he answered them, "You give them something to eat." They said to him, "Are we to go and buy two hundred denarii worth of bread and give it to them to eat? *38.* And he said to them, "How many loaves have you? Go and see." When they had found out, they said, "Five, and two fish." *39.* Then he ordered them to get all the people to sit down in groups on the green grass. *40.* So they sat down in groups of hundreds and of fifties. *41.* Taking the five loaves and the two fish, he looked up to heaven, and blessed and broke the loaves, and gave them to his disciples to set before the people; and he divided the two fish among them all. *42.* And all ate and were filled; *43.* and they took up twelve baskets full of broken pieces and of the fish. *44.* Those who had eaten the loaves numbered five thousand men.

Note: The Jesus miracle of the multiplication of loaves and fish, in comparison with the heroes of Jewish scripture

One has only to read these Jewish hero stories to see that they are the backdrop intended by the formulators of these Jesus stories. While the Moses account is most frequently associated with Jesus' multiplication of loaves, it is really the Elisha story that is closest. The food is already there but is insufficient in amount; the miracle is that the food goes round and that there are leftovers. If this is the story that the Christians have in mind, then their comment is to emphasize Jesus' much greater status than that of the revered Elisha. In the Markan account, Mark 6:30–44, there are only five loaves and two fish for five thousand men, while in the second account, Mark 8:1–10, seven loaves "and a few fish" must feed four thousand men. The Johannine version, 6:1–14, holds that Jesus has only five loaves and two fish to feed "a large crowd." Thus Jesus stands beside Elisha but clearly outshines him.

OTHER NATURE MIRACLES OF JESUS

Jesus causes a miraculous catch of fish

Jesus promises Simon such a catch of people

3.60. Then Jesus Said to Simon, "Do not be Afraid; from Now on you will be Catching People"

Luke 5:1–11

1. Once while Jesus was standing beside the lake of Gennesaret, and the crowd was pressing in on him to hear the word of God, *2.* he saw two boats there at the shore of the lake; the fishermen had gone out of them and were washing their nets. *3.* He got into one of the boats, the one belonging to Simon, and asked him to put out a little way from the shore. Then he sat down and taught the crowds from the boat. *4.* When he had finished speaking, he said to Simon, "Put out into the deep water and let down your nets for a catch." *5.* Simon answered, "Master, we have worked all night long but have caught nothing. Yet if you say so, I will let down the nets." *6.* When they had done this, they caught so many fish that their nets were beginning to break. *7.* So they signaled their partners in the other boat to come and help them. And they came and filled both boats, so that they began to sink. *8.* But when Simon Peter saw it, he fell down at Jesus' knees, saying, "Go away from me, Lord, for I am a sinful man!" *9.* For he and all who were with him were amazed at the catch of fish that they had taken; *10.* and so also were James and John, sons of Zebedee, who were partners with Simon. Then Jesus said to Simon, "Do not be afraid; from now on you will be catching people." *11.* When they had brought their boats to shore, they left everything and followed him.

The resurrected Jesus reveals himself to his disciples in the miraculous catch of fish

3.61 That Disciple Whom Jesus Loved Said to Peter, "It is the Lord!"

John 21:1–14

1. After these things Jesus showed himself to his disciples by the Sea of Tiberias; and he showed himself in this way. *2.* Gathered there together were Simon Peter, Thomas called the Twin, Nathanael of Cana in Galilee, the sons of Zebedee, and two others of his disciples. *3.* Simon Peter said to them, "I am going fishing." They said to him, "We will go with you." They went out and got into the boat, but that night they caught nothing.

4. Just after daybreak, Jesus stood on the beach; but the disciples did not know that it was Jesus. *5.* Jesus said to them, "Children, you have no fish, have you?" They answered him, "No." *6.* He said to them, "Cast the net to the right side of the boat, and you will find some." So they cast it, and now they were not able to haul it in because there were so many fish. *7.* That disciple whom Jesus loved said to Peter, "It is the Lord!" When Simon Peter heard that it was the Lord, he put on some clothes, for he was naked, and jumped into the sea. *8.* But the other disciples came in the boat, dragging the net full of fish, for they were not far from the land, only about a hundred yards off.

9. When they had gone ashore, they saw a charcoal fire there, with fish on it, and bread. *10.* Jesus said to them, "Bring some of the fish that you have just caught." *11.* So Simon Peter went aboard and hauled the net ashore, full of large fish, a hundred fifty-three of them; and though there were so many, the net was not torn. *12.* Jesus said to them, "Come and have breakfast." Now none of the disciples dared to ask him, "Who are you?" because they knew it was the Lord. *13.* Jesus came and took the bread and gave it to them, and did the same with the fish. *14.* This was now the third time that Jesus appeared to the disciples after he was raised from the dead.

Jesus curses the fig tree

3.62. When He Came to It, he Found Nothing But Leaves, For It was Not the Season for Figs. He Said to it, "May No One Ever Eat Fruit From You Again"

Mark 11:12–14, 20–24 (Matt. 21:18–22)

12. On the following day, when they came from Bethany, he was hungry. *13.* Seeing in the distance a fig tree in leaf, he went to see whether perhaps he would find anything on it. When he came to it, he found nothing but leaves, for it was not the season for figs. *14.* He said to it, "May no one ever eat fruit from you again." And his disciples heard it. . . . *20.* In the morning as they passed by, they saw the fig tree withered away to its roots. *21.* Then Peter remembered and said to him, "Rabbi, look! The fig tree that you cursed has withered." *22.* Jesus answered them, "Have faith in God. *23.* Truly I tell you, if you say to this mountain, 'Be taken up and thrown into the sea,' and if you do not doubt in your heart, but believe that what you say will come to pass, it will be done for you. *24.* So I tell you, whatever you ask for in prayer, believe that you have received it, and it will be yours."

Jesus pays tax with a shekel from a fish's mouth

3.63. "Go to the Sea and Cast a Hook; Take the First Fish that Comes Up; and When You Open its Mouth, You Will Find a Coin; Take That and Give It to Them for You and Me"

Matt. 17:24–27

24. When they reached Capernaum, the collectors of the temple tax came to Peter and said, "Does your teacher not pay the temple tax?" *25.* He said, "Yes, he does." And when he came home, Jesus spoke of it first, asking, "What do you think, Simon? From whom do kings of the earth take toll or tribute? From their children or from others?" *26.* When Peter said, "From others," Jesus said to him, "Then the children are free. *27.* However, so that we do not give offense to them, go to the sea and cast a hook; take the first fish that comes up; and when you open its mouth, you will find a coin; take that and give it to them for you and me."

Part IV

MAGIC AND MIRACLES

8

MAGIC IN THE ANCIENT WORLD

4.1. Sorcerers and those taught by the Egyptians profess to do wonderful miracles

> Sorcerers who profess to do wonderful miracles, and the accomplishments of those who are taught by the Egyptians, who for a few obols make known their sacred law in the middle of the market place and drive daemons out of men and blow away diseases and invoke the souls of heroes . . .
>
> (Celsus: Origen, *Contra Celsum* 1.68)

INTRODUCTION

The purpose of this chapter is to recognize that certain elements found in the Jesus miracles invited associations with magic. Older scholarship presumed that there were certain elements of "magic" that clearly distinguished it from "miracle." Today, we recognize that the subject of magic is far more complex.

Harold Remus' monograph *Pagan–Christian Conflict Over Miracle in the Second Century*[1] illustrates how "magic" may be used as a negative label for an action that others positively label "miracle."

The demarcation of magic and miracle (or religion) involves social and cultural judgments, on the part both of ancients

---

1 Harold Remus, *Pagan–Christian Conflict over Miracle in the Second Century* (Patristic Monograph Series 10; Cambridge, MA: The Philadelphia Patristic Foundation, 1983).

and moderns. This does not necessarily mean there are no "objective" criteria, i.e. canons mutually agreed upon between social groupings or at least within such groupings. It does mean that attention to the social and cultural conditioning of the terminology and the way its referents are viewed cannot be ignored, and, indeed, deserve more systematic treatment than has usually been given them.[2]

When magic is viewed pejoratively, it can become a negative label to explain the successful supernatural deeds of any hero, as Charles Robert Phillips observes:

> A charge of magic represented a persuasive way to denigrate one's theological opposition: the opposition would have to "prove" that its alleged powers derived from the "right" cosmic forces.[3]

Evidence supports the fact that magic was a force relied upon by many people from various strata of Greco-Roman society. And to be successful in magical power was no small accomplishment, even though the blueblood *literati* would mock such ideas. The fact that such arguments were even launched tells us that it was an issue of some pertinence to the age. Moreover, the laws against sorcery can only mean that it was taken seriously as a force that carried the potential for real danger.

Howard Kee has chastised John M. Hull because to his mind, Hull has ignored the difference between the apocalyptic worldview (which Kee presupposes for all Christian communities) and the worldview which supports magic.

> What Hull has ignored is that there is a fundamental difference between the apocalyptic worldview, which sees the cosmos as the place of struggle between God and his opponents, but which awaits the triumph of God and the vindication of his faithful people, and the magical view which regards the gods and all other powers as fair game for exploitation and manipulation by those shrewd enough

---

2 Ibid., 54.
3 Charles Robert Phillips, "The Sociology of Religious Knowledge in the Roman Empire to A.D. 284," *ANRW* II 16/3 (1986) 2677–2773, p. 2711.

to achieve thereby their own ends or the defeat of their enemies. There is no hint of the latter outlook – which is the essence of magic – in the synoptic Traditions or in its apocalyptic antecedents, but it becomes a pervasive factor of life in the Roman world from the Antonine period onward. It is precisely to this epoch that Hall must turn in his effort to document his position.[4]

But Hull does not have to wait until the Antonine epoch for evidence. The redaction of Matthew and Luke on Markan exorcism stories removes features that might suggest a magical association for Jesus' miracles. The deep sighs of Jesus and his pronouncing of foreign phrases in Mark have been removed by these evangelists precisely because they seem to fit so well into a magical tradition of healing.

The point that needs to be made is this: there is no suggestion in any Christian material that magic was considered as anything but completely negative, no matter where it occurred. If our purpose is to interpret the intended meaning of the Jesus miracle stories, then, a suggestion of a magical power, such as was understood in the Greco-Roman world, is completely unsupported. For the Christian community, "magic" was a negative label for Jesus' heavenly empowerment by the Holy Spirit.

If, however, we wish to understand how certain elements of the miracle stories might well lead the Greco-Roman listener to wonder if a magical meaning was intended, we need to be aware of the most common features of magical cures and exorcisms among the people of the Greco-Roman world.

The chapter is divided into three sections. In the first the nature of magic and magicians is described by Pliny the Elder, Plutarch and Seneca. The second section features examples of certain people who were thought to have magical powers. Empedocles the Pythagorean is one example. Apuleius discusses a man who he thinks is really just suffering from epilepsy. Lucian's satirical portrayal of the "Hyperboreans" walking on water illustrates the mockery that Jesus' walking on the sea would have engendered in many.

The third section is a selection of texts from the Greek Magical

---

4 Howard Clark Kee, *Medicine, Miracle and Magic in New Testament Times* (Cambridge: Cambridge University Press, 1986), 114.

Papyri, which are supposed to cure the very troubles that Jesus does in his miracles. They illustrate just what features of Jesus' miracles would have been easily and innocently judged as magical by a Greco-Roman listener.

Throughout the three sections, the Jesus miracles are placed wherever the subject under discussion creates a fair association. This is not to categorize the intended meaning for the Jesus miracle, but only to illustrate the element that could have invited such a linkage.

THE NATURE OF MAGIC

Pliny the Elder (23–79 CE)

4.2.1. Magic, the Most Fraudulent of Arts, has Held Complete Sway Throughout the World

Pliny the Elder, *Natural History* 30.1[5]
In the previous part of my work I have often indeed refuted the fraudulent lies of the Magi, whenever the subject and the occasion required it, and I shall continue to expose them. In a few respects, however, the theme deserves to be enlarged upon, were it only because the most fraudulent of arts has held complete sway throughout the world for many ages.

4.2.2. Magic Subjects to Itself Three Other Arts: Medicine, Religion and Astrology. Holding the Emotions in a Three-Fold Bond, Magic Rose to Such a Height that Even Today it Has Sway Over a Great Part of Humankind, and in the East Commands the King of Kings

Pliny the Elder, *Natural History* 30.1.2
Nobody should be surprised at the greatness of its influence, since alone of the arts it has embraced three others that hold supreme dominion over the human mind, and made them subject to itself alone. Nobody will doubt that it first arose from medicine and that professing to promote health it insidiously advanced under the disguise of a higher and holier system; that to the most seductive and welcome promises it added the power of religion, about which even today the human race is quite in the dark; that again meeting with success it made a further addition of astrology, because there is nobody who is not eager to learn his destiny,

---

5 All quotations are taken from Pliny the Elder, *Natural History*, vol. 8 (trans. W. H. S. Jones; 1963).

or who does not believe that the truest account of it is that gained by watching the skies. Accordingly, holding men's emotions in a three-fold bond, magic rose to such a height that even today it has sway over a great part of mankind, and in the East commands the Kings of Kings.

Note

The fact that Jesus was known to be a man from the East would invite the prejudicial view seen here, that magic flourishes there.

The power of words

Both Pliny the Elder and Plutarch include chants, personal prayers, ritual prayers and also "charms" and other good-luck formulae. Pliny illustrates how difficult it is to establish external criteria to separate magic, medicine and miracle.

Pliny the Elder

4.3.1. Have Words and Formulated Incantation any Effect? As a Body, the Public at All Times Believes in Them Unconsciously

Pliny the Elder, *Natural History* 28.3.10
Of the remedies derived from man, the first raises a most important question, and one never settled: have words and formulated incantations any effect? If they have, it would be right and proper to give the credit to mankind. As individuals, however, all our wisest men reject belief in them, although as a body the public at all times believes in them unconsciously.

4.3.2. Signs of Public Belief that Incantations which are Performed Perfectly Do Have their Effect

Pliny the Elder, *Natural History* 28.3.11
In fact the sacrifice of victims without a prayer is supposed to be of no effect; without it too the gods are not thought to be properly consulted. Moreover, there is one form of words for getting favourable omens, another for averting evil, and yet another for a commendation. We see also that our chief magistrates have adopted fixed formulas for their prayers; that to prevent a word's being omitted or out of place a reader dictates beforehand the prayer from a script; that another attendant is appointed as a guard to keep watch, and yet another is put in charge to maintain a strict silence; that a piper plays so that nothing but the prayer is heard. Remarkable instances of both kinds of interference are on record: cases when the noise of actual ill omens

179

has ruined the prayer, or when a mistake has been made in the prayer itself; then suddenly the head of the liver, or the heart, has disappeared from the entrails, or these have been doubled, while the victim was standing. There has come down to us a striking example of ritual in that to which the Decii, a father and son, devoted themselves; extant too is the plea of innocence uttered by the Vestal Tuccia when, accused of unchastity, she carried water in a sieve, in the year of the City six hundred and nine. Our own generation indeed even saw buried alive in the Cattle Market a Greek man and a Greek woman, and victims from other peoples with whom at the time we were at war. The prayer used at this ceremony is wont to be dictated by the Master of the College of the Quindecimviri, and if one reads it one is forced to admit that there is power in ritual formulas, the events of eight hundred and thirty years showing this for all of them. It is believed today that our Vestal Virgins by a spell root to the spot runaway slaves, provided they have not left the City bounds, and yet, if this view is once admitted, that the gods hear certain prayers, or are moved by any form of words, the whole question must be answered in the affirmative.

4.3.3. Our Ancestors Often Utilized the Power of the Spoken Word

Pliny the Elder, *Natural History* 28.3.13–4.14
Even lightning can be brought by charms from the sky
Our ancestors, indeed, reported such wonders again and again, and that, most impossible of all, even lightning can be brought by charms from the sky, as I have mentioned on the proper occasion.[6]

Lucius Piso in the first Book of his *Annals* tells us that King Tullus Hostilius used the same sacrificial ritual as Numa, which he found in Numa's books, in an attempt to draw Jupiter down from the sky, and was struck by lightning because he made certain mistakes in the ceremony.

4.3.4. By Words the Destinies and Omens of Mighty Events are Changed

Pliny the Elder, *Natural History* 28.4.14–16
Many indeed assure us that by words the destinies and omens of mighty events are changed. During the digging of the foundations for a shrine on the Tarpeian Hill there was discovered a human head. For an interpretation envoys were sent to Olenus of Cales, the most distinguished seer of Etruria. Perceiving that the sign portended glory and success, Olenus tried by questioning to divert the blessing to his own people. He first traced with his staff the outline of the temple on the ground in front of

---

6   2.140.

him, and then asked: "Is this then, Romans, what you say? 'Here will be the temple of Jupiter, All-good and Almighty; here we found the head?'" The *Annals* most firmly insists that the destiny of Rome would have passed to Etruria, had not the Roman envoys, forewarned by the seer's son, replied: "Not exactly here, but it was in Rome that we say the head was found." It is said that the same thing happened again when a clay four-horse chariot, designed for the roof of the same shrine, grew larger in the furnace, and once more in a similar way was the happy augury retained.

4.3.5. Neither Evil Omens nor Auspices Affect Those Who at the Outset of any Undertaking Declare That They Take No Notice of Them

Pliny the Elder, *Natural History* 28.4.17–18

Let these instances suffice to show that the power of omens is really in our own control, and that their influence is conditional upon the way we receive each. At any rate, in the teaching of the augurs it is a fundamental principle that neither evil omens nor any auspices affect those who at the outset of any undertaking declare that they take no notice of them; no greater instance of the divine mercy could be found than this boon. Again, in the actual laws of the Twelve Tables we find also these words: "Whoever shall have bewitched the crops," and in another place: "whoever shall have cast an evil spell." Verrius Flaccus[7] cites trustworthy authorities to show that it was the custom, at the very beginning of a siege, for the Roman priests to call forth the divinity under whose protection the besieged town was, and to promise him the same or even more splendid worship among the Roman people. Down to the present day this ritual has remained part of the doctrine of the Pontiffs, and it is certain that the reason why the tutelary deity of Rome has been kept a secret is to prevent any enemy from acting in a similar way.

4.3.6. There is Indeed Nobody Who Does Not Fear to be Spell-Bound by Imprecations

Pliny the Elder, *Natural History* 28.4.19

There is indeed nobody who does not fear to be spell-bound by imprecations. A similar feeling makes everybody break the shells of eggs or snails immediately after eating them, or else pierce them with the spoon that they have used. And so Theocritus among the Greeks, Catullus and quite recently Virgil among ourselves, have represented love charms in their poems. Many believe that by charms pottery can be crushed, and not a few even serpents; that these themselves can break the spell, this being the only kind of intelligence they possess; and by the charms of the Marsi [a German tribe] they are gathered together even when asleep at night.

---

7 Roman historian who died in the reign of Tiberius.

4.3.7. It is Not Easy to Say Whether Our Faith is More Violently Shaken by the Foreign, Unpronounceable Words, or by the Unexpected Plain Ones

Pliny the Elder, *Natural History* 28.4.19–20

On walls too are written prayers to avert fires. It is not easy to say whether our faith is more violently shaken by the foreign, unpronounceable words, or by the unexpected plain ones, which our mind forces us to consider absurd, being always on the look-out for something big, something adequate to move a god, or rather to impose its will on his divinity.

4.3.8. Magic Formulae Cure and Keep One Safe

Pliny the Elder, *Natural History* 28.4.21

Homer said that by a magic formula Ulysses stayed the haemorrhage from his wounded thigh;[8] Theophrastus that there is a formula to cure sciatica; Cato handed down one to set dislocated limbs, Marcus Varro one for gout. The dictator Caesar, after one serious accident to his carriage, is said always, as soon as he was seated, to have been in the habit of repeating three times a formula of prayer for a safe journey, a thing we know that most people do today.

Plutarch

4.4. Sorcerers Advise those Possessed by Demons to Recite "the Ephesian Letters" (Magical Formulae)

Plutarch, *Table Talk, Moralia* 5.706D[9]

(*From "Question 5": That "one should guard especially against the pleasures derived from degenerate music, and how to do so"*)

Replied Lamprias [Plutarch's brother], Whenever we fall among the Sirens, we must call upon the Muses and take refuge in the Helicon of olden times. If a man has a passion for a costly harlot, we cannot bring Penelope on stage, nor marry Pantheia[10] to him; but it is possible to take a man who is enjoying mimes and tunes and lyrics that are bad art and bad taste, and lead him back to Euripides and Pindar and Menander, "washing the brine from the ears with the clear fresh water of reason", in Plato's words.[11]

---

8 Trans. note: *Odyssey* 19.457, where it is not Odysseus, but Autolycus and his sons who effect the cure.

9 Plutarch, *Table Talk, Moralia*, vol. 9 (trans. Edwin L. Minar, F. H. Sandbach and W. C. Helmbold; London: Heinemann, 1961), 5.706D.

10 The wife of a Persian grandee in Xenophon's historical novel *Cyropaedeia*.

11 Plato, *Phaedrus* 243D.

For just as sorcerers advise those possessed with demons to recite and name over to themselves the Ephesian letters,[12] so we, in the midst of such warblings and caperings,

> Stirred by frenzies and whoops to the tumult of tossing heads,[13]

if we bethink ourselves of those hallowed and venerable writings and set up for comparison songs and poems and tales of true nobility, shall not be altogether dazed by these performances, nor shall we surrender ourselves, as it were, to float reclining on the gentle stream of music.

Superstitious actions

Pliny the Elder

4.5. Superstitious Customs and Actions

4.5.1. Superstitious Social Customs are Thought to Protect Us

Pliny the Elder, *Natural History* 28.5.22–24

Why on the first day of the year do we wish one another cheerfully a happy and prosperous New Year? Why do we also, on days of general purification, choose persons with lucky names to lead the victims? Why do we meet the evil eye by a special attitude of prayer, some invoking the Greek Nemesis, for which purpose there is at Rome an image of the goddess on the Capitol, although she has no Latin name? Why on mentioning the dead do we protest that their memory is not being attacked by us? Why do we believe that in all matters the odd numbers are more powerful, as is implied by the attention paid to critical days in fevers? Why at the harvest of the first-fruits do we say: "These are old," and pray for new ones to take their place? Why do we say, "Good health" to those who sneeze? This custom according to report even Tiberius Caesar, admittedly the most gloomy of men, insisted on even in a carriage, and some think it more effective to add to the salutation the name of the sneezer. Moreover, according to an accepted belief absent people can divine by the ringing in their ears that they are the object of talk. Attalus assures us that if on seeing a scorpion one says "Two," it is checked and does not strike. The mention of scorpions[14] reminds me that in Africa nobody decides on anything without first saying "Africa," whereas among all other peoples a man prays first for the approval of the gods.

---

12 The Ephesian letters are a magical formula: "askion, kataskion, lix, tetrax, damnameneus, aisia." The translators refer us to W. Schultz, *Philologus* 68 (1909), 210–228.

13 Pindar, *Fragments* 208.

14 Trans. note: "Africa was personified, in the time of Hadrian, as a woman, represented in divers ways on bronze coins, with a scorpion in her hand or on her head," p. 16.

4.5.2 Superstitious Customs at Table and at Worship

Pliny the Elder, *Natural History* 28.5.24–27

But when a table is ready it is a universal custom, we see, to take off one's ring, since it is clear that scrupulous actions, even without words, have their powers. Some people, to calm mental anxiety, carry saliva with the finger to behind the ear. There is even a proverb that bids us turn down our thumbs to show approval.[15] In worshipping we raise our right hand to our lips and turn round our whole body, the Gauls considering it more effective to make the turn to the left. All peoples agree in worshipping lightning by clucking with the tongue. If during a banquet fires have been mentioned we avert the omen by pouring water under the table. It is supposed to be a most unlucky sign for the floor to be swept while a diner is leaving the banquet, or for a table or dumb-waiter to be removed while a guest is drinking. Servius Sulpicius,[16] a noble Roman, has left an essay on why we should not leave the table; for in his day it was not the custom to have more tables than there were guests; for if a course or a table is recalled by a sneeze and nothing of it tasted afterwards, it is considered an evil portent, as is to eat nothing at all. These customs were established by those of old, who believed that gods were present on all occasions and at all times, and therefore left them to us reconciled even in our faults.

4.5.3. The Special Danger when Food Falls from the Table

Pliny the Elder, *Natural History* 28.5.27

Moreover, it has been remarked that a sudden silence falls on a banquet only when the number of those present is even, and that it portends danger to the reputation of each of them. Food also that fell from the hand used to be put back at least during courses, and it was forbidden to blow off, for tidiness, any dirt; auguries have been recorded from the words or thoughts of the diner who dropped food, a very dreadful omen being if the Pontiff should do so at a formal dinner. In any case putting it back on the table and burning it before the Lar counts as expiation.

4.5.4. Health Concerns Prompt Superstitious Actions

Pliny the Elder, *Natural History* 28.5.28–29

Medicines set down by chance on a table before being used are said to lose their efficacy. To cut the nails on the market days at Rome in silence, beginning with the forefinger, is a custom many people feel binding on them; while to cut the hair on the seventeenth day of the month and on

---

15 See Juvenal 3.36.

16 Trans. note: "A contemporary of Cicero, who took part in the troublous politics of the period."

the twenty-ninth prevents its falling out as well as headaches. A country rule observed on most Italian farms forbids women to twirl their spindles while walking along the road, or even to carry them uncovered, on the ground that such actions blight the hopes of everything, especially the hope of a good harvest. Marcus Servilius Nonianus,[17] a leading citizen of Rome, who was not so long ago afraid of ophthalmia, used to tie round his neck, before he mentioned the disease himself or any one else spoke to him about it, a sheet of paper fastened with thread, on which were written the two Greek letters rho and alpha; Mucianus,[18] three times consul, following the same observance, used a living fly in a white linen bag. Both avowed that by these remedies they themselves were kept free from ophthalmia.

4.5.5. I Am Shy of Quoting Charms, because of the Widely Different Feelings They Arouse

Pliny the Elder, *Natural History* 28.5.29

We certainly still have formulas to charm away hail, various diseases, and burns, some actually tested by experience, but I am very shy of quoting them, because of the widely different feelings they arouse. Wherefore everyone must form his own opinion about them as he pleases.

The powers of those who practice witchcraft

Pliny the Elder

4.6. Persons who Practice Witchcraft are Able to Handle Snakes and Cure Snakebite

Pliny the Elder, *Natural History* 28.6.30–33

Persons possessed of powers of witchcraft and of the evil eye, along with many peculiar characteristics of animals I have spoken of[19] when dealing with the marvels of the nations; it is superfluous to go over the ground again. Of certain men the whole bodies are beneficent, for example the members of those families that frighten serpents. These by a mere touch or by wet suction relieve the bitten victims. In this class are the Psylli, the Marsi, and the Ophiogenes, as they are called, in the island of Cyprus. And

---

17 Trans. note: "consul A.D. 35, died 59, and known personally to Pliny, who mentions him several times," p. 21.

18 Trans. note: "C. Licinius Mucianus was consul for the third time in A.D. 72. In 68–69 he was governor of Syria with a command of four legions. See Tacitus *Histories*, 1.10."

19 7.13ff.

envoy from this family, by name Evagon, was at Rome thrown by the consuls as a test into a cask of serpents, which to the genral amazement licked him all over. A feature of this family, if it still survives, is the foul smell of its members in the spring. Their sweat also, not only their saliva, had curative powers. But the natives of Tentyris, an island on the Nile, are such a terror to the crocodiles that these run away at the mere sound of their voice. All these peoples, so strong their natural antipathy, can, as is well known, effect a cure by their very arrival, just as wounds grow worse on the entry of those who have ever been bitten by the tooth of snake or dog. The latter also addle the eggs of a sitting hen, and make cattle miscarry; so much venom remains from the injury once received that the poisoned are turned into poisoners. The remedy is for their hands to be first washed in water, which is then used to sprinkle on the patients. On the other hand, those who have once been stung by a scorpion are never afterwards attacked by hornets, wasps or bees. He may be less surprised at this who knows that moths do not touch a garment that has been worn at a funeral, and that snakes are with difficulty pulled out of their holes except with the left hand.

Followers of Jesus

4.7. "They will Pick up Snakes in their Hands"

Mark 16:17–18

17. "And these signs will accompany those who believe: by using my name they will cast out demons; they will speak in new tongues; *18.* they will pick up snakes in their hands, and if they drink any deadly thing, it will not hurt them; they will lay their hands on the sick, and they will recover."[20]

Seneca

In this passage from Seneca's tragedy *Hercules Oetaeus* the nurse delivers the following speech to her mistress, Deïanira, wife of Hercules, who is afraid that she has lost the love of her husband. The nurse gives us an illustration of ways in which nature is vulnerable to "magic" in the Greco-Roman imagination.

---

20 His text is recognized by scholars as a secondary addition to Mark's gospel.

4.8. Magic Arts and Prayers are Used to Alter Nature

Seneca, *Hercules Oetaeus* 453–463[21]

By magic arts and prayers commingled do wives oft hold fast their husbands. I have bidden the trees grow green in the midst of winter's frost, and the hurtling lightning stand; I have stirred up the deep, though the winds were still, and have calmed the heaving sea; the parched earth has opened with fresh fountains; rocks have found motion; the gates have I rent asunder and the shades of Dis, and at my prayer's demand the spirits talk, the infernal dog is still; midnight has seen the sun, and day, the night; the sea, land, heaven and Tartarus yield to my will, and naught holds to law against my incantations. Bend him we will; my charms will find the way.

Cf. Mark 4:35–41 (Matt. 8:23–27//Luke 8:22–25); Mark 6:45–52 (Matt. 14:22–32, cf. John 6:15–21); Mark 11:12–24 (Matt. 21:18–22).

Pliny the Elder

4.9. The Potency of Human Saliva

Pliny the Elder, *Natural History* 28.7

4.9.1. Saliva from a Person who is Fasting Prevents Snakebite

Pliny the Elder, *Natural History* 28.7.35

I have however pointed out that the best of all safeguards against serpents is the saliva of a fasting human being, but our daily experience may teach us yet other values of its use. We spit on epileptics in a fit, that is, we throw back infection.

4.9.2. We Ward off Witchcraft by Spitting

Pliny the Elder, *Natural History* 28.7.35–36

In a similar way we ward off witchcraft and the bad luck that follows meeting a person lame in the right leg. We also ask forgiveness of the gods for a too presumptuous hope by spitting into our bosom; the same reason again accounts for the custom, in using any remedy, of spitting on the ground three times by way of ritual, thus increasing its efficacy, and 'of marking early incipient boils three times with fasting saliva. It is surprising, but

---

21 Seneca, *Hercules Oetaeus*, *Tragedies*, vol. 2 (trans. Frank Justus Miller; London: Heinemann, 1917), 453–463.

easily tested, that if one is sorry for a blow, whether inflicted by hand or by a missile, and at once spits into the palm of the hand that gave the wound, the resentment of the victim is immediately softened.

4.9.3. Lichens and Leprous Sores are Kept in Check by Fasting Saliva

Pliny the Elder, *Natural History* 28.7.37–38
Let us therefore believe that lichens too and leprous sores are kept in check by continual application of fasting saliva, as is also ophthalmia by using saliva every morning as eye ointment, carcinomata by kneading earth apple with saliva, and pains in the neck by applying fasting saliva with the right hand to the right knee and with the left hand to the left knee; let us also believe that any insect that has entered the ear, if spat upon, comes out. It acts as a charm for a man to spit on the urine he has voided; similarly to spit into the right shoe before putting it on, also when passing a place where one has run into some danger. Marcion of Smyrna, who wrote on the virtues of simples, tells us that the sea scolopendra bursts if spat upon, as do also bramble and other toads. Ofilius says that serpents too burst if one spits into their open mouths.

4.9.4. Upper Eyelids are Restored to Sensation if Touched with Saliva

Pliny the Elder, *Natural History* 28.7.38
. . . and Salpe[22] [says] that sensation in any numbed limb is restored by spitting into the bosom, or if the upper eyelids are touched with saliva.

4.9.5. Spitting Three Times into the Bosom Protects from the Stranger or from Giving the Sleeping Baby the Evil Eye

Pliny the Elder, *Natural History* 28.7.39
If we hold these beliefs, we should also believe that the right course, on the arrival of a stranger, or if a sleeping baby is looked at, is for the nurse to spit three times at her charge. And yet the baby is further under the divine protection of Fascinus,[23] guardian not only of babies but of generals, a deity whose worship, part of the Roman religion, is entrusted to the

---

22 Trans. note, "A woman of Lemnos who wrote on the disease of women," p. 29.
23 "Fascinus was the spirit of daemon or the phallus, an emblem of which was hung round the neck of infants to keep away evil influences. An image was also attached to the ear of a triumphant general, in which, too was a slave, who bade him look back, saying: *respice post te, hominem te memento.* See Juvenal X.41," W. H. S. Jones, p. 30n.

Vestals; hanging under the chariots of generals at their triumphs he defends them as a physician from jealousy, and the similar physic of the tongue bids them look back, so that at the back Fortune, destroyer of fame, may be won over.

Cf. Mark 7:31–37 (Matt. 15:29–31); Mark 8:22–26.

HEROES WITH THE POWER OF MAGIC

Empedocles (484–424 BCE)

Empedocles was a student of Pythagoras, and known for his strange powers. Because Diogenes reports that Gorgias referred to Empedocles' powers as "magical," the entry belongs here. But Empedocles is also considered a healer (see Chapter 2) and a worker of nature miracles (see Chapter 6).

4.10. Gorgias Apollodorus, Student of Empedocles, Testifies to Empedocles' Magical Power and His Claims to Give Magical Power

Diogenes Laertius, *Empedocles*, *Lives of Eminent Philosophers* 8.58–59[24]
Gorgias of Leontini, a man pre-eminent in oratory and the author of a treatise on the art, had been his [Empedocles'] pupil. Of Gorgias, Apollodorus says in his *Chronology* that he lived to be one hundred and nine. Satyrus quotes this same Gorgias as saying that he himself was present when Empedocles performed magical feats. Nay more: he contends that Empedocles in his poems lays claim to this power and to much besides when he says:

> And thou shalt learn all the drugs that are a defence to ward off ills and old age, since for thee alone, shall I accomplish all this. Thou shalt arrest the violence of the unwearied winds that arise and sweep the earth, laying waste the cornfields with their blasts; and again, if thou so will, thou shalt call back winds in requital. Thou shalt make after the dark rain a seasonable drought for men, and again after the summer drought thou shalt cause tree-nourishing streams to pour from the sky. Thou shalt bring back from Hades a dead man's strength.

---

24 Diogenes Laertius, *Empedocles*, *The Lives of Eminent Philosophers*, vol. 2 (trans. R. D. Hicks; London: Heinemann, 1925), 8.58–59.

Apuleius

Apuleius (circa 155 CE) had to defend himself against legal charges that he had seduced his wealthy wife into marrying him through the powers of magic. As part of his defense (*apologia*) he agrees that there are spirits who can cause divinations and "the miracles of magicians," but pronounces that the trouble with young Thallus is not possession by a magical power, but the disease epilepsy.

4.11. Certain Divine Powers Possessing a Character Midway between Gods and Men Control the Miracles of Magicians

Apuleius, *Apologia* 43[25]

I have read this [stories about divination among a certain group of boys] and the like concerning boys and the art-magic in several authors, but I am in doubt whether to admit the truth of such stories or no, although I believe Plato when he asserts that there are certain divine powers holding a position and possessing a character midway between gods and men, and that all divination and the miracles of magicians are controlled by them.

Satire: the Hyperborean Who Flies Through Air and Walks on Water

Lucian

In this satirical essay, *The Lover of Lies*, Lucian of Samosata spoofs the credulousness of his society in the matter of the supernatural. Here, his character Cleodemus is urging his friend to believe in wonders by giving testimony about a stranger from the land of the Hyperboreans whom he saw flying through air and walking on water. The Pythagoreans had a tradition that Abaris, a Hyperborean, had been given a sacred arrow by the god Apollo, and that he could fly over water on this holy shaft. Lucian is winking at such stories.

Two other texts bring attention to Lucian's dismissal of miracles as ridiculous magic for the credulous. Cleodemus goes on with a list of "trivial feats" which include miracles of healing and raising from the dead. Lucian shows us his opinion of such persons in the concluding tale, where the Hyperborean, described as a magician by Cleodemus, charges Glaucias a fee to be paid immediately' after which he uses his conjuring powers so that Glaucias might commit adultery with another man's wife.

---

25 Apuleius, *The Apologia and Florida of Apuleius of Madaura* (trans. H. E. Butler; Oxford: Clarendon Press, 1909), 78–80.

For Lucian, "miracle workers" are charlatans who will do anything for money.

4.12. I Saw a Hyperborean Magician Walk on Water (see Mark 6:45–52)

Lucian of Samosata (circa 120–190 CE), *The Lover of Lies* 13[26]

Said Cleodemus, "I myself was formerly more incredulous than you in regard to such things [wonders]; for I thought it in no way possible that they could happen; but when first I saw the foreign stranger fly – he came from the land of the Hyperboreans, he said –, I believed and was conquered after long resistance. What was I to do when I saw him soar through the air in broad daylight and walk on the water and go through fire slowly on foot?" "Did you see that?" said I – "the Hyperborean flying, or stepping on the water?" "Certainly," said he, "with brogues[27] on his feet such as people of that country commonly wear."

4.13. Other "Trivial" Feats the Magician Could Do Like Bringing Mouldy Corpses to Life

Lucian, *The Lover of Lies* 13

As for the trivial feats, what is the use of telling all that he performed, sending Cupids after people, bringing up supernatural beings, calling mouldy corpses to life, making Hecate herself appear in plain sight, and pulling down the moon?
(See John 11:1–46.)

THE MAGICAL PAPYRI

The texts that are presented here are all inscriptions from the Magical Papyri Collection.[28] I have chosen those that address the same diseases and daimon/demon-possession problems that Jesus cures through his miracles. These texts are important because they represent a facet of magic that was well known in antiquity, but was *not* attached to Jesus. Nevertheless, the foreign commands

---

26 All quotations are taken from Lucian, *The Lover of Lies, Lucian*, vol. 3 (trans. A. M. Harmon; London: Heinemann, 1921), 13.

27 The translator is referring to a shoe that is made of unfinished, rough leather.

28 All texts in this section are taken from *The Greek Magical Papyri in Translation Including the Demotic Spells*, ed. Hans Dieter Betz (Chicago and London: University of Chicago Press, 1986), vol. 1. Hereafter the volume will be referred as *GMPT*.

Jesus gives in two of his miracles ("Talitha cum" in Mark's raising of Jairus' Daughter [Mark 5:21–43//Matt. 9:18–26//Matt. 9:18–26//Luke 8:40–56] and "Ephthatha" in Mark's Healing of the Deaf Man with a Speech Impediment [Mark 7:31]) would sound very much like a magical spell. Interestingly, in Matthew and Luke's version of the raising of Jairus' daughter "Talitha cum" has been excised, and Mark's story of the healing of the deaf man with the speech impediment is not found in either evangelist's gospel.

Magical spells

Texts designated PGM are translated from Greek, while those designated PDM are translated from demotic (Egyptian).

For excellent health

4.14 PGM XCIV.7–9[29]

*[30] *For excellent health*:[31] Write on an amulet: "ABRAŌ[32] ... ARŌN BARA BAR ... A ... Ō."

For direct vision

4.15. PGM V.54–69[33]

* **Direct vision spell**: "EEIM TO EIM ALALĒP BARBAIATH/ MENEBREIO ARBATHIAŌTH IOUĒL IAĒL OUĒNĒIIE MESOMMIAS, let the god who prophesies to me come and let him not go away until I dismiss him. OURNAOUR SOUL ZASOUL/OUGOT NOOUMBIAOU THABRAT BERIAOU ACHTHIRI MARAI ELPHĒON TABAŌTH KIRASINA LAMPSOURĒ IABOE ABLAMATHANALBA AKRAMMACHAMAREI."

29 Trans. Roy Kotanski, *GMPT*, 304.
30 "An asterisk introduces an independent spell or a spell that contains most of the constituent parts necessary to effect the whole charm, though organic connections with adjacent spells can be recognized (e.g. spells entitled 'Another' ... or the like," *GMPT*, xxxii.
31 "Phrases set in italic boldface type refer to various subtitles and a number of types of rubrics (subsumed under the main title) that function in a titular sense to introduce a component feature of a spell." Ibid.
32 "Small capital letters indicate magical names which are usually untranslatable and often meaningless to the reader." Ibid.
33 Trans. W. C. Grese, ibid., 102.

In a bronze cup over oil. Anoint/[34] your right eye with water from a shipwreck and the left with Coptic eyepaint, with the same water. If you cannot find water from a shipwreck, then from a sunken skiff.

Against ophthalmia

4.16. PDM xiv.1097–1103[35]

*To heal ophthalmia in a man: "O Amoun, this lofty male, this male of Ethiopia who came down from Meroe to Egypt and who found my son Horus hurrying on his feet. He beat (?) him on his head with three spells in the Ethiopian language. When he finds NN,[36] whom NN bore, he will hurry on/ his feet, and he will beat (?) him on his head with three spells in the Ethiopian language: "GENTINI tentina qyqybi [ak]khe[37] akha."

[Say it] to a little oil; add salt and nasturtium seed to it, anoint the man who has ophthalmia with it, also write this on a new papyrus, and make it into a papyrus roll on his body: "You are the eye of heaven," in the writings . . . [38]

Against headache

4.17. PGM VII.199–201[39]

For migraine headache: Take oil in your hands and utter the spell/ "Zeus sowed a grape seed: it parts the soil; he does not sow it; it does not sprout."

---

34 "A diagonal slash indicates every fifth line of translated text." Ibid.

35 Trans. Janet H. Johnson, ibid., 247.

36 "In the magical formularies, this abbreviation stands for a name or names to be inserted by the reader, the names of the person against or for whom the magic is to be carried out." Ibid., xxxiii.

37 "Brackets enclosing words indicate that the words are not preserved in the original text. These include (1) suggested restoration of lacunae; (2) editorial expansions of the text to elucidate the sense of the original language; and (3) phrases traditionally set off by pointed brackets ⟨ ⟩, namely modern corrections to scribal omissions or errors." Ibid.

38 "What is left blank here is written in the papyrus as the hieroglyph of an eye with rays rising up from it." Note by Janet H. Johnson, ibid., 277, n. 593.

39 Trans. John Scarborough, ibid., 121.

4.18. PGM XVIIIb.1–7[40]

"GORGŌPHŌNAS[41]"I conjure you all by the
ORGŌPHŌNAS sacred name to heal Dionysius
RGŌPHŌNAS or Anys, whom Heraklia bore,
GŌPHŌNAS from every shivering fit and fever,
ŌPHŌNAS whether daily or intermittent [fever]
PHŌNAS by night or day, or quartan fever,
ONAS immediately, immediately, quickly,
NAS quickly."
AS
S"

Against fever

4.19. PGM VII.211–212[42]

*For fever with shivering fits:[43] Take oil in your hands and say 7 times,
"SABAŌTH" (add the usual, twice). And spread on oil from the sacrum to
the feet.

4.20. PGM VII.213–214[44]

*For daily fever and nightly fever: On the shiny side of an olive leaf
write . . . ,[45] and on the dark side write. . . . and wear it as an emulet.[46]

---

40 Trans. John Scarborough, ibid., 255. The words form a triangle, with the
ever-decreasing name GORGŌPHŌNAS in the center, and the words of the
charm written around, forming three lines, and moving from inside to outside
the triangular shape.
41 Note by John Scarborough, "The name GORGŌPHŌNAS, here apparently femi-
nine accusative plural, may refer to the epithet of Athena, 'Gorgo-slayer.'"
42 Trans. John Scarborough, *GMPT*, 121.
43 "Phrases set in roman boldface type refer to general titles of charms which
usually stand at the beginning of the spell and which are often followed by
one or more subtitles. Many spells do not possess a title, either because of a
scribal omission or because it has been lost in a lacuna in the text." Ibid.,
xxxii.
44 Trans. John Scarborough, ibid.
45 Here a small figure is drawn, a circle held by two slanted lines that meet at
a point outside, like the sun being held between two beams emanating from
a point in space.
46 Here a crescent moon curved to the left (i.e. a new moon) is drawn.

4.21. PDM xiv.1219–1227[47]

*Horus . . . went up the mountain at midday during the season of inun-
dation, mounted on a white horse . . . on a black horse,/ the papyrus rolls
[of . . .] being on (?) him, those of the Great of Five in his breast. He
found all the gods seated at the place of judgment eating [of the produce]
of the Nile, my great one. Said they, "Horus, come and eat! Horus, come!
Are you going to eat?

He said, "Go away from me! I have no [way] to eat. My head hurts;
my body hurts. A fever has taken hold of me; a south wind has seized
me. Does Isis [stop] making magic? Does Nephthys stop curing? Are the
sixteen those of the avenger? Is my one a divine power of a god? Are [the
365] gods sitting down to eat the produce of the fields of the Nile (?),
my great one, until they remove the fever/ from the head of the son of
Isis, from the head of NN, whom NN bore, being the fever of night, the
fever of midday, headache, this burning, this heat of the fevers of those
below the brow to his feet, [until they] remove [it] from the head of NN,
whom NN bore?"

[Say it] over genuine oil, seven times; anoint his hand, his body, his
feet; and speak to him.

4.22. PGM LXXXIII.1–20[48]

*For [fever with shivering fits]: GŌBA . . . S . . . MŌ . . . NOUSĒA . . .
EIEGE . . . OSARK . . . AUSE fever with shivering fits,/ I conjure you,
MICHAĒL, archangel of the earth; [whether] it is daily or nightly/ or
quartan fever; I conjure you, the Almighty SABAOTH, that it no longer
touch the soul of the one who carries [this], nor [touch] his whole body;
also the dead, deliver . . . the distress IDOT . . . YGRSBŌNŌE. . . . /"

"He who dwells in the help of the Most High shall abide in the shadow
of the God of heaven. He will say of God, 'thou art my refuge and my
help; I will put my trust in him."[49]

"Our Father who art in heaven, hallowed be thy will;/ our daily bread."[50]

"Holy, holy is the Lord SABBAOTH, heaven is full of justice, holy is
the one of glory."[51]

"ANIAADA . . . IA, MIGAĒL[52] of lords, Abraham Isaac Jacob ELŌEI
ELŌE Solomon (?)/ SABAŌTH ŌĒL."

---

47 Trans. Janet H. Johnson, *GMPT*, 250–251.
48 Trans. Roy Kotansky, ibid., 300.
49 LXX Ps. 90:1–2 with variations.
50 Note by R. Kotansky, "This is a somewhat confused quotation of the Lord's
   Prayer, Mt 6:9–11. The papyrus may read 'your father.'"
51 An allusion to LXX Isa. 6:3.
52 Note by R. Kotansky, "Read Michael."

Note

Roy Kotansky, translator of the text, comments here:

> This fever amulet is of special interest because it cites
> several biblical verses. Despite the writer's use of these cita-
> tions, the character of the spell shows it is syncretistic rather
> than distinctively Christian. In fact, the incoherent manner
> in which the verses are quoted suggests that the writer was
> ignorant of their context and meaning.[53]

To stop a flux in a woman

4.23. PDM xiv. 978–980[54]

Another, after it: Juice of a cucumber which has been rubbed, one
measure; water of the ear of a . . . animal, one measure, in accordance with
the measure of a wine cup; you should add a measure of good wine to
them and she should drink it at midday without having/ eaten anything
at all after bathing in the bath, which she did beforehand. When evening
comes, you should put the rag with honey up in her as above for seven
days.

4.24. PDM xiv. 981–984[55]

Another, after it: You should bring a new dish; you should put ten
measures of old sweet wine in it; and you should put a drachma of fresh
rue in it from dawn until midday. She should wash in the bath, come
out, and drink it. When evening comes, you should put honey up in her
as above again for seven days.

Dealing with the daimonic

For restraining

4.25. PGM VII. 429–458[56]

*A restraining [rite] for anything, works even on chariots. It also causes
enmity / and sickness, cuts down, destroys, and overturns, for [whatever]

---

53 *GMPT*, 300.
54 Trans. Janet H. Johnson, *GMPT*, 243.
55 Ibid.
56 Trans. Morton Smith, ibid., 129–130.

you wish. The spell [in it], when said, conjures daimons [out] and makes them enter [objects or people]. Engrave in a plate [made] of lead from a cold-water channel what you want to happen, and when you have consecrated it with bitter aromatics such as myrrh, bdellium, styrax, and aloes and thyme, / with river mud, late in the evening or in the middle of the night, where there is a stream or the drain of a bath, having tied a cord [to the plate] throw it into the stream – or into the sea – [and let it] be carried along. Use the cord so that, when you wish, you can undo [the spell]. Then should you wish to break [the spell], untie the plate. Say the formula 7 times and you will see something wonderful. Then go away without turning back / or giving an answer to anyone, and when you have washed and immersed yourself, go up to your own [room] and rest, and use [only] vegetable food. Write [the spell] with a headless bronze needle.

The text to be written is: "I conjure you, lord Osiris, by your holy names OUCHIŌCH OUSENARATH, Osiris, OUSERRANNOUPHTHI OSORNOUPHĒ/ Osiris-Mnevis, OUSERSETEMENTH AMARA MACHI CH ŌMASŌ EMMAI SERBŌNI EMER Isis,[57] ARATŌPHI ERACHAX ESEOI ŌTH ARBIŌTHI AMEN CH[N]OUM (?) MONMONT OUZATHI PĒR OUNNEPHER EN ŌŌŌ, I give over to you, lord Osiris, and I deposit with you this matter/" (add the usual).

But if you cause [the plate] to be buried or [sunk in] river or land or sea or stream or coffin or in a well, write the Orphic formula, saying "ASKEI KAI TASKEI" and, taking a black thread, make 365 knots and bind [the thread] around the outside of the plate, saying the same formula again and, "Keep him who is held" (or "bound"), or whatever you do. And thus [the plate]/ is deposited. For Selene, when she goes through the underworld, breaks whatever [spell] she finds. But when this [rite] has been performed, [the spell] remains [unbroken] so long as you say over [the formula] daily at this spot [where the plate is deposited]. Do not hastily share [this information] with anyone, for you will find [its like (?) only] with much labor.

For meeting your daimon

4.26. PGM VII. 505–528[58]

*Meeting with your own daimon: "Hail, Tyche, and you, the daimon of this place, and you, the present hour, and you, the present day – and every day as well. Hail, Universe, that is, earth and heaven. Hail, Helios, for you are the one who has established yourself in invisible light over the holy firmament/ ORKORĒTHARA.[59]

57 "EMER Isis is Egyptian for 'whom Isis loves,'" Morton Smith, ibid., 130, n. 60.

58 Trans. Hubert Martin, Jr., ibid., 131–132.

59 Note by Hubert Martin, Jr., "For the magical name ORKORĒTHARA, see Bousset, *Religionsgeschichtliche Studien*, 203."

"You are the father of the reborn Aion ZARACHTHŌ, you are the father of awful Nature *Thortchophanō*;[60] you are the one who has in yourself the mixture of universal nature and who begot the five wandering stars of the planets,[61] which are the entrails of heaven, the guts of earth, the fountainhead of the waters, and the violence/ of fire AZAMACHAR ANAPHANDAŌ EREYA ANEREYA PHENPHENSŌ IGRAA; you are the youthful one, highborn, scion of the holy temple, kinsman to the holy mere called Abyss which is located beside the two pedestals SKIATHI and MANTŌ. And the earth's 4 basements were shaken, O master of all, / holy Scarab, AŌ SATHREN ABRASAX IAŌAI AEŌ EŌA ŌAĒ IAO IĒO EY AĒ EY IE IAŌAI."

Write the name in myrrh ink on two male eggs.[62] You are to cleanse yourself thoroughly with one; then lick off the name, break it, and throw it away. Hold the other in your partially open right hand and show it to the sun at dawn and ... / olive branches; raise up your right hand, supporting the elbow with your left hand. Then speak the formula 7 times, crack the egg open, and swallow its contents.

Do this for 7 days, and recite the formula at sunset as well as sunrise.

To make a daimon depart

4.27. PGM XCIV.17–21[63]

For those possessed by daimons " ... T ... Y ... depart ... YT ... ". The things prescribed below ... / "ATR ... Y SOLŌMŌN ... is washed ... ".

---

60 Note by Hubert Martin, Jr., "Written in Coptic."
61 Note by Hubert Martin, Jr., "That is, the planets."
62 Note by Hubert Martin, Jr.: "That is, eggs from which male chicks would be hatched. The ancients believed that one could predict the sex of the chick from the shape of the egg, though there appears to be some uncertainty as to which shape produced which sex. See Aristotle, *Historia Animalium* VI.2 (559a); Pliny, *NH* 10.74; Columella, *De Re Restica* VIII.5." Cf. the comments by P. Louis in vol. 2 (Paris: Les belles lettres, 1968) of his Budé translation of the same treatise, p. 225, n.a; also the reference at PGM XII.100 to an egg that will produce a male chick.
63 Trans. Roy Kotansky, *GMPT*, 304.

Against daimons that bring epilepsy and muteness

4.28. PGM CXIV.1–14[64]

*"[Protect] her, NN, O lord, [from all] evil acts [and from every] demonic visitation [and] . . . of Hekate and from . . . / attack and [from every onslaught (?)] in sleep . . . [from] mute daimons [and from every] epileptic fit [and from all] epilepsy/ and . . . and . . . "

To do something spectacular and to be free of danger

4.29. PGM XII.160–178[65]

*[Charm to release from bonds:][66] If you want to do something spectacular and want to free yourself from danger, stand at the door and say the spell, and having said it, go out, adding: "Let the bonds of him, NN, be loosened, and let the doors be opened for him, and let no one see him."

You may even prove that it happens. Bind someone securely and shut him in a house. Stand outside and say the spell six or seven times thus: "I call upon you great gods, with a loud voice,/ AISAR AIŌTH OUAIGNŌR MARSABŌOUTŌRTHE LABATH ERMOU CHOŌRTHEN MANACHTHŌRPH PECHRĒPH TAOPHPŌTHTHOCHO THARŌCH BALETHAN CHEBRŌOUTHAST ADŌNAI HARMIŌTH."

Whenever [you say] this spell, and he has been released, say this besides, in order that the doors might open: "OCHLOBARACHŌ LAILAM DARIDAM [DARDAM] DARDARAMPTOU IARTHA IERBA DIERBA BAROTHA THIARBA ARBITHO . . . O MAAR SEMESILAM MARMARACHNEU MANE THŌTH; holy one, enter and release him, NN, and give him a way/ of escape, SESENGENBARPHARAGGĒS, you who loosen all bonds and you who loosen the iron fetter that has been placed around him, NN, because the great, unutterable, holy, righteous, awful, powerful, unspeakable, fearful and not-to-be-despised daimon of the great god commands you, SOROERMER [PHERGAR] BAX MAMPHRI OURIXG."

When the bonds break, say: "I thank you, lord, [because] the holy spirit, the unique one, the living one, has [released] me."

And say this spell again: /"Star-grouping god, you thunderbolt-with-great-clap-Zeus-confining-world-flashing-abundant-bolt-bestowing

---

64 Trans. Roy Kotansky, ibid., 313.
65 Trans. R. F. Hock, ibid., 159–160.
66 "This title for the spell does not appear in the papyrus manuscript and has been supplied by Preisendanz. It is, however, typical of other spells to begin with the phrase, 'If you wish to do (this and this), . . . ' " Note by R. F. Hock, ibid., 159, n. 5.

daimon, cracking-through-the-air, ray-producing, mind-piercing, you who [produce] cunning."

And use also the name of Helios for everything: "Fiery, EPHAIĒ, Hephaistos, who is shining with fire, brightly moving, ANANŌCHA AMARZA MARMARAMŌ.

APPENDIX A

Diseases and doctors

And there was a woman who had had a flow of blood for twelve years, and who had suffered much under many physicians, and had spent all that she had, and was no better but rather grew worse.

(Mark 5:25–26)

INTRODUCTION

The miraculous cure of any disease is measured for greatness by the gravity of the illness itself. But another factor in our appreciating the immensity of the "salvation" in the eyes of a Greco-Roman audience is the treatments to which sufferers would have been otherwise subjected.

I have chosen the title "Diseases and Doctors" rather than "Medicine" for this appendix because in the Greco-Roman world, the concept of "medicine" was easily blurred with "magic." In this appendix, we focus on the way the doctors of antiquity would have understood the seriousness of diseases, and on the treatments their training would have prescribed. The texts are drawn from three sources: Hippocrates, Celsus (the first-century author as distinct from the second-century polemicist against Christianity), and Pliny the Elder. Hippocrates (469–399 BCE) was held in great regard as the father of medicine, and even though some of his theories would be disputed by famous physicians such as Asclepiades, or the great Galen, Hippocrates remained the measuring rod against which all theories and practices among doctors of the first century were discussed. Thus, Hippocrates' ideas can represent with some fairness the basic ideas that would have been known to generations of doctors.

201

Aulus Cornelius Celsus (wrote 14–37 CE) was a contemporary of Jesus, and his treatise represents the medical learning considered reliable in his age. Pliny the Elder (24–79 CE) offers a larger range of popular medical remedies among the people. This obvious blend of folk remedies and formal medicine illustrates the mixture of medicine and magic in those "cures" common to the Greco-Roman world.

We cannot suppose that the medical knowledge represented here was readily available to everyone, least of all the destitute. However, the texts here show us a large set of medical ideas and treatments that must have been reasonably familiar to many people in the Greco-Roman world. The writers of the miracle stories would have had some idea of the seriousness of a complaint, and have witnessed for themselves some of the treatments for the most common of these diseases. The writers of the Jesus miracle stories had every reason to expect that the communities for whom they formulated the stories would have had such knowledge in order to appreciate the claim being made for Jesus. Indeed Abraham Malherbe's *Social Aspects of Early Christianity*,[1] Wayne Meeks' *The First Urban Christians*,[2] and more recently, Richard Horsley's *Sociology and the Jesus Movement*[3] all conclude that the membership of Christian communities included a broad cross-section of Greco-Roman society. This selection of texts is meant to allow us to join those audiences and to see the miracle stories through their lens.

---

1 Abraham, J. Malherbe, *Social Aspects of Early Christianity* (Baton Rouge and London: Louisiana State University Press, 1977).
2 Wayne A. Meeks, *The First Urban Christians: The Social World of the Apostle Paul* (New Haven: Yale University Press, 1983).
3 Richard A. Horsley, *Sociology and the Jesus Movement*, (2nd ed.; New York: Continuum, 1994).

THE GRECO-ROMAN WORLD AND THE DOCTOR

Medicaments are "the hands of the gods"

A.1. Marcellus[4] Supports the View of Herophilus[5] that Medicaments are "The Hands of the Gods"

Marcellus, *Epistula Cornelii Celsi De Medicamentis* 5.36[6]
They say, Gaius Julius Callistus, that Herophilus, who was once held to be among the greatest physicians, said that medicaments are the hands of the gods, and indeed not without reason, in my opinion. For certainly what divine touch can effect, medicaments tested by use and experience also accomplish.

A.2. Plutarch[7] Claims that Erasistratus[8] Exposes the Absurdity of Herophilus' Opinion

Plutarch, *Quaestiones Symposicae* 4.1.3[9]
When [Philo] mixes those regal and potent substances – which Herophilus[10] used to call 'hands of gods' – mixing together into the same compound mineral, vegetable, and animal products from both land and sea, Erasistratus exposes his absurdity and excessive elaboration.

---

4 A physician and poet who flourished during the reign of Hadrian and Antoninus Pius, and whose works can be dated fairly circa 160 CE.

5 Herophilus was active as physician in Alexandria about 300 BCE.

6 Marcellus, *De Medicamentis*, ed. [Max] Niedermann, 2nd ed. E. Liechtenhan. Trans. J. Kollesch and D. Nickel. *Corpus Medicorum Latinorum* (Berlin and Leipzig: 1915). This reference is owed to Heinrich von Staden, ed. and trans., *Herophilus: The Art of Medicine in Early Alexandria* (Cambridge: Cambridge University Press, 1989), 417.

7 Philosopher and biographer, he flourished in the late first and early second century CE.

8 Erasistratus was a contemporary of Herophilus, a physician in the court of Seleucus Nicator of Antioch. For a meticulous discussion of the dating of both Herophilus and Erasistratus, see von Staden, *Herophilus*, 43–49.

9 Ibid., 417.

10 Trans. note: "The MSS read 'Erasistratus'; Max Wellmann, Karl Deichgräber, and others have suggested emending the text to read 'Herophilus . . . [lacuna], Erasistratus'" (ibid.).

Jibes at the doctor's expense

A.3. The Doctors' Examination Gave me my Fever

Martial, *Epigrams* 5.9[11]

I was sickening; but you at once attended me, Symmachus, with a train of a hundred apprentices. A hundred hands frosted by the North wind have pawed me: I had no fever before, Symmachus; now I have.

A.4. The Doctor Turned Undertaker

Martial, *Epigrams* 1.47[12]

Lately was Diaulus a doctor, now he is an undertaker. What the undertaker now does the doctor too did before.

A.5. The Oculist Turned Gladiator

Martial, *Epigrams* 8.74[13]

You are now a gladiator; you were an eye-specialist before. You did as doctor what you do now as gladiator.

A.6. The Doctor Caught Stealing Pretends He Does So to Protect Me

Martial, *Epigrams* 9.96[14]

Doctor Herodes had stolen a drinking-ladle from a sick patient. When detected he said, "You fool, why then do you drink?" (He pretends to have taken the object which made the patient ill)

A.7. The Avarice of the Doctor

Plutarch, *Sayings of Kings and Commanders*, *Moralia* 3.177f. (9)[15]

When the keybone of his [Philip's] shoulder had been broken in battle, and the attending physician insistently demanded a fee every day, he said, "Take as much as you wish; for you have the key in your charge."

("Key" represents wordplay on *kleis*, which means both "key" and "collarbone.")

---

11 Martial, *Epigrams*, vol. 1 (trans. Walter C. A. Kerr; London: Heinemann, 1919), 5.9.
12 Ibid., 1.47.
13 Martial, *Epigrams*, vol. 2 (trans. Walter C. A. Kerr; London: Heinemann, 1920), 8.74.
14 Ibid., 9.96.
15 I am indebted for this text and note to Vernon Robbins, *Ancient Quotes and Anecdotes* (Sonoma, CA: Polebridge, 1989), 297.

A.8. Pliny the Elder Deplores Greek Physicians: Greeks Practice Medicine for a Fee, to Gain Credit and to Destroy Us Romans

Pliny the Elder, *Natural History* 29.7[16]

I shall speak about those Greek fellows in their proper place, son Marcus, and point out the result of my enquiries at Athens, and convince you what benefit comes from dipping into their literature, and not making a close study of it. They are quite a worthless people, and an intractable one, and you must consider my words prophetic. When that race gives us its literature it will corrupt all things, and even all the more if its sends hither its physicians. They have conspired together to murder all foreigners with their physic, but this very thing they do for a fee, to gain credit and to destroy us easily. They are also always dubbing us foreigners, and to fling more filth on us than on others they give us the foul name of Opici.[17] I have forbidden you to have dealings with physicians.

Proper conduct of a physician

A.9. The Doctor and the Philosopher Should Never Advertise Services, but Always Be Petitioned

(Notice that all miracles of Jesus, with the exception of Mark 3:1–6 [Matt 12:9–12; Luke 6:6–11]: The Healing of the Man with the Withered Hand, and two miracles Luke drew from that story [Luke 13:10–17: The Woman Bent for Eighteen Years, and Luke 14:16: The Man with Dropsy] are petitioned, not "advertised" or imposed.)

Epictetus, *Discourses* 3.23.27–28[18]

Does a philosopher invite people to a lecture? – Is it not rather the case that, as the sun draws its own sustenance to itself, so he also draws to himself those to whom he is to do good? What physician ever invites a patient to come and be healed by him? Although I am told that in these days the physicians in Rome *do* advertise; however, in my time they were called in by their patients. "I invite you to come and hear that you are in a bad way, and that you are concerned with anything rather than what you should be concerned with, and that you are ignorant of the good and the evil, and are wretched and miserable." That's a fine invitation! And yet if the philosopher's discourse does not produce this effect, it is lifeless and so is the speaker himself.

---

16 Pliny the Elder, *Natural History*, vol. 8 (trans. W. H. S. Jones; London: Heinemann, 1963), 29.7.

17 "An uncultivated Italian tribe," Jones, ibid., 192, n. a.

18 Epictetus, *Epictetus*, vol. 2 (trans. W. A. Oldfather; London: Heinemann, 1928), 3.23.27–28.

AVAILABILITY OF PHYSICIANS: PUBLIC DOCTORS

There is evidence that towns hired certain physicians, *archiatroi*, to provide the indigent with free services in order to avert disease and epidemic.[19]

A.10. Massilia's [Marseilles's] Hiring of Public Physicians is Another Example of the "Civilizing" Roman Influence on the Barbarians as They Also Hire Public Sophists

Strabo, *Geography* 4.1.5 (C 180–181)[20]

Since, on account of the overmastery of the Romans, the barbarians who are situated beyond the Massiliotes became more and more subdued as time went on, and instead of carrying on war have already turned to civic life and farming, it may also be the case that the Massiliotes themselves no longer occupy themselves so earnestly with the pursuits aforementioned. Their present state of life makes this clear; for all the men of culture turn to the art of speaking and the study of philosophy; so that the city, although a short time ago it was given over as merely a training school for the barbarians and was schooling the Galatae to be fond enough of the Greeks to write even their contracts in Greek, at the present time has attracted also the most notable of Romans, if eager for knowledge, to go to school there instead of making their foreign sojourn at Athens. Seeing these men and at the same time living at peace, the Galatae are glad to adapt their leisure to such modes of life, not only as individuals, but also in a public way; at any rate, they welcome sophists, hiring some at private expense, but others in common, as cities, just as they do physicians.

19 See inscription in "Arabia," *Inscriptiones Graecae ad Res Romanas Pertinentes* (trans. René Cagnat and Georges Louis Lafaye; 4 vols.; Rome: L'Erma di Bretschneider, 1964), vol. 3, inscription 1333, p. 475: "from the ability to foreknow the path the disease will take ... indeed Claudius Andromache, principal doctor [head doctor] ... ".

20 Strabo, *The Geography of Strabo*, vol. 2 (trans. Horace Leonard Jones; London: Heinemann, 1923), 4.1.5 (c 180–181).

PRESCRIPTIONS AND PROGNOSES

A.11. "What drugs will not cure, the knife will;

What drugs will not cure, the knife will;
what the knife will not cure, the cautery will;
what the cautery will not cure must be considered
incurable.

(Hippocrates, *Aphorisms* 7.87)[21]

Certainly not everyone was able to see a physician on a regular basis, but the formulators of the healing miracle stories may be presumed to be conversant with the illness they name to their audience.

For the regular, traditional medical position I quote Hippocrates, who was, of course, the major reference of physicians. Yet, Hippocrates belongs to the pre-Hellenistic world. For the first-century evidence of that tradition and its modifications, I quote from Celsus (circa 34 CE) and Pliny the Elder (1 BCE–79 CE).

Deafness

Pliny the Elder

A.12. Treatments for Pains in the Ears

Pliny the Elder, *Natural History* 28.48[22]
Pain in the ears and ear affections[23] are cured by the urine of a wild boar kept in a glass vessel, by the gall of a wild boar, pig, or ox, with citrus oil and rose oil in equal proportions, but best of all by warm bull's gall with leek juice, or with honey should there be suppuration, and for foul odour the gall by itself warmed in a pomegranate rind. Ruptures in this region are thoroughly healed by the gall with woman's milk. Some hold that for hardness of hearing also the ears should be rinsed out with this wash, others add serpents' slough and vinegar (they insert the mixture on wool), the ears being first rinsed with warm water, or, if the hardness of hearing amounts to deafness, they pour in bull's gall with myrrh and rue warmed in pomegranate rind, also fat bacon; or fresh ass's dung with rose

---

21 G. E. R. Lloyd (ed.) *Hippocratic Writings* (trans. J. Chadwick, W. N. Mann, I. M. Lonie and E. T. Withington; Harmondsworth: Penguin, 1978), 266.

22 Pliny the Elder, *Natural History*, vol. 8 (trans. Jones), 28.48.

23 "Affections" is a term used to describe "a bodily state due to any influence" (*OED*).

oil is inserted in drops, all being warmed. More useful is the foam of a horse, or fresh horse-dung reduced to ash and mixed with rose-oil, fresh butter, beef suet with goose grease, she-goat's or bull's urine, or that used by fullers, stale, and warmed until the steam rises up the neck of the jar (a third part of vinegar is added and little myrrh), the dung, mixed with the gall, of a calf that has not tasted grass added to the slough of snakes, the ears being first warmed; these medicaments are inserted into the ears on wool. Beneficial is also veal suet, with goose grease and juice of ocimum; the marrow of a calf mixed with pounded cummin and poured into the ear; and for ear pains the seminal fluid of a hog, caught as it drips from a sow before it can touch the ground; for fractures of the ears the glue made from the genitals of calves and melted in water; for other affections the fat of foxes, goat's gall with warm rose-oil or with leek juice, or, if any part of the ear has been ruptured, with woman's milk; if there is hardness of hearing, ox gall with the urine of a goat, male or female, or if there is pus. But whatever the use may be, it is thought that these remedies are much more efficacious if they are smoke-dried for twenty days in a goat's horn. Another approved treatment is a third of a denarius of hare's rennet and half a denarius of sacopenium in Amminean wine. Parotid swellings are reduced by bear's grease with an equal weight of wax and bull suet (some add hypocisthis), and an application of butter by itself after previous fomentation with a decoction of fenugreek, more efficaciously with the addition of strychnos. Beneficial also are the testicles of foxes and bull's blood dried and pounded, she-goat's urine warmed and poured by drops into the ear, and an application of she-goat's dung with axle-grease.

Dropsy

Hippocrates

A.13. All Cases of Dropsy Arising from Acute Diseases are Bad

Hippocrates, *Prognosis* 8[24]
All cases of dropsy arising from acute diseases are bad. For, besides not getting rid of the fever, they are particularly painful and liable to cause death.

---

24 Lloyd (ed.) *Hippocratic Writings*, 174.

Celsus

A.14. Symptoms of Dropsy

Celsus, *On Medicine* 2.7.5[25]

Dropsy is impending, when with prolonged diarrhoea the feet swell; when there is pain in the lower belly and hips; but this class of disease is wont to arise from the flanks. There is danger, the same as just stated, to those in whom, when there is a desire for stool, the bowels yield nothing unless a forced hard motion; also in whom there is a swelling in the feet, and a swelling in turn in the right and then the left half of the abdomen which rises and subsides: but this disease appears to begin from the liver. It is a sign of the same disease, when intestines in the umbilical region undergo twisting (the Greeks call it *strophus*), when pains in the hips persist, which are not dispersed either by time or by medicaments.

A.15.1. The Treatment is Easier for Slaves because it Demands Deprivation and Confinement

Celsus, *On Medicine* 3.21.2–3

It is relieved more easily in slaves than in freemen, for since it demands hunger, thirst, and a thousand other troublesome treatments and prolonged endurance, it is easier to help those who are easily constrained than those who have an unserviceable freedom. But even those who are in subjection, if they cannot exercise complete self-control, are not brought back to health.

A.15.2. A Story to Show that the Patient's Temperament is More Important in the Cure than the Treatments Are

Hence a not undistinguished physician, a pupil of Chrysippus, at the court of King Antigonus, held that a certain friend of the king, noted for intemperance, could not be cured, although but moderately affected by that malady; and when another physician, Philip of Epirus, promised that he would cure him, the pupil of Chrysippus replied that Philip was regarding the disease, he the patient's spirit. Nor was he mistaken. For although the patient was watched with the greatest diligence, not only by his physician but by the king as well, by devouring his poultices and by drinking his own urine, he hurried himself headlong to his end.

---

25 All quotations are taken from Celsus, *On Medicine*, vol. 1 (trans. W. G. Spencer; London: Heinemann, 1935).

A.16. Treatments for Dropsy

Pliny the Elder, *Natural History* 28.68[26]

Good for dropsy is urine from the bladder of a wild boar given little by little in the drink, that being more beneficial which has dried up with its bladder, the ash of bull's dung especially but also that of oxen – herd animals I mean; it is called bolbiton – three spoonfuls in a hemina of honey wine, cow dung for women, bull dung for men (the Magi have made a sort of mystery of this distinction), the dung of a bull calf applied locally, ash of calf dung with staphylinus seed in equal proportions taken in wine, and goat's blood with goat's marrow. That of a he-goat is considered more beneficial, especially if he has browsed on lentisk.

Epilepsy

A.17.1. Epilepsy from Childhood is Typified by Erratic Seizures[27]

Hippocrates, *The Sacred Disease* 14

When the disease has been present from childhood, a habit develops of attacks occurring at any change of wind and specially when it is southerly. This is hard to cure because the brain has become more moist than normal and is flooded with phlegm. This renders discharges more frequent. The phlegm can no longer be completely separated out; neither can the brain, which remains wet and soaked, be dried up.

A.17.2. These Observations Result from the Study of Goats, a Species Liable to this Disease[28]

Hippocrates, *The Sacred Disease* 14

This observation results specially from a study of animals, particularly of goats which are liable to this disease. Indeed, they are peculiarly susceptible to it. If you cut open the head you will find that the brain is wet, full of fluid and foul-smelling, convincing proof that disease and not the deity is harming the body. It is just the same with man, for when the malady becomes chronic, it becomes incurable. The brain is dissolved by phlegm and liquefies; the melted substance thus formed turns into water which surrounds the brain on the outside and washes round it like the

---

26 Pliny the Elder, *Natural History*, vol. 8 (trans. Jones), 28.68.
27 Lloyd *Hippocratic Writings*, 246.
28 Ibid., 247.

sea round an island. Consequently, fits become more frequent and require less to cause them. The disease therefore becomes very chronic as the fluid surrounding the brain is dilute because its quantity is so great, and as a result it may be quickly overcome by the blood and warmed.

Celsus

Celsus nowhere uses the Greek name [epilepsy] perhaps because it was held to be ill omened. The name *comitialis morbus* was given to the disease because a meeting of the *comitia* was adjourned if anyone was attacked by it, since it was looked upon as a divine manifestation.[29]

A.18. Treatment after a Seizure

Celsus, *On Medicine* 3.23.2–4[30]

If a man falls into a fit without the addition of spasms, certainly he should not be bled; if there are spasms, at any rate he should not be bled unless there are other indications for the bleeding. But it is necessary to move the bowels by a clyster, or by a purge of black hellebore, or by both if the strength allows of it. Next, the head should be shaved and oil and vinegar poured over it, the patient should be given food on the third day, as soon as the hour has passed at which he had a fit. But neither gruels, nor other soft and easily digested food, nor meat, least of all pork, are suitable for such patients, but food materials of the second class: for there is need to give strength and indigestion is to be avoided; in addition he should avoid sunshine, the bath, a fire, all heating agents; also cold wine, venery, overlooking a precipice, and everything terrifying, vomiting, fatigue, anxiety and all business.

When food has been given upon the third day, it should be omitted on the fourth, and then on alternate days, observing the same hour for the meal, until fourteen days have elapsed. When the malady lasts beyond this period, it loses its acute character, and if it persists, it is now to be treated as chronic.

---

29 Celsus, *On Medicine*, vol. 3 (trans. W. G. Spencer; London: Heinemann, 1938), 332, n. b.
30 Celsus, *On Medicina*, vol. 1 (trans. Spencer), 3.23–24.

Pliny the Elder

A.19. Treatments for Epilepsy

Pliny the Elder, *Natural History* 28.63[31]

For epilepsy it is beneficial to eat a bear's testes or to take those of a wild boar in mare's milk or water, likewise wild-boar's urine in oxymel, with increased efficacy if it has dried in his bladder. There are also given the testicles of pigs dried and pounded in sow's milk, abstinence from wine preceding and following for [ten] days. There are also given the lungs of a hare preserved in salt, with a third part of frankincense, taken in white wine for thirty days; likewise a hare's rennet, an ass's brain in hydromel, first smoked on burning leaves, half an ounce a day for [five] days, or an ass's hoofs reduced to ash and two spoonfuls taken in drink for a whole month, likewise his testes preserved in salt and sprinkled on drink, preferably on ass's milk, or on water. The odour of the after-birth of she-asses, especially if they have had a male foal, inhaled on the approach of a fit, repels it. There are some who recommend eating with bread the heart of a black jackass in the open air on the first or second day of the moon, some the flesh, others drinking for forty days the blood diluted with vinegar. Certain people mix an ass's urine with smithy water in which hot iron has been dipped, and use the same drought to treat delirious raving. To epileptics is also given mare's milk to drink, the excrescence on a horse's leg taken in oxymel; there is given too goat's flesh roasted on a funeral pyre, as the Magi would have it, goat suet boiled down with an equal weight of bull's gall stored in the gall bladder without touching the earth, and taken in water with the patient standing upright. The disease itself is detected by the fumes of burnt goat's horn or deer's horn.[32] Rubbing with the urine of an ass's foal mixed with nard is said to be beneficial to the planet-struck.[33]

Apuleius

Apuleius (circa 155 CE) had to defend himself against legal charges that he had used magic to bewitch a wealthy woman into marrying

---

31 Pliny the Elder, *Natural History*, vol. 8 (trans. W. H. S. Jones), 28.63.

32 "Neither Lettré nor the Bohn translator comments on this vague sentence. It is not clear how the presence of epilepsy is detected by this test. Possibly a fit is diagnosed as epileptic according as it reacts to the treatment," Jones, p. 152, n. c.

33 "Sometimes sunstroke may be referred to by this term. Many expressions in this chapter are curious. Why for instance both *testes* and *testiculi*? *Morbo comitialium* is strange and so is the apparent omission on two occasions of a numeral," Jones, pp. 152–153, n. d.

him. As part of his defense (apologia) he explains a misdiagnosis of the condition of young Thallus, who does not need the ministrations of any magician, but the attentions of a doctor because his trouble is medical, not spiritual. Thallus has epilepsy.

A.20. Thallus' Troubles do Not Require a Magician. He has Epilepsy and Needs a Doctor

Apuleius, *Apologia* 43[34]

As a matter of fact, Thallus, whom you mentioned, needs a doctor rather than a magician. For the poor wretch is such a victim to epilepsy that he frequently has fits twice or thrice in one day without the need for any incantations, and exhausts all his limbs with his convulsions. His face is ulcerous, his head bruised in front and behind, his eyes are dull, his nostrils distended, his feet stumbling. He may claim to be the greatest of magicians in whose presence Thallus has remained for any considerable time upon his feet. For he is continually lying down, either a seizure or mere weariness causing him to collapse.

Eye ailments and unguents

Though the medical descriptions of various eye ailments and their treatments is quite copious, there is little hope for anyone who is actually blind. These entries deal with physicians' efforts to save the eyes of their patients. They are included here to give us a better idea of the treatments that an audience of Christian listeners would have supposed might have been suffered all in vain by the blind petitioners in the gospels. And they help us to measure the weight of the Jesus miracle itself.

Hippocrates

A.21. Cures for Pains in the Eyes

Hippocrates, *Aphorisms* 6.31[35]

Pains in the eyes are cured by drinking neat wine, by bathing, by vapour baths, by bleeding or by the administration of certain drugs.

---

34 Apuleius, *The Apologia and Florida of Apuleius of Madaura* (trans. H. E. Butler; Oxford: Clarendon Press, 1909), 79–80.
35 Lloyd, *Hippocratic Writings*, p. 229.

Pliny the Elder

A.22. Ophthalmia is Kept in Check by Applications of Fasting Saliva

Pliny the Elder, *Natural History* 28.7.37–38[36]
Let us therefore believe that lichens too and leprous sores are kept in check by continual application of fasting saliva, as is also ophthalmia by using saliva every morning as eye ointment, carcinomata by kneading earth apple with saliva, and pains in the neck by applying fasting saliva with the right hand to the right knee and with the left hand to the left knee; let us also believe that any insect that has entered the ear, if spat upon, comes out.

A.23.1. Eye Fluxes Require Applications of Beef Suet

Pliny the Elder, *Natural History* 28.47.167
To eye fluxes is applied beef suet boiled with oil; scabrous eyes are smeared with the same and deer's horn reduced to ash, but the tips by themselves are thought to be more efficacious.

A.23.2. Eyefluxes are Relieved by a Solution of Warm Water and Goat's Cheese

Pliny the Elder, *Natural History* 28.47.170
Eyefluxes are relieved by an application in warm water of soft cheese made from goat's milk, or if there is swelling, in honey; in both cases there should be fomentation with warm whey.

A.23.3. Dry Ophthalmia is Cured by Paste of Burnt Pork Loins, or a Pastille of Goat Dung Swallowed at New Moon

Pliny the Elder, *Natural History* 28.47.170
Dry ophthalmia is cured by taking the small loins of pork, burning and pounding, and then placing them on the eyes. She-goats are said never to suffer from ophthalmia, because of certain herbs they eat, and likewise gazelles; for this reason it is recommended that at the new moon their dung should be swallowed, coated with wax.

---

36 All quotations are taken from Pliny the Elder, *Natural History*, vol. 8 (trans. S. Jones).

A.23.4. Eyes are Benefited by Fumigation with Steam from a She-Goat's Boiled or Roasted Liver

Pliny the Elder, *Natural History* 28.47.170–171

Some smear the eyes with the gravy from a she-goat's roasted liver, or with its gall; they prescribe its meat as food, and fumigation of the eyes with the steam that arises from cooking; they also consider it important for the animal to have been of a red colour. They also wish the eyes to be fumigated with the steam of the liver boiled in a clay pot; some say that it should be roasted.

A.23.5. Valued Eye Remedies Include Ointments of Goat's Dung; Hare's Lung; Wolf's Fat, or a Bracelet holding a Fox's Tongue

Pliny the Elder, *Natural History* 28.47.172

Goat's dung with honey is a not unvalued ointment for eye fluxes, or the marrow for eye pains, or a hare's lung, and for dimness its gall with raisin wine or honey. Wolf's fat also or pig's marrow is prescribed as an ointment for ophthalmia. But it is said that those who carry a fox's tongue in a bracelet will never suffer from ophthalmia.

Fever

Celsus

A.24. A Physician Must Consider the Patient's Safety First

Celsus, *On Medicine* 3.4.1[37]

Asclepiades said that it is the office of the practitioner to treat safely, speedily, and pleasantly. That is our aspiration, but there is generally danger both in too much haste and too much pleasure. But what moderation must be shown, in order that as far as possible all those blessings may be attained, the patient's safety being always kept first, will be considered among the actual details of the treatment.

A.25. Asclepiades Taught that the Patient should be Refused Water and Sleep in the First Days

Celsus, *On Medicine* 3.4.2–4

Before everything is the question as to what regimen the patient should keep to during the first days. The ancients tried to ensure assimilation by

---

37 All quotations are taken from Celsus, *On Medicine*, vol. 1 (trans. Spencer).

administering certain medicaments, because they dreaded indigestion most of all; next by the repetition of clysters they extracted the matter which appeared to be doing harm. Asclepiades did away with medicaments; he did not clyster the bowel with such frequency but still he generally did this in every disease; but the actual fever, he professed to use as a remedy against itself: for he deemed that the patient's forces ought to be reduced by daylight, by keeping awake, by extreme thirst, so that during the first days he would not allow even the mouth to be swilled out. Therefore those are quite wrong who believe his regimen was a pleasant one in all respects; for in the later days he allowed even luxuries to his patient, but in the first days of the fever he played the part of the torturer.

Hemorrhage

Pliny the Elder

A.26.1. A Woman's Monthly Flux is Regulated by an Internal, Inanimate Mole

Pliny the Elder, *Natural History* 7.15.63[38]
Woman is, however, the only animal that has monthly periods; consequently she alone has what are called moles in her womb. This mole is a shapeless and inanimate mass of flesh that resists the point and the edge of a knife; it moves about, and it checks menstruation, as it also checks births: in some cases causing death, in others growing old with the patient, sometimes when the bowels are violently moved being ejected. A similar object is also formed in the stomach of males, called a tumour, as in the case of the praetorian Oppius Capito.

A.26.2. Contact with a Woman's Monthly Flux is Harmful

Pliny the Elder, *Natural History* 7.15.64
But nothing could easily be found that is more remarkable than the monthly flux of women. Contact with it turns new wine sour, crops touched by it become barren, grafts die, seeds in gardens are dried up, the fruit of trees falls off, the bright surface of mirrors in which it is merely reflected is dimmed, the edge of steel and the gleam of ivory are dulled, hives of bees die, even bronze and iron are at once seized by rust, and a horrible smell fills the air; to taste it drives dogs mad and infects their bites with an incurable poison.

---

38 All quotations are taken from Pliny the Elder, *Natural History*, vol. 2 (trans. H. Rackham; London: Heinemann, 1942).

A.26.3. For Female Complaints

Pliny the Elder, *Natural History* 28.77.246, 248, 249, 250, 251, 252, 254, 255, 256[39]

246 The purgings of women are aided by bull's gall applied as a pessary in unwashed wool – Olympias, a woman of Thebes, added suet and soda – by ash of deer's horn taken in drink, and uterine troubles by an application also of this, and by two-oboli pessaries of bull's gall and poppy juice. ... 248 The hare is also of great use to women. The uterus is benefited by the dried lung taken in drink, fluxes by the liver taken in water with Samian earth. ... 249 For inflation of the uterus it is beneficial to make with oil a liniment of wild boar's dung or pig's. More efficacious is the dried dung reduced to powder to sprinkle in the drink, even if the woman is suffering the pains of pregnancy or child-birth. ... 250 Ulcerations also of the uterus are healed by the dried suet of the same animal [the ass], which applied in raw wool as a pessary softens uterine indurations; while by itself either fresh or dried suet, applied in water, acts as a depilatory. 251 Dried ass's spleen, applied in water to the breasts, produces an abundant supply of milk, and used in fumigation corrects displacement of the uterus. ... 252 Ass's dung applied fresh is said to be a wonderful reliever of fluxes of blood, as is also the ash of the same dung, an application which is also beneficial to the uterus. ... 253 Calf's gall also checks the flow if rubbed on the navel, and is generally beneficial to the uterus. 254 A bull-calf's gall beaten up with half the quantity of honey is stored away for uterine complaints. ... 255 Midwives assure us that a flux, however copious, is stayed by drinking the urine of a she-goat, or if an applications is made of her dung. ... 256 To fumigate the uterus with the hairs of kids is thought to be beneficial, and it is so for a flux of blood if kid's rennet is taken in drink, or applied locally with seed of hyoscyamus.

Leprosy

There is controversy about what the word *lepra* is meant to convey in the Jesus stories because it could be used in two ways. *Lepra* was used as a synonym for a number of skin diseases, such as a serious eczema or psoriasis, and indeed, it is this classification which would hold for the description of leprosy in the Hebrew scriptures. The disease we call leprosy today was designated *elephantiasis* by the doctors of the ancient world. This is a "nodular" leprosy, in which tumors disfigure the body.

---

39 Pliny the Elder, *Natural History*, vol. 8 (trans. Jones), 28.77.

Of course, the more serious of the two is the "nodular" leprosy, and it is perhaps the grotesque, frightful and terrible character of this *elephantiasis* that convinces some scholars that surely it is this disease which is intended by the author of the Jesus story in Mark 1:40–45. However, in the story of Jesus' cure of the leper, Jesus tells the cured man to go and show himself to the priest and offer what Moses commanded the people (Mark 1:44). Those regulations can be found in Appendix B, texts B3–B4. The leprosy in Mark 1:40–45, then, is the type referred to in Leviticus, i.e. the skin disease.

Hippocrates

A.27. Leprosy is a Disfigurement and Not a Disease

Hippocrates, *Affections* 35[40]
"Lepra",[41] prurigo, psora, lichen, alphos, and alopecia arise because of phlegm. These are disfigurements rather than diseases.

Pliny the Elder

A.28. Leprous Sores are Often Kept from Worsening by the Application of Fasting Saliva

Pliny the Elder, *Natural History* 28.7
Let us therefore believe that lichens too and leprous sores are kept in check by continual applications of fasting saliva, as is also ophthalmia by using saliva every morning as eye ointment, carcinomata by kneading earth apple with saliva, and pains in the neck by applying fasting saliva with the right hand to the right knee and with the left hand to the left knee; let us also believe that any insect that has entered the ear, if spat upon, comes out.

---

40 Hippocrates, *Affections, Hippocrates*, vol. 5 (trans. Paul Potter; London: Heinemann, 1988), 35.

41 The quotation marks are mine to draw attention to the fact that the translator chooses a transliteration of the Greek word rather than the word "leprosy."

Bowed spine

Hippocrates

A.29. The Majority of the Afflicted are Short-Lived

Hippocrates, *On Joints* 41[42]

When the spinal vertebrae are drawn into a hump by diseases, most cases are incurable, especially when the hump is formed above the attachment of the diaphragm. Some of those lower down are resolved when varicosities form in the legs, and still more when these are in the vein at the back of the knee. . . . And where the hump is above the diaphragm, the ribs do not enlarge in breadth, but forwards, and the chest becomes pointed instead of broad; the patients also get short of breath and hoarse, for the cavities which receive and send out the breath have smaller capacity. Besides, they are also obliged to hold the neck concave at the great vertebra, that the head may not be thrown forwards. This, then, causes great constriction in the gullet, since it inclines inwards; for this bone, if it inclines inwards, causes difficult breathing even in undeformed persons, until it is pushed back. In consequence of this attitude, such persons seem to have the larynx more projecting than the healthy. They have also, as a rule, hard and unripened tubercles in the lungs; for the origin of the curvature and contraction is in most cases due to such gatherings, in which the neighbouring ligaments take part. Cases where the curvature is below the diaphragm are sometimes complicated with affections of the kidneys and parts about the bladder, and besides there are purulent abscessions in the lumbar region and about the groins, chronic and hard to cure; and neither of these causes resolution of the curvatures. The hips are still more attenuated in such cases than where the hump is high up; yet the spine as a whole is longer in these than in high curvatures. . . . When curvature comes on in persons whose bodily growth is complete, its occurrence produces an apparent crisis in the disease then present.

Many patients, too, have borne curvature well and with good health up to old age, especially those whose bodies tend to be fleshy and plump; but few even of these survive sixty years, and the majority are rather short-lived.

---

42 Hippocrates, *On Joints*, *Hippocrates*, vol. 3 (trans. E. T. Withington; London: Heinemann, 1928), 41.

Paralysis

Celsus

A.30.1. Relaxing of the Sinew is a Frequent Disease Everywhere

Celsus, *On Medicine* 3.27[43]

Relaxing of the sinews is a frequent disease everywhere. It attacks at times the whole body, at times part of it. Ancient writers named the former apoplexy, the latter paralysis: I see that now both are called paralysis. Those who are gravely paralyzed in all their limbs are as a rule quickly carried off, but if not so carried off, some may live a long while, yet rarely however regain health. Mostly they drag out a miserable existence, their memory lost also. The disease, when partial only, is never acute, often prolonged, generally remediable.

A.30.2. If All the Limbs are Gravely Paralyzed Withdrawal of Blood Either Kills or Cures. Any Other Treatment Merely Postpones Death

If all the limbs are gravely paralyzed withdrawal of blood either kills or cures. Any other kind of treatment scarcely ever restores health, it often merely postpones death, and meanwhile makes life a burden. If after blood-letting, neither movement nor the mind is recovered, there is no hope left; if they do return, health also is in prospect.

REVIVING PERSONS APPARENTLY DEAD

Asclepiades

A.31. Asclepiades the Physician (first century BCE) Revives a Man Carried Out to Burial

Apuleius, *Florida* 19[44]

The famous Asclepiades, who ranks among the greatest of doctors, indeed, if you except Hippocrates, as the very greatest, was the first to discover the use of wine as a remedy. It requires, however, to be administered at the proper moment, and it was in the discovery of the right moment that

---

43 All quotations are taken from Celsus, *On Medicine*, vol. 1 (trans. Spencer).
44 Apuleius, *The Apologia and Florida of Apuleius of Madaura* (trans. Butler), 207–208.

he showed special skill, noting most carefully the slightest symptom of disorder or undue rapidity of the pulse. It chanced that once, when he was returning to town from his country house, he observed an enormous funeral procession in the suburbs of the city. A huge multitude of men who had come out to perform the last honours stood round about the bier, all of them plunged in deep sorrow and wearing worn and ragged apparel. He asked whom they were burying, but no one replied; so he went nearer to satisfy his curiosity and to see who it might be that was dead, or, it may be, in the hope to make some discovery in the interests of his profession. Be this as it may, he certainly snatched the man from the jaws of death as he lay there on the verge of burial. The poor fellow's limbs were already covered with spices, his mouth filled with sweet-smelling unguent. He had been anointed and was all ready for the pyre. But Asclepiades looked upon him, took careful note of certain signs; handled his body again and again, and perceived that the life was still in him, though scarcely to be detected. Straightway he cried out, "He lives! Throw down your torches, take away your fire, demolish the pyre, take back the funeral feast and spread it on his board at home." While he spoke, a murmur arose: some said that they must take the doctor's word, others mocked at the physician's skill. At last, in spite of the opposition offered even by his relations, perhaps because they had already entered into possession of the dead man's property, perhaps because they did not yet believe his words, Asclepiades persuaded them to put off the burial for a brief space. Having thus rescued him from the hands of the undertaker, he carried the man home, as it were from the very mouth of hell, and straightaway revived the spirit within him, and by means of certain drugs called forth the life that still lay hidden in the secret places of the body.[45]

A.32.1. Aesclepiades' Revival of the Dead Man Shows that Medicine Can Deceive

Celsus, *On Medicine* 2.6.16–18[46]

Asclepiades, when he met a funeral procession, recognized that a man who was being carried out to burial was alive; and it is not primarily a fault of the art if there is a fault on the part of its professor. But I shall more modestly suggest that the art of medicine is conjectural, and such is the characteristic of a conjecture, that though it answers more frequently, yet it sometimes deceives. A sign therefore is not to be rejected if it is deceptive in scarcely one out of a thousand cases, since it holds good in countless patients. I state this, not merely in connexion with noxious signs, but as to salutary signs as well; seeing that hope is disappointed now and again,

---

45 Asclepiades was known to prefer diet as a treatment. His use of drugs here represents a resort in special circumstances.

46 All quotations are taken from Celsus, *On Medicine*, vol. 1 (trans. Spencer).

and that the patient dies whom the practitioner at first deemed safe; and further that measures proper for curing now and again make a change into something worse. Nor, in the face of such a variety of temperaments, can human frailty avoid this.

A.32.2. It is Rather in Acute Diseases that Signs, Whether of Recovery or of Death, May be Fallacious

Nevertheless the medical art is to be relied upon, which more often, and in by far the greater number of patients, benefits the sick. It should not be ignored, however, that it is rather in acute diseases that signs, whether of recovery or of death, may be fallacious.

APPENDIX B

Jesus, Torah and Miracles

INTRODUCTION

Issues of Jewish ritual purity and Sabbath observance occur in some of the Jesus stories, and some conversance with the significance of these issues is clearly required. With the journey of the miracle story to its final stages of composition, non-Jewish formulators and redactors might be rather unsure about the problem relative to Torah observance with this or that action of Jesus. This appendix contains a selection of texts from Jewish scripture, from Josephus, but also from the Mishnah. While it is true that the Mishnah was only finalized at the end of the second century CE, we cannot suppose that the applications of Torah that we find there only began with the destruction of the Temple (70 C.E.)! The religious sensibilities that are expressed in the Mishnah help us to appreciate the conflict and tension in some of the stories about Jesus and to see better the particular face of the Christ who performs each miracle.

LEPROSY

Scripture

Jesus heals a leper

B.1. Go, Show Yourself to the Priest and Offer for your Cleansing what Moses Commanded

Mark 1:40–45//Matt. 8:1–4//Luke 5: 12–16

40. A leper came to him begging him, and kneeling he said to him, "If you choose, you can make me clean." 41. Moved with pity, Jesus stretched out his hand and touched him, and said to him, "I do choose. Be made

clean!" *42.* Immediately the leprosy left him, and he was made clean. *43.* After sternly warning him he sent him away at once, *44.* saying to him, "See that you say nothing to anyone; but go, show yourself to the priest, and offer for your cleansing what Moses commanded, as a testimony to them." *45.* But he went out and began to proclaim it freely, and to spread the word, so that Jesus could no longer go into a town openly, but stayed out in the country; and people came to him from every quarter.

Jesus heals ten lepers

B.2. Jesus Said to Ten Lepers: "Go Show Yourselves to the Priests." And as they Went they Were Cleansed

Luke 17:11–19

11. On the way to Jerusalem Jesus was going through the region between Samaria and Galilee. *12.* As he entered a village, ten lepers approached him. Keeping their distance, *13.* they called out, saying, "Jesus, Master, have mercy on us!" *14.* When he saw them, he said to them, "Go and show yourselves to the priests." And as they went, they were made clean. *15.* Then one of them, when he saw that he was healed, turned back, praising God with a loud voice. *16.* He prostrated himself at Jesus' feet and thanked him. And he was a Samaritan. *17.* Then Jesus asked, "Were not the ten made clean? But the other nine, where are they? *18.* Was none of them found to return and give praise to God except this foreigner?" *19.* Then he said to him, "Get up and go on your way; your faith has made you well."

B.3. The Appearance of Leprosy

Lev. 13:9–17

9. When a person contracts a leprous disease, he shall be brought to the priest. *10.* The priest shall make an examination, and if there is a white swelling in the skin that has turned the hair white, and there is quick raw flesh in the swelling, *11.* it is a chronic leprous disease in the skin of his body. The priest shall pronounce him unclean; he shall not confine him, for he is unclean. *12.* But if the disease breaks out in the skin, so that it covers all the skin of the diseased person from head to foot, so far as the priest can see, *13.* then the priest shall make an examination, and if the disease has covered all his body, he shall pronounce him clean of the disease; since it has all turned white, he is clean. *14.* But if raw flesh ever appears on him, he shall be unclean; *15.* the priest shall examine the raw flesh and pronounce him unclean. Raw flesh is unclean, for it is a leprous disease. *16.* But if the raw flesh again turns white, he shall come to the priest; *17.* the priest shall examine him, and if the disease has turned white, the priest shall pronounce the diseased person clean. He is clean.

B.4. Showing Oneself to the Priest and Offering for One's Cleansing from Leprosy what Moses Demanded, for a Proof to the People

B.4.1. The Offering on the First Day

Lev. 14:1–9

1. The Lord spoke to Moses, saying: *2.* This shall be the ritual for the leprous person at the time of his cleansing:

He shall be brought to the priest; *3.* the priest shall go out of the camp, and the priest shall make an examination. If the disease is healed in the leprous person, *4.* the priest shall command that two living clean birds and cedarwood and crimson yarn and hyssop be brought for the one who is to be cleansed. *5.* The priest shall command that one of the birds be slaughtered over fresh water in an earthen vessel. *6.* He shall take the living bird with the cedar wood and the crimson yarn and the hyssop, and dip them and the living bird in the blood of the bird that was slaughtered over the fresh water. *7.* He shall sprinkle it seven times upon the one who is to be cleansed of the leprous disease; then he shall pronounce him clean, and he shall let the living bird go into the open field. *8.* The one who is to be cleansed shall wash his clothes, and shave off all his hair, and bathe himself in water, and he shall be clean. After that he shall come into the camp, but shall live outside the tent seven days. *9.* On the seventh day he shall shave all his hair: of head, beard, eyebrows; he shall shave all his hair. Then he shall wash his clothes, and bathe his body in water, and he shall be clean.

B.4.2. The Offering on the Eighth Day

Lev. 14:10–20

10. On the eighth day he shall take two male lambs without blemish, and one ewe lamb in its first year without blemish, and a grain offering of three tenths of an ephah[1] of choice flour mixed with oil, and one log of oil. *11.* And the priest who cleanses shall set the person to be cleansed, along with these things, before the Lord, at the entrance of the tent of meeting. *12.* The priest shall take one of the lambs, and offer it as a guilt offering, along with the log of oil, and raise them as an elevation offering before the Lord. *13.* He shall slaughter the lamb in the place where the sin offering and the burnt offering are slaughtered in the holy place; for the guilt offering, like the sin offering, belongs to the priest; it is most holy. *14.* The priest shall take some of the blood of the guilt offering and put it on the lobe of the right ear of the one to be cleansed, and on the

---

1 About a bushel.

thumb of his right hand, and on the big toe of the right foot. *15*. The priest shall take some of the log of oil and pour it into the palm of his own left hand, *16*. and dip his right finger in the oil that is in his left hand and sprinkle some oil with his finger seven times before the Lord. *17*. Some of the oil that remains in his hand the priest shall put on the lobe of the right ear of the one to be cleansed, and on the thumb of the right hand, and on the big toe of the right foot, on top of the blood of the guilt offering. *18*. The rest of the oil that is in the priest's hand he shall put on the head of the one to be cleansed. Then the priest shall make atonement on his behalf before the Lord: *19*. the priest shall offer the sin offering, to make atonement for the one to be cleansed from his uncleanness. Afterward he shall slaughter the burnt offering; *20*. and the priest shall offer the burnt offering and the grain offering on the altar. Thus the priest shall make atonement on his behalf and he shall be clean.

Greco-Roman writers

B.5. Moses Forbids Lepers Either to Stay in a Town Or to Reside in a Village

Josephus, *Against Apion* 1.31.281–282[2]

[Moses] forbids lepers either to stay in a town or to reside in a village; they must be solitary vagrants, with their clothes rent; anyone who touches or lives under the same roof with them he considers unclean. Moreover, even if the malady is cured and the victim returns to his normal condition, Moses prescribes certain rites of purification – to cleanse himself in a bath of spring-water and to cut off all his hair- and requires him to offer a numerous variety of sacrifices before entering the holy city.

Mishnah

B.6. The Appearance of Leprosy

Mishnah: Negaim (Leprosy [literally: Plagues]) 8.7[3]
(Commentary on Lev. 13:9–17)

If a man came [before the priest in the beginning] with his whole body white, he must be shut up; if, then, white hair arose he must be certified

---

2 Josephus, *The Life; Against Apion, Josephus*, vol. 1 (trans. H. St. J. Thackeray; London: Heinemann, 1926).

3 *The Mishnah* (trans. Herbert Danby; London: Oxford University Press, 1933), 686.

unclean; if [afterward] both hairs or one of them turned black, if both of them or one of them became short, if a boil joined both hairs or one of them, if the boil encompassed both hairs or one of them, or if they were sundered by a boil or the quick flesh of a boil, or a burning or the quick flesh of a burning, or by a tetter, and then there arose quick flesh or white hair, he is unclean. ... If it broke out abroad and covered but part of his skin, he is unclean; if it broke out abroad and covered all his skin, he is clean.

B.7. Contracting Uncleannness by Passing a Leper who is Stationary Outside

Mishnah: Negaim 13.7[4]

If a man unclean [from leprosy] stood beneath a tree and one that was clean passed by, he becomes unclean; if he that was clean stood beneath the tree and he that was unclean passed by, he remains unclean. So, too, if a man carried [beneath a tree] a stone afflicted with leprosy, he [that was standing beneath the tree] remains clean; but if he set it down the other becomes unclean.[5]

B.8. The Cleansing of the Leper

Mishnah: Negaim 14.1–3[6]

1. How did they cleanse the leper?[7] He brought a new earthenware flask and put therein a quarter-log[8] of living water; and he brought two birds that had lived in freedom. The priest slaughtered one of them over the earthenware vessel and over the living water, and dug a hole and buried it in his presence. He took cedarwood and hyssop and scarlet wool and bound them together with the ends of the strips [of wool]; and brought near to them the tips of the wings and the tip of the tail of the second bird; and dipped them [in the blood of the slaughtered bird] and sprinkled [the blood] seven times on the back of the leper's hand; and some say, also on his forehead. So likewise used they to sprinkle the lintel of the house from outside.

2. He then came to set free the living bird. He used not to turn his face toward the sea or toward the city or toward the wilderness, for it is written, *But he shall let go the living bird out of the city into the open field.*[9] He then

---

4 Ibid., 694.

5 The leper must not be stationary just as the unclean stone must not be allowed to be set down in the presence of the clean.

6 Danby, *The Mishnah*, 695.

7 Lev. 14:2–14.

8 "A 'log' is equal to the contents of six eggs." Danby, *The Mishnah*, Appendix II, p. 798.

9 Lev. 14:33.

came to cut off the hair of the leper. He passed the razor over the whole of his skin and washed his garments and immersed himself; and thus he became so clean that he no more conveyed uncleanness by entering in, yet he [still] conveyed uncleanness like a creeping thing:[10] he could enter within the city wall but he was forbidden to enter into his house for seven days, and he was not allowed marital connexion.

3. On the seventh day he cut off his hair a second time after the manner of the first cutting. He washed his garments and immersed himself; and thus he became clean so that he no more conveyed uncleanness like a creeping thing but was become like one that had immersed himself the selfsame day [because of uncleanness] and so could eat of [Second] Tithe. After he had awaited sunset he could eat of Heave-offering;[11] and after he had brought his offering of atonement he could eat of the Hallowed Things. Thus there are three stages in the purification of the leper; so, too, there are three stages in the purification of a woman after childbirth.

"THEY THAT SUFFER A FLUX"[12]

Scripture

Jesus heals a woman suffering from hemorrhage for twelve years

B.9. Mark 5:21–34 (//Matt. 9:18–26//Luke 8:40–48)

21. And when Jesus had crossed again in the boat to the other side, a great crowd gathered about him; and he was by the sea. 22. Then one of the leaders of the synagogue named Jairus came and, when he saw him, fell at his feet 23. and begged him repeatedly, "My little daughter is at the point of death. Come and lay your hands on her, so that she may be made well, and live." 24. So he went with him.

And a large crowd followed him and pressed in on him. 25. Now there was a woman who had been suffering from hemorrhages for twelve years. 26. She had endured much under many physicians, and had spent all that she had; and she was no better, but rather grew worse. 27. She had heard about Jesus, and came up behind him in the crowd and touched his cloak, 28. for she said, "If I but touch his clothes, I will be made well." 29. Immediately her hemorrhage stopped; and she felt in her body that she

---

10 Lev. 11:29–31.

11 This refers to the particular type of ritual followed at a sacrifice. The right thigh of the sacrificial animal was "heaved" before the Lord.

12 The following cases are grouped together in the Mishnah: a man or a woman with a flux, a menstruant, a woman after childbirth, a leper and a corpse. See in particular Nazirite 9.4; Sotah 1.5; Kerinoth 2.1; Parah 6.5 and Zabim 5.6.

was healed of her disease. *30*. Immediately aware that power had gone forth from him, Jesus turned about in the crowd and said, "Who touched my clothes?" *31*. And his disciples said to him, "You see the crowd pressing in on you; how can you say, 'Who touched me?' " *32*. He looked all around to see who had done it. *33*. But the woman, knowing what had happened to her, came in fear and trembling, fell down before him, and told him the whole truth. *34*. He said to her, "Daughter, your faith has made you well; go in peace, and be healed of your disease."

B.10. All the Days of her Discharge of Blood She Shall Continue in Uncleanness

Lev. 15:25–30

25. If a woman has a discharge of blood for many days, not at the time of her impurity [menstruation], or if she has a discharge beyond the time of her impurity, all the days of the discharge she shall continue in uncleanness; as in the days of her impurity, she shall be unclean. *26*. Every bed on which she lies during all the days of her discharge shall be treated as the bed of her impurity; and everything on which she sits shall be unclean, as in the uncleanness of her impurity. *27*. And whoever touches these things shall be unclean, and shall wash his clothes, and bathe in water, and be unclean until the evening. *28*. If she is cleansed of her discharge, she shall count seven days, and after that she shall be clean. *29*. On the eighth day she shall take two turtledoves or two pigeons and bring them to the priest, to the entrance of the tent of meeting. *30*. The priest shall offer one for a sin offering and the other for a burnt offering; and the priest shall make atonement on her behalf before the Lord for her unclean discharge.

Mishnah

B.11. All are Susceptible to Uncleanness by reason of a Flux

Mishnah: Zabim (They That Suffer a Flux): 2.1[13]

All are susceptible to uncleanness by reason of a flux, even proselytes, even slaves, whether freedmen or not, a deaf-mute, an imbecile or a minor, a eunuch of man's making or a eunuch by nature. To one that is of doubtful sex or of double sex the stringencies that bear in the case of a man and the stringencies that bear in the case of a woman both apply: they convey uncleanness through blood like a woman, and through semen like a man; but their uncleanness remains in doubt.

---

13 Danby, *The Mishnah*, 768.

B.12.1. Touching Them or Objects They Touched Incurs Uncleanness

Mishnah: Zabim 5.1[14]

If a man touched a Zab or if a Zab touched him, if a man shifted a Zab or if a Zab shifted him, he conveys uncleanness by contact, but not by carrying, to foodstuffs and liquids and vessels that can be made clean by immersing. Rabbi Joshua laid down a general rule: All they that convey uncleanness to garments while they have contact with them, convey first-grade uncleanness to foodstuffs and liquids, and second-grade uncleanness to the hands, but they do not convey uncleanness to a man or to an earthenware vessel; after they are severed from what had rendered them unclean they convey first-grade uncleanness to foodstuffs and liquids, and second-grade uncleanness to the hands, but they do not convey uncleanness to garments.

B.12.2. Mishnah: Zabim 5.6[15]

If a man touched a man or a woman that had a flux, or a menstruant or a woman after childbirth, or a leper, or aught that these had lain upon or sat upon, he conveys uncleanness at a first remove and at a second remove and renders [Heave-offering] invalid at a third remove. It is all one whether he touched, or shifted, lifted, or was lifted. R. Eliezer says: Or if he lifted it.

B.13. Touching a Menstruant is More Grave Suffering than Corpse Uncleanness

Mishnah: Zabim 5.11[16]

He that has suffered a pollution is like to one that has touched a creeping thing, and he that has connexion with a menstruant is like to one that suffers corpse uncleanness; howbeit it is more grave for him that has connexion with a menstruant in that he conveys a lesser uncleanness to what he lies upon or sits upon so that this renders foods and liquids unclean.

B.14. Gradations of Uncleanness Among the Unclean

Mishnah: Kelim (Vessels) 1.4[17]

[The uncleanness of] the man that has a flux is exceeded by the uncleanness of the woman that has a flux, for she conveys uncleanness to him

---

14 Danby, *The Mishnah*, 771.
15 Ibid., 772.
16 Ibid., 773.
17 Ibid., 601–605.

that has connexion with her. [The uncleanness of] the woman that has a flux is exceeded by [the uncleanness of] the leper, for he renders [a house] unclean by entering into it. [The uncleanness of] the leper is exceeded by [the uncleanness of] a barleycorn's bulk of bone [from a corpse], for it conveys seven-day uncleanness. These are all exceeded by [the uncleanness of] a corpse, for it conveys uncleanness by overshadowing.[18]

TOUCHING A CORPSE

Scripture

Jesus raises a twelve-year-old girl from the dead

B.15. Mark 5:21–43 (//Matt. 9:18–26//Luke 8:40–56)

21. When Jesus had crossed again in the boat to the other side, a great crowd gathered around him; and he was by the sea. *22.* Then one of the leaders of the synagogue named Jairus came and when he saw him, fell at his feet *23.* and begged him repeatedly, "My little daughter is at the point of death. Come and lay your hands on her, so that she may be made well, and live." *24.* So he went with him.

And a large crowd followed him and pressed in on him. *25.* Now there was a woman who had been suffering from hemorrhages for twelve years. *26.* She had endured much under many physicians, and had spent all that she had; and she was no better, but rather grew worse. *27.* She had heard about Jesus, and came up behind him in the crowd and touched his cloak, *28.* for she said, "If I but touch his clothes, I will be made well." *29.* Immediately her hemorrhage stopped; and she felt in her body that she was healed of her disease. *30.* Immediately aware that power had gone forth from him, Jesus turned about in the crowd and said, "Who touched my clothes?" *31.* And his disciples said to him, "You see the crowd pressing in on you; how can you say, 'Who touched me?'" *32.* He looked all around to see who had done it. *33.* But the woman, knowing what had happened to her, came in fear and trembling, fell down before him, and told him the whole truth. *34.* He said to her, "Daughter, your faith has made you well; go in peace, and be healed of your disease."

18 Danby, "Literally tents or overshadowings. From Num 19:14 it is inferred that all (men and utensils) who are under the same tent or roof as a corpse (i.e. a dead human body or a part of it), or who are overshadowed by something which also overshadows a corpse (and the same also applies to a person or utensil which overshadows or is overshadowed by a corpse) suffer corpse-uncleanness and remain unclean for seven days." *The Mishnah*, 649, n. 3.

35. While he was still speaking, some people came from the leader's house to say, "Your daughter is dead. Why trouble the teacher any further?" *36.* But overhearing what they said, Jesus said to the leader of the synagogue, "Do not fear, only believe." *37.* He allowed no one to follow him except Peter, and James, and John, the brother of James. *38.* When they came to the house of the leader of the synagogue, he saw a commotion, people weeping and wailing loudly. *39.* When he had entered, he said to them, "Why do you make a commotion and weep? The child is not dead but sleeping." *40.* And they laughed at him. Then he put them all outside, and took the child's father and mother and those who were with him, and went in where the child was. *41.* He took her by the hand and said to her, "Talitha cum," which means, "Little girl, get up!" *42.* And immediately the girl got up and began to walk about (she was twelve years of age). At this they were overcome with amazement. *43.* He strictly ordered them that no one should know this, and told them to give her something to eat.

Jesus raises the only son of a widow from the dead

B.16. Luke 7:11–17

11. Soon afterwards he went to a town called Nain, and his disciples and a large crowd went with him. *12.* As he approached the gate of the town, a man who had died was being carried out. He was his mother's only son, and she was a widow; and with her was a large crowd from the town. *13.* When the Lord saw her, he had compassion on her and said to her, "Do not weep." *14.* Then he came forward and touched the bier, and the bearers stood still. And he said, "Young man, I say to you, rise!" *15.* The dead man sat up and began to speak, and Jesus gave him to his mother. *16.* Fear seized all of them and they glorified God, saying, "A great prophet has risen among us!" and "God has looked favorably on his people!" *17.* This word about him spread throughout Judea and all the surrounding country.

B.17. He who Touches the Dead Body of Any Person shall be Unclean Seven Days

Num. 19:11–13

11. Those who touch the dead body of any human being shall be unclean seven days. *12.* They shall purify themselves with the water on the third day and on the seventh day, and so be clean; but if they do not purify themselves on the third day and on the seventh day, they will not become clean. *13.* All who touch a corpse, the body of a human being who has died, and do not purify themselves, defile the tabernacle of the Lord; such persons shall be cut off from Israel. Since water for cleansing was not dashed on them, they remain unclean; their uncleanness is still on them.

Mishnah

B.18. If a Man Touches a Corpse He Contracts Seven-Day Uncleanness

Oholoth (Tents) 1.1[19]

[Sometimes] two things contract uncleanness from a corpse, one of them seven-day uncleanness and the other evening-uncleanness: [sometimes] three things contract uncleanness from a corpse, two of them seven-day uncleanness and the third evening-uncleanness; [sometimes] four things contract uncleanness from a corpse, three of them seven-day uncleanness and the fourth evening-uncleanness. How [does this befall] the two things? If a man touches a corpse he contracts seven-day uncleanness, and if a man touches him he contracts evening-uncleanness.[20]

B.19. Kelim (Vessels) 1.1[21]

These Fathers of Uncleanness, [namely,] a [dead] creeping thing, male semen, he that has contracted uncleanness from a corpse, a leper in his days of reckoning, and Sin-offering water too little in quantity to be sprinkled, convey uncleanness to men and vessels by contact and to earthenware vessels by [presence within their] air-space; but they do not convey uncleanness by carrying.

B.20. All Forms of Uncleanness Are Exceeded by the Uncleanness of a Corpse, For it Conveys Uncleanness by Overshadowing

Kelim 1.4[22]

[The uncleanness of] the man that has a flux is exceeded by the uncleanness of the woman that has a flux, for she conveys uncleanness to him that has connexion with her. [The uncleanness of] the woman that has a flux is exceeded by [the uncleanness of] the leper, for he renders [a house] unclean by entering into it. [The uncleanness of] the leper is exceeded by [the uncleanness of] a barleycorn's bulk of bone [from a corpse], for it conveys seven-day uncleanness. These are all exceeded by [the uncleanness of] a corpse, for it conveys uncleanness by overshadowing, which uncleanness is conveyed by naught else.

19 Ibid., 649–50.
20 "The corpse itself is a 'father of fathers of uncleanness'; what it touches becomes itself a 'father of uncleanness', and what touches this suffers 'derived uncleanness' ('first-grade uncleanness' or 'uncleanness at a first remove'). But if the third party touched the second while the second was still in contact with the corpse, the third party also counts as a 'father of uncleanness.' " Ibid., 650.
21 Ibid., 604.
22 Ibid., 604–605.

THE SABBATH OBSERVANCE

Jesus heals on the sabbath

Five particular stories of Jesus' healing on the sabbath mark out this theme as a prominent one for early Christians. In all these stories, the Christian listener would receive the idea that Jewish Law was inhumane or was interpreted in inhumane ways by the Jewish leadership, especially when the healer is one of whom they are jealous. Jesus is focused on the needs of the sick, and his various defenses for his actions shine with irresistible *humanitas*. The injunctions against "healing" on the sabbath seem unfair when the possibility of Jesus' proximity offers a complete release for the sick from their bondage. The sick move us with their immediate need either because they are incapacitated for work (such as The Man with the Withered Hand [Mark 3:1–6]) or suffer from a ghastly disease (The Man with Dropsy [Luke 14:1–6]) or from so many years of illness that one more moment in such slavery seems unthinkable (such as The Woman Bent for Eighteen years [Luke 13:10–17]; The Man Paralyzed for Thirty-eight Years [John 5:1–18] and The Man Born Blind [John 9:1–41]).

Of course, applications of the Law could not be expected to provide for the case of a miracle worker healing on the sabbath! Rather they presuppose activities associated with "healing" such as regular types of therapies. The Law ensured that therapists too could rest on the sabbath. However, there was always provision for a life-threatening situation. Even the Mishnah, the codification of Pharisaic and rabbinic prescriptions, makes accommodation for such emergencies.

The Jewish perspective on sabbath observance

Scripture

B.21. The Seventh Day is a Sabbath to the Lord Your God; In It You Shall Not Do Any Work

Exod. 20:8–11
[And the Lord spoke] 8. "Remember the sabbath day, and keep it holy. 9. Six days you shall labor and do all your work. 10. But the seventh day is a sabbath to the Lord your God; you shall not do any work – you, your son, or your daughter, your male or female slave, your livestock, or the alien resident in your towns. 11. For in six days the Lord made heaven

and earth, the sea, and all that is in them, but rested the seventh day; therefore the Lord blessed the sabbath day and consecrated it."

B.22. You shall Keep the Sabbath because it is Holy for you

Exod. 31:12–17

12. The Lord said to Moses: *13.* You yourself are to speak to the Israelites: 'You shall keep my sabbaths, for this is a sign between me and you throughout your generations, given in order that you may know that I, the Lord, sanctify you. *14.* You shall keep the sabbath, because it is holy for you; everyone who profanes it shall be put to death; whoever does any work on it shall be cut off from among the people. *15.* Six days shall work be done, but the seventh day is a sabbath of solemn rest, holy to the Lord; whoever does any work on the sabbath day shall be put to death. *16.* Therefore the Israelites shall keep the sabbath, observing the sabbath throughout their generations, as a perpetual covenant. *17.* It is a sign forever between me and the people of Israel that in six days the Lord made heaven and earth, and on the seventh day he rested, and was refreshed."

Mishnah

Sabbath injunctions

B.23. If he was Mindful of the Sabbath, His Works Make Him Culpable for Every Sabbath [Which He Profaned]

Mishnah: Shabbath, 7.1[23]

A great general rule have they laid down concerning the Sabbath: whosoever, forgetful of the principle of the Sabbath, committed many acts of work on many Sabbaths, is liable only to one Sin-offering; but if, mindful of the principle of the Sabbath, he yet committed many acts of work on many Sabbaths, he is liable for every Sabbath [which he profaned]. If he knew that it was the Sabbath and he yet committed many acts of work on many Sabbaths, he is liable for every main class of work [which he performed]; if he committed many acts of work of one main class, he is liable only to one Sin-offering.

23 Ibid., 106.

B.24. There are Thirty-Nine Classes of "Work"

Mishnah: Shabbath 7.2[24]

The main classes of work are forty save one: sowing, ploughing, reaping, binding sheaves, threshing, winnowing, cleansing crops, grinding, sifting, *kneading*,[25] baking, shearing wool, washing or beating or dying it, spinning, weaving, making two loops, weaving two threads, separating two threads, tying [a knot], loosening [a knot], sewing two stitches, tearing in order to sew two stitches, hunting a gazelle, slaughtering or flaying or salting it or curing its skin, scraping it or cutting it up, writing two letters, erasing in order to write two letters, building, pulling down, putting out a fire, lighting a fire, striking with a hammer and *taking out aught from one domain into another*.[26] These are the main classes of work: forty save one.

B.25. On the Sabbath Water May Not be Drawn to Rub Off Eye Plaster[27]

Mishnah: Shabbath 8.1[28]

[He is culpable] that takes out wine enough to mix the cup, or milk enough for a gulp, or honey enough to rub off eye-plaster, or a quarter-*log* of any other liquid or a quarter-*log* of liquid refuse. Rabbi Simeon says: The prescribed measure is a quarter-*log* in every case; and they have enjoined these [several] measures only on them that keep the like of these things stored.

B.26. Chronic Ailments Should Not Receive Special Treatments

Mishnah, Shabbath 14.3–4[29]

3. Greek hyssop[30] may not be eaten on the Sabbath since it is not the food of them that are in health, but a man may eat pennyroyal[31] or drink

---

24 Ibid.
25 My italic. See John 9:6, where the mixing of the spit and mud constitutes activity technically unnecessary of the sabbath.
26 My italic. See John 5:9, where Jesus instructs the man to pick up his pallet and walk.
27 See John 9:7, 11, where the blind man follows instructions to go bathe his eyes in the pool of Siloam to wash off the "eye-plaster" Jesus has made from his own saliva and mud.
28 Ibid., 107.
29 Ibid., 113.
30 For stomach worms. Ibid., 113, n. 6.
31 For liver worms. Ibid., 113, n. 7.

knotgrass-water.[32] He may eat any foodstuffs that serve for healing or drink any liquids except purgative water or a cup of root-water, since these serve to cure jaundice; but he may drink purgative water to quench his thirst, *and he may anoint himself with root-oil if it is not used for healing.*[33] 4. If his teeth pain him he may not suck vinegar through them but he may take vinegar after his usual fashion,[34] *and if he is healed, he is healed.*[35] If his loins pain him he may not rub thereon wine or vinegar, yet he may anoint them with oil but not with rose-oil. Kings' children may anoint their wounds with rose-oil since it is their custom to do so on ordinary days. Rabbi Simeon says: All Israelites are kings' children!

B.27. On the Sabbath a Dislocated Hand or Foot May Not be Set

Mishnah: Shabbath 22.6[36]

They may anoint or rub their stomach[37] but not have themselves kneaded or scraped. They may not go down to Kordima, and they may not use artificial emetics; they may not straighten a [deformed] child's body or set a broken limb. If a man's hand or foot is dislocated he may not pour cold water over it, but he may wash it after his usual fashion, and if he is healed, he is healed.

B.28. When Life is in Danger, This Overrides the Sabbath

Mishnah: Yoma (Day of Atonement) 8.6[38]

If ravenous hunger seized a man he may be given even unclean things to eat until his eyes are enlightened.[39] If a mad dog bit him he may not be given the lobe of its liver to eat; but Rabbi Mattithiah b. Heresh[40] permits it. Moreover Rabbi Mattithiah b. Heresh said: If a man has a pain in his throat they may drop medicine into his mouth on the Sabbath, since there is doubt whether life is in danger, and whenever there is doubt whether life is in danger this overrides the Sabbath.

---

32 "An antidote to harmful liquids. The two latter were both taken by those in health." Ibid., 113, n. 8.

33 My italic. See John 9:6–7, where Jesus anoints the man's eyes with the salve he has made, which is also an action forbidden on the sabbath.

34 At a meal. Ibid., 113, n. 9.

35 My italic. Notice that the idea is that God will see to the healing on that day if there is one to occur.

36 Ibid., 119.

37 "Some texts omit 'their stomach.' " Ibid., 119, n. 11.

38 Ibid., 172.

39 1 Sam. 14:27.

40 It should be noted that Rabbi Mattithiah b. Heresh belongs to the third generation of Rabbis (i.e. 120–140 CE) and thus postdates the formation of the New Testament writings, but since it is readily admitted among Biblical

B.29. If a Building Fall on a Man and there is Doubt Whether he is Alive or Dead, they may Clear Away the Ruin to Check

Mishnah: Yoma 8.7[41]

If a building fell down upon a man and there is doubt whether he is there or not, or whether he is alive or dead, or whether he is a gentile or an Israelite, they may clear away the ruin from above him. If they find him alive they may clear it away [still more] from above him; but if dead, they leave him.

JEWISH DEALINGS WITH GENTILES

Jesus exorcizes the daughter of the Syrophoenician woman

B.30. Jesus Said to her "Let the Children be Fed First, for it is Not Fair to Take the Children's Food and Throw it to the Dogs"

Mark 7: 24–30 Matt. 15:21–28

24. From there he set out and went away to the region of Tyre. He entered a house and did not want anyone to know he was there. Yet he could not escape notice, 25. but a woman whose little daughter had an unclean spirit immediately heard about him and she came and bowed down at this feet. 26. Now the woman was a Gentile, of Syrophoenician origin. She begged him to cast the demon out of her daughter. 27. He said to her, "Let the children be fed first, for it is not fair to take the children's food and throw it to the dogs." 28. But she answered him, "Sir, even the dogs under the table eat the children's crumbs." 29. Then he said to her, "For saying that, you may go – the demon has left your daughter." 30. So she went home, found the child lying on the bed, and the demon gone.

This miracle story illustrates a gentile mother's "winning" a miracle from the Jewish Jesus by her wit. It raises the whole question of Jewish and gentile relationships. From the Jewish sources we draw on a selection of texts from Josephus' apology to Apion and from the teachings of the "Fathers," Pirke Aboth, in the Mishnah about a righteous Jew's relationship with the world.

scholars that the attributions of rulings are not necessarily accurate in the Mishnah, his ruling is reproduced here as a possible articulation of a policy that predates him.

41 Danby, *The Mishnah*, 172.

Jewish witness

Josephus (37–95? CE)

B.31. Apion's Accusation that We Take an Oath Against Showing Goodwill towards Others is Completely Imaginary

Josephus, *Against Apion* 2.121–122[42]

Then he attributes to us an imaginary oath, and would have it appear that we swear by the God who made heaven and earth and sea to show no goodwill to a single alien, above all to Greeks. Having once started false accusations, he should have said, "show no goodwill to a single alien, above all to Egyptians"; for then this reference to the oath would have been in keeping with his original fiction, if, as we are given to understand, the cause of the expulsion of our forefathers by their Egyptian "kinsmen" was not their malice, but their misfortunes.

B.32. Plato Himself Agrees with Our Lawgiver Moses on the Caution to Be Observed in Preventing Foreigners from Mixing with Them

Josephus, *Against Apion* 2.257

In two points, in particular, Plato followed the example of our legislator [Moses]. He prescribed as the primary duty of the citizens a study of their laws, which they must all learn word for word by heart. Again he took precautions to prevent foreigners from mixing with them at random, and to keep the state pure and confined to law-abiding citizens.[43]

B.33. Unlike the Discourteous Lacedaemonians We Gladly Welcome Any who Wish to Share Our Customs

Josephus, *Against Apion* 2.259

The Lacedaemonians made a practice of expelling foreigners and would not allow their own citizens to travel abroad, in both cases apprehensive of their laws being corrupted. *They* might perhaps be justly reproached for discourtesy, because they accorded to no one the rights either of citizenship or of residence among them. We, on the contrary, while we have no desire to emulate the customs of others, yet gladly welcome any who wish to share our own. That, I think, may be taken as a proof both of humanity and magnanimity.

---

42 All quotations are from Josephus, *The Life; Against Apion* (trans. Thackeray).

Mishnah

Berachoth (Blessings)

B.34. At the End of the Sabbath Observance, the Lamp and Spices of the Community are Blessed, but Not Those of Gentiles, or the Deceased, or Those Used for Idolatry

Berachoth 8.5–6[44]

5. The School of Shammai say: [The order of saying the Benedictions at the outgoing of the sabbath is] the lamp, the food, the spices and the *Habdalah*.[45] . . . 6. No Benediction may be said over the lamp or the spices of gentiles, or over a lamp or spices used for the dead, or over a lamp or spices used for idolatry. No Benediction may be said over a lamp until one can enjoy its light.

Shebith (The Seventh Year)

B.35. No Israelite May Help Another Israelite Break Laws of the Seventh Year, but He May Help a Gentile in his Fields, and Offer Him Greetings in the Interests of Peace

Shebith 4.3[46]

Newly ploughed land may be hired in the Seventh Year from a gentile but not an Israelite; and gentiles may be helped [when labouring in the fields] in the Seventh Year, but not Israelites. Moreover, greetings may be offered to gentiles in the interests of peace.

Hallah (Dough-offerings)

B.36. Gentile Bread Dough is Not Acceptable for Offerings

Hallah 3.5[47]

If a gentile gave dough to an Israelite to prepare for him it is exempt from Dough-offering. If he gave it to him as a gift and [it was given] before it was rolled out, it is liable; if after it was rolled out, it is exempt.

---

43 Plato, *Laws*, esp. 12.949E ff.
44 Ibid., 9.
45 The *Habdalal* is a ceremony to bring the sabbath to a close. Ibid., Appendix I.9, p. 793.
46 Ibid., 43.
47 Ibid., 86.

If a man prepared his dough together with [dough belonging to] a gentile, and the portion belonging to the Israelite was less than the measure liable to Dough-offering, it is exempt from Dough-offering.

Yebamoth (Sisters-in-law)

B.37. Evidence Given by a Gentile Concerning a Man's Death is Not Valid, Although that of Women's "Hear-Say" and Children's Talk Is

Yebamoth 16.5[48]

Even if a man [only] heard women saying, "Such-a-one is dead," that suffices to justify him in giving evidence of death or in marrying the widow.[49] Rabbi Judah says: Even if he [only] heard children saying, "We are going to bewail and bury such-a-one," that suffices, whether or not he had an intention [to give evidence thereof]. Rabbi Judah ben Baba says: if it was an Israelite, even though he had the intention [to give evidence, his evidence would be valid]; but if it was a gentile and he had the intention [to give evidence], his evidence would not be valid.

Nedarim (Vows)

B.38. Hateful is Uncircumcision; Great is Circumcision

Nedarim 3.11[50]

[If he said,] "Konam![51], if I have any benefit from the children of Noah!" he is permitted [to have benefit] from Israelites, but not from other nations; [but if he said, "Konam!] if I have any benefit from the seed of Abraham!" he is forbidden to have benefit from Israelites but not from other nations. . . . [If he said, "Konam!] if I have benefit from the circumcised!" he is forbidden to have benefit [even] from the uncircumcised in Israel but he is permitted to have benefit from the circumcised among the nations of the world, since "uncircumcised" is but used as a name for the gentiles, as it is written, For all the other nations are uncircumcised, and all the house of Israel are uncircumcised in heart.[52] Again it says, This uncircumcised Philistine.[53] Again it says, Lest the daughters of the Philistines rejoice, lest the daughters of the uncircumcised triumph. Rabbi Eleazar ben Azariah says:

---

48 Ibid., 244.
49 Ibid., 244, n. 1.
50 Ibid., 267–268.
51 "Sacred offering to the Lord!"
52 Jer. 9:26.
53 1 Sam. 17:36.

Hateful is the uncircumcision, whereby the wicked are held up to shame, as it is written, *For all the nations are uncircumcised.* Rabbi Ishmael says: Great is circumcision, whereby the covenant was made thirteen times.[54] Rabbi Jose says: Great is circumcision which overrides even the rigour of the Sabbath. (Shabbath 19:1) Rabbi Joshua ben Karha says: Great is circumcision which even for the sake of Moses, the righteous, was not suspended so much as an hour. (Exodus 4.24ff.) Rabbi Nehemiah says: Great is circumcision which overrides the laws of leprosy-signs. Rabbi says: Great is circumcision, for despite all the religious duties which Abraham our father fulfilled, he was not called "perfect" until he was circumcised, as it is written, *Walk before me and be thou perfect.*[55] After another fashion [it is said], Great is circumcision: but for it the Holy One, blessed is He, had not created his world, as it is written, *Thus saith the Lord, but for my covenant day and night, I had not set forth the ordinances of heaven and earth.*[56]

Gittin (Bills of Divorce)

B.39. All are Qualified to Bring a Bill of Divorce Except a Deaf-Mute, an Imbecile, a Minor, a Blind Man, or a Gentile

Gittin 2.5[57]

All are qualified to write a bill of divorce, even a deaf-mute, an imbecile, or a minor. A woman may write her own bill of divorce and a man may write his own quittance,[58] since the validity of the writ depends on them that sign it. All are qualified to bring a bill of divorce except a deaf-mute, an imbecile, a minor, a blind man, or a gentile.

Note: "dog's dough" in Palestine

In the NRSV Jesus' harsh statement to the Syrophoenician woman is translated so that the Greek word "bread" is rendered "food." "It is not fair to take the children's food [bread] and throw it to the dogs" (Mark 7:27). The image of bread, however, may be a refer-

---

54 Danby's note: "The word 'covenant' is used thirteen times in the book of Genesis."
55 Gen. 17:1.
56 Jer. 33:25.
57 Danby, *The Mishnah*, 308.
58 "Which the woman signs and leaves with him on receipt of her ketubah." The ketubah was a written document "in which the bridegroom pledges himself to assign a certain sum of money to the bride in the event of his death or his divorcing her." Ibid., 308, n. 4 and Appendix I, p. 794, n. 16.

ence to the distinction that is testified in the Mishnah between ordinary bread and a rough heavy bread made of bran called "dog's dough." The fact that the Mishnah addresses the question of whether "dog's dough" could qualify for the dough-offering to the Lord shows that people ate it, especially, we can imagine, the poor who had nothing else. The qualifying criterion that the bread had to be "edible by herdsmen" suggests that even poorer qualities were made, and this was likely for the dogs.

Hallah (Dough offering)

B.40. Dog's Dough may be Offered if Herdsmen are Able to Eat It

Mishnah: Hallah 1.8[59]

Dog's-dough,[60] if herdsmen can eat of it, is liable to Dough-offering, and it may be used for *Erub* and *Shittuf*[61] and Benedictions and the Common Grace must be said over it; it may be made on a Festival-day, and by [eating unleavened an olive's bulk of] it a man can fulfil his obligation at Passover. But if herdsmen cannot eat of it it is not liable to Dough-offering; nor may it be used for *Erub* and *Shittuf*, and Benedictions and Common Grace need not be said over it; it may not be made on a Festival day, and by [eating unleavened an olive's bulk of] it a man does not fulfil his obligation at Passover. In either case it is susceptible to food-uncleanness.

THE DEAF-MUTE AND TORAH

The Mishnah most frequently groups deaf-mutes with "imbeciles" and "minors." The perception of a similarity in the limitations of all three is probably a reflection of the ordinary views held throughout the Greco-Roman world. Consciousness of the humiliating social circumstances of deaf-mutes allows an increase in understanding the huge implications of Jesus' curing a person with this affliction in Mark 7:31–37.

---

59 Ibid., 84.
60 Dog's dough has a large portion of bran. Ibid., 84, n. 1.
61 *Shittuf* is food contributed to a common table for sabbath to obfuscate the need to work or travel. Ibid., 84, n. 2 and Appendix I, pp. 795–796, nn. 8, 39.

Scripture

Jesus heals a man who is deaf and has a speech impediment

B.41. Jesus Put his Fingers into his Ears, Spat and Touched his Tongue; and Looking up to Heaven, he Sighed and Said to him, "Ephphatha"

Mark 7:31–37 Matt. 15:29–31[62]

31. Then he returned from the region of Tyre, and went by way of Sidon towards the Sea of Galilee, in the region of the Decapolis. 32. They brought to him a deaf man who had an impediment in his speech; and they begged him to lay his hand on him. 33. He took him aside in private, away from the crowd, and put his fingers into his ears, and he spat and touched his tongue. 34. Then looking up to heaven, he sighed and said to him, "Ephphatha," that is, "Be opened." 35. And immediately his ears were opened, his tongue was released, and he spoke plainly. 36. Then Jesus ordered them to tell no one; but the more he ordered them, the more zealously they proclaimed it. 37. They were astounded beyond measure, saying, "He has done everything well; he even makes the deaf to hear and the mute to speak."

Jesus casts out the demon that causes a man to be a deaf-mute

Notice that the Sayings Source (i.e. Q) also carries a tradition about Jesus curing a deaf-mute. However, in this case, the illness is caused by a demon, and the cure of the man needs only the expulsion of that demon. In Q, other sayings were attached to defend Jesus from the charge of collusion with Satan. I include the cluster because that is the way this miracle carries its own interpretation at an early stage in Christian tradition.

---

62 While Matt. 15:29–31 is cited as a parallel, it is more a brief summary: "29. After Jesus had left that place, he passed along the Sea of Galilee, and he went up the mountain, where he sat down. 30. Great crowds came to him, bringing with them the lame, the maimed, the blind, the mute, and many others. They put them at his feet, and he cured them, 31. so that the crowd was amazed when they saw the mute speaking, the maimed whole, the lame walking, and the blind seeing. And they praised the God of Israel." By incorporating the Markan story in this summary, Matthew honors the traditions he received, but avoids the problematic character of the Markan story where Jesus is shown using spittle, deep sighing, and then foreign-sounding utterances, the combination of which would risk suggesting a magical rite to many people of the Greco-Roman world.

B.42. Luke 11:14–23//Matt. 12:22–30

14. Now he was casting out a demon that was mute; when the demon had gone out, the one who had been mute spoke, and the crowds were amazed. *15.* But some of them said, "He casts out demons by Beelzebul, the ruler of demons." *16.* Others, to test him, kept demanding from him a sign from heaven. *17.* But he knew what they were thinking and said to them, "Every kingdom divided against itself becomes a desert, and house falls on house. *18.* If Satan also is divided against himself, how will his kingdom stand? – for you say that I cast out demons by Beelzebul. *19.* Now if I cast out demons by Beelzebul, by whom do your exorcists cast them out? Therefore, they shall be your judges. *20.* But if it is by the finger of God that I cast out demons, then the kingdom of God has come upon you. *21.* But when a strong man, fully armed, guards his castle, his property is safe; *22.* But when one stronger than he attacks him and overpowers him, he takes away his armor in which he trusted and divides his plunder. *23.* Whoever is not with me is against me, and whoever does not gather with me scatters."

Mishnah

B.43. Deaf-Mutes, Imbeciles and Minors May Not Lay on Hands at the Sacrifice

Mishnah: Menahoth (Meal Offerings) 9.8[63]
All may perform the laying on of hands[64] excepting a deaf-mute, an imbecile, a minor, a blind man, a gentile, a slave, an agent, or a woman. The laying on of hands is a residue of the commandment. Both hands must be laid upon the head; and in the place where they lay on the hands there they slaughter the beast and the slaughtering straightaway follows the laying on of hands.

B.44. Deaf-Mutes, Imbeciles and Minors May Not Slaughter Validly Without Supervision

Mishnah: Hullin (Animals Killed for Food) 1.1[65]
All may slaughter and what they slaughter is valid, save only a deaf-mute, an imbecile and a minor, lest they impair what they slaughter; but if any among these slaughtered while others beheld them,[66] what they slaughter

---

63 Ibid., 505.
64 This refers to the laying on of hands over the victim to be sacrificed for atonement (Lev. 1:4).
65 Danby, *The Mishnah*, 513.
66 "To testify that the manner of slaughtering was according to the rules prescribed." Ibid., 513, n. 8.

is valid. What is slaughtered by a gentile is deemed carrion,[67] and it conveys uncleanness by carrying. If a man slaughtered by night (so, too, if a blind man slaughtered) what he slaughters is valid. If he slaughterd on the Sabbath or on the Day of Atonement, although he is guilty against his own soul,[68] what he slaughters is valid.

B.45. Deaf-Mutes, Imbeciles and Minors may Not Represent the Community

Mishnah: Rosh Hashanah (New Year) 3.8[69]

A deaf-mute, an imbecile, or a minor cannot fulfil an obligation [i.e. blow the *shofar* at the New Year] on behalf of the many. This is the general rule: any on whom an obligation is not incumbent cannot fulfill that obligation on behalf of the many.

UTTERING A CHARM OVER A WOUND

Nowhere in the Jesus miracles is Jesus said to utter a "charm" over any wound. However, the following injunction about such practices alerts us to their frequency in magic. For this reason, we shall see the early Church supplying Greek translations of the Aramaic commands of Jesus that were included in a few of the miracle stories and could invite a connection with magical charms:

1   *Mark 5:41 is omitted in Matt. 9:22 and Luke 8:54.*
    Mark 5:41: He took her [the dead girl] by the hand and said to her, "Talitha cum," which means, "Little girl, get up!"
2   *Mark 7:34 is omitted in Matt. 15:29–31.*
    Mark 7:34: Then looking up to heaven, he sighed and said to him, "Ephphatha," that is, "Be opened."

67   "Like the flesh of a beast that has died of itself." Ibid., 513, n. 9.
68   "By performing work which is forbidden on such days and which, if done deliberately, is punishable by Extirpation." (Extirpation is exclusion from the community.) Ibid., 5, n. 11.
69   Ibid., 397.

Mishnah

B.46. To Utter a Charm Over a Wound is to Forfeit the World to Come

Mishnah: Sanhedrin 10:1[70]

All Israelites have a share in the world to come, for it is written, *Thy people also shall be all righteous, they shall inherit the land for ever; the branch of my planting, the work of my hands that I may be glorified.*[71] And these are they that have no share in the world to come: he that says that there is no resurrection of the dead prescribed in the Law,[72] and [he that says] that the Law is not from Heaven, and an Epicurean.[73] Rabbi Akiba[74] says: Also he that reads the heretical books,[75] or that utters charms over a wound and says, *I will put none of the diseases upon thee which I have put upon the Egyptians: for I am the Lord that healeth thee.*[76] Abba Saul[77] says: Also he that pronounces the Name with its proper letters.

70 Ibid., 397.
71 Isa. 60:21.
72 Danby notes, "Some manuscripts omit, 'prescribed in the Law,'" *Mishnah*, 397, n. 3.
73 Danby's note, "A frequent epithet applied both to gentiles and Jews opposed to the rabbinical teachings. It is in no way associated with teachings supposed by the Jews to emanate from the philosopher Epicurus; to Jewish ears it conveys the sense of the root *pakar*, 'be free from restraint,' and so, licentious and sceptical," *The Mishnah*, 397, n. 4.
74 Rabbi Akiba belongs to the third generation of Rabbis (120–140 CE), but the uncertainty of rabbinic attributions in the Mishnah does not disqualify this teaching from its possible formulation and observance contemporary with evolution of New Testament materials.
75 Literally, 'external books,' books excluded from the canon of Hebrew scriptures." Ibid., 397, n. 5.
76 Exod. 15:26. In this verse, the Lord makes a promise to the people after he has sweetened the waters at Marah. He promises, "If you will diligently hearken to the voice of the Lord your God, and do that which is right in his eyes, and give heed to his commandments and keep all his statues, I will put none of the diseases upon you which I put upon the Egyptians; for I am the Lord your healer."
77 Abba Saul is dated among the fourth generation of Rabbis (140–165 CE).

BIBLIOGRAPHY

Writings from antiquity

Aelius Aristides. *The Complete Works*. Trans. Charles A. Behr. Leiden: Brill, 1981.

Apollodorus. *The Library*. Trans. Sir James George Frazer. 2 vols. London: Heinemann, 1921.

Apollonius Rhodius. *Argonautica*. Trans. R. C. Seaton. London: Heinemann, 1912.

Apuleius. *Apologia and Florida*. Trans. H. E. Butler. Oxford: Clarendon Press, 1909.

—— *De Deo Socratis*. Trans. Emma J. Edelstein and Ludwig Edelstein, in *Asclepius*. 2 vols. Baltimore: The Johns Hopkins Press, 1945.

—— *Metamorphoses*. vol. 2. Trans. J. Arthur Hanson. Cambridge, MA: Harvard University Press, 1989.

Artemidorus. *The Interpretation of Dreams: Oneirocritica*. Trans. and commentary by Robert J. White. Park Ridge, NJ: Noyes Press, 1975.

Athenaeus. *Deipnosophistae*. vol. 7. Trans. C. B. Gulick. London: Heinemann, 1941.

Celsus. *On Medicine*. Trans. W. G. Spencer. 3 vols. London: Heinemann, 1935–1938.

Cicero. *Pro Lege Manilia; De Imperio Cn. Pompei*, in *Selected Political Speeches of Cicero*. Trans. Michael Grant. Harmondsworth: Penguin, 1969.

Dio Cassius. *Roman History*. Trans. Earnest Cary. 9 vols. London: Heinemann, 1914–1925.

Dio Chrysostom. *Third Discourse on Kingship*. Trans. J. W. Cohoon and H. L. Crosby. 5 vols. London: Heinemann. 1932–1951.

Diodorus Siculus. *The Library of History*. Trans. C. H. Oldfather *et al.* 12 vols. London: Heinemann, 1933–1968.

Diogenes Laertius. *The Lives of Eminent Philosophers*. Trans. R. D. Hicks. 2 vols. London: Heinemann, 1925.

Epictetus. *Discourses*, in *Epictetus*. vol. 2. Trans. W. A. Oldfather. London: Heinemann, 1928.

Euripides. *The Bacchae*. Trans. Gilbert Murray. London: George Allen & Unwin; New York: Longmans, Green & Co., 1904.

—— *Euripides*. Trans. Arthur S. Way. 4 vols; London: Heinemann, 1912.

—— *Iphigenia at Aulis*. Trans. W. S. Merwin and G. Dimock. New York: Oxford University Press, 1978.

Eusebius. *The Treatise of Eusebius against the Life of Apollonius*, In Philostratus, *The Life of Apollonius of Tyana*. Trans. F. C. Conybeare. 2 vols. London: Heinemann, 1912–1950.

Herodotus. *Herodotus*. Trans. A. D. Godley. 4 vols. London: Heinemann, 1922–1938.

Hesiod. *The Homeric Hymns and Homerica*. Trans. H. G. Evelyn-White. London: Heinemann, 1914.

Hippocrates. *On Joints* in *Hippocrates*. Trans. E. T. Withington 3 vols. London: Heinemann, 1928.

—— *On Affections*. vol. 5. Trans. Paul Potter. London: Heinemann, 1988.

Homer. *Iliad*. Trans. A. T. Murray. 2 vols. London: Heinemann, 1924–1925.

—— *Odyssey*. Trans. A. T. Murray. 2 vols. London: Heinemann, 1919.

Iamblichus. *The Life of Pythagoras*, in *The Pythagorean Sourcebook*. Compiled and translated by Kenneth Sylvan Guthrie. Michigan: Phanes, 1987.

Josephus. *Against Apion*, in *Josephus*. vol. 1. Trans. H. St. J. Thackeray. London: Heinemann, 1926.

—— *Jewish Antiquities*, in *Josephus*. vols 4–5. Trans. Ralph Marcus *et al*. London: Heinemann, 1930–1934.

—— *Jewish Antiquities*, in *Josephus*. vol. 9. Trans. L. H. Feldman, 1965.

—— *The Jewish War*, in *Josephus*. vol. 3. Trans. H. St. J. Thackeray. London: Heinemann, 1928.

Lucian. *Lucian*. Trans. A. M. Harmon *et al*. 8 vols. London: Heinemann, 1913–1967.

Marcellus. *De Medicamentis*. ed. [Max] Niedermann, 2nd ed. E. Liechtenhan. Trans. J. Kollesch and D. Nickel. *Corpus Medicorum Latinorum*. Berlin and Leipzig, 1915.

Martial. *Epigrams*. Trans. Walter C. A. Kerr. 2 vols. London: Heinemann, 1919–1920.

Origen. *Contra Celsum*. Trans. Henry Chadwick. London: Cambridge University Press, 1953 repr. 1965.

Pausanius. *Description of Greece*. Trans. W. H. S. Jones and H. A. Ormerod. 4 vols. London: Heinemann, 1918–1935.

Petronius. *Satyricon*. Trans. W. H. D. Rouse. London: Heinemann, 1936.

Philo. *Philo*. Trans. F. H. Colson, G. H. Whitaker *et al*. 10 vols. (and two supplementary volumes). London: Heinemann, 1929–1962.

Philodemus. *De Pietate*. Ed. Th. Gomperz. *Herkulanische Studien*. II. 1866. Trans. J. M. Edmonds. *Lyra Graeca*. vol. 3. London: Heinemann, 1927.

Philostratus. *Imagines*. Trans. Arthur Fairbanks. London: Heinemann, 1931.

—— *The Life of Apollonius of Tyana*. Trans. F. C. Conybeare. 2 vols. London: Heinemann, 1912–1950.

Pindar. *The Odes of Pindar*. Trans. Richard Lattimore. Chicago and London: Phoenix Books and University of Chicago Press, 1947.

Pliny the Elder. *Natural History*. vol. 5 Trans. H. Rackham *et al*. 10 vols. London: Heinemann, 1938–1963.

Plutarch. *Lives*. Trans. Bernadotte Perrin. 11 vols. London: Heinemann, 1914–1926.

—— *Moralia; De Defectu Oraculorum*. Vol. 5 Trans. Frank Cole Babbit *et al*. 15 vols. London: Heinemann, 1927–1969.

Porphyry. *Life of Pythagoras*, in *The Pythagorean Sourcebook*. Compiled and translated by Kenneth Sylvan Guthrie. Michigan: Phanes, 1987.

Select Epigrams from the Greek Anthology. Trans. J. W. Mackail. London: New York and Bombay: Longmans, Green and Co., 1906.

Seneca. *Hercules Oetaeus. Tragedies*. Trans. Frank Justus Miller. 2 vols. London: Heinemann, 1917–1929.

Sextus Empiricus. *Against the Professors*. Trans. R. G. Bury. London: Heinemann, 1949.

Strabo. *The Geography of Strabo*. Trans. Horace Leonard Jones. 8 vols. London: Heinemann, 1923–1932.

Suetonius. *The Lives of the Caesars*. Trans. J. C. Rolfe. 2 vols. London: Heinemann, 1914.

Tacitus. *The Histories and the Annals*. vol. 2. Trans. Clifford H. Moore. London: Heinemann, 1931.

Theocritus. *The Hymn to the Dioscuri*, in *The Greek Bucolic Poets*. Trans. J. M. Edmonds. London: Heinemann, 1912.

Virgil. *The Aeneid. Virgil*. Trans. H. Rushton Fairclough. 2 vols. London: Heinemann, 1916–1918.

Texts and tools

Bible: New Revised Standard Version.

Aland, Kurt. *Synopsis Quattuor Evangeliorum*. 10th ed. Stuttgart: Deutsche Bibelstiftung, 1976.

Aune, D. E. ed. *Greco-Roman Literature and the New Testament*. SL5BS 21. Atlanta: Scholars Press, 1988.

Bauer, W. *A Greek English–Lexicon of the New Testament and Other Early Christian Literature*. Trans. and adaptation by W. F. Arndt and F. W. Gingrich. 2nd ed. revised and augmented by F. W. Gingrich and F. W. Danker from W. Bauer's 5th ed. Chicago and London: University of Chicago Press, 1979.

Billerbeck, P. and H. L. Strack. *Kommentar zum Neuen Testament aus Talmud und Midrasch*. 4 vols. Munich: Beck, 1961.

Charlesworth, James H., ed. *The Old Testament Pseudepigrapha*. 2 vols. New York: Doubleday, 1983.

Danby, Herbert. *The Mishnah*. London: Oxford University Press, 1933.

Edelstein, Emma J. and Ludwig Edelstein. *Asclepius*. 2 vols. Baltimore: The Johns Hopkins Press, 1945.

Epstein, I. *The Babylonian Talmud*. 35 vols. London: Soncino, 1935.

Feldman, Louis H. and Meyer Reinhold. *Jewish Life and Thought Among Greeks and Romans: Primary Readings*. Minneapolis: Fortress Press, 1996.

Fiebig, P., ed. *Antike Wundergeschichten zum Studien der Wunder des Neuen Testaments*. *Kleine Texte für Vorlesungen und Übungen 79*. Bonn: Marcus and Weber, 1911; 2nd ed., ed. G. Delling. *Antike Wundertexte*. Berlin: Walter de Gruyter, 1949.

—— *Rabbinische Wundergeschichte*. Berlin: Walter de Gruyter, 1933.

Fitzmyer, Joseph. *The Genesis Apocryphon of Qumran Cave 1: A Commentary*. *Biblica et Orientalia* 18A; 2nd ed. revised; Rome: Biblical Institute Press, 1971.

Giannini, A., ed. and trans. *Paradoxographorum Graecorum Reliquiae*. *Classici Greci e Latini*. *Sezione Testi e Commenti* 3. Milan: Instituto Editoriale Italiano, 1965.

Grenfell, B. P. and A. S. Hunt, eds. *The Oxyrhynchus Papyri*. London, 1898–1927.

Guthrie, Kenneth Sylvan, compiler and trans. *The Pythagorean Sourcebook and Library: An Anthology of Ancient Writings which Relate to Pythagoras and Pythagorean Philosophy*. Michigan: Phanes, 1987.

Hammond, N. G. L. and H. H. Scullard. *Oxford Classical Dictionary*. 2nd ed. Oxford: Clarendon Press, 1970.

Hunt, A. S., ed. *Catalogue of the Greek Papyri in the John Rylands Library, Manchester*. Manchester, 1911–1915.

Lloyd, G. E. R., ed. *Hippocratic Writings*. Trans. J. Chadwick, W. N. Mann, I. M. Lonie and E. T. Withington. Harmondsworth: Penguin, 1978.

Neusner, Jacob, trans. *The Babylonian Talmud: An American Translation*. Atlanta, GA: Scholar's Press, 1990. Vol. 21B.

Robbins, Vernon, ed. and comp. *Ancient Quotes and Anecdotes*. Foundations and Facets Reference Series. Sonoma, CA: Polebridge Press, 1989.

Staden, Heinrich von. *Herophilus: The Art of Medicine in Early Alexandria*. Cambridge: Cambridge University Press, 1989.

Vanderlip, Vera F. *The Four Hymns of Isidorus and the Cult of Isis*. American Studies in Papyrology 12. Toronto: Hakkert, 1972.

Weinreich, Otto. *Antike Heilungswunder: Untersuchungen zum Wunderglauben der Griechen und Römer*. Berlin: Walter de Gruyter: Verlag von Alfred Töpelmann (vormals J. Ricker). Photomechischer Nachdruck. Berlin: Walter de Gruyter, 1969.

Wettstein, Jacob. *Novum Testamentum Graecum*. 2 vols. Amsterdam: Dommerian, 1752. Repr. Gräz: Druck, 1962.

Wright, M. R. *Empedocles: The Extant Fragments*. New Haven and Condon: Yale University Press, 1981.

Papyri and inscriptions

Ägyptische Urkunden aus den königlichen Museen zu Berlin: Griechische Urkunden. Berlin, 1895–1926.

Corpus Inscriptionum Graecarum. Berlin, 1828–1897.

Greek Magical Papyri in Translation including the Demotic Spells. Ed. Hans Dieter Betz. Chicago and London: University of Chicago Press, 1986.

Inscriptiones Graecae. Ed. cons. et auct. Academiae Regiae Borussicae. Berlin, 1873.

Inscriptiones Graecae ad Res Romanas Pertinentes Auctoritate et Impensis Academiae Inscriptionum et Litterarum Humaniorum Collectae et Editae. Trans. René Cagnat et Georges Louis Lafaye. 4 vols. Rome: L'Erma de Bretschneider, 1964. Vol. 3.

Memphis Text. Trans. R. Harder. *Abhandlungen der Preussischen Akademie der Wissenschaften zu Berlin.* Berlin, 1934.

Orientis Graeci Inscriptiones Selectae. Ed. W. Dittenberger. Leipzig, 1903–1905.

Papyrus Berolinensis. R. Reitzenstein, *Hellenistische Wundererzählungen.* First published 1906; repr. Darmstadt: Wissenschaftliche Buchgesellschaft, 1963.

Books and theses

Aune, David E. *The New Testament in its Literary Environment.* Library of Early Christianity 8. Philadelphia: Westminster, 1987.

Barrett, A. *Caligula: The Corruption of Power.* London: B. T. Batsford, 1989.

Branham, R. Bracht. *Unruly Eloquence: Lucian and the Comedy of Traditions.* Cambridge, MA: Harvard, University Press, 1989.

Budge, E. A. *The Alexander Book in Ethiopia.* London: Oxford University Press, 1933.

Bultmann, Rudolf. *The History of the Synoptic Tradition.* Trans. John Marsh from 1931 German ed. Revised ed. Oxford: Basil Blackwell, 1972.

Burnett, John. *Early Greek Philosophy.* London: Adam and Charles Black, 1930.

Cohn, Norman R. C. *Cosmos, Chaos and the World to Come: The Ancient Roots of Apocalyptic Faith.* New Haven: Yale University Press, 1993.

Cole, Susan Guettel. *Theoi Megaloi: The Cult of the Great Gods at Samothrace.* Leiden: Brill, 1984.

Collins, Adela Yarbro. *Cosmology and Eschatology in Jewish and Christian Apocalypticism.* Leiden: E. J. Brill, 1996.

Collins, John. *Between Athens and Jerusalem: Jewish Identity in the Hellenistic Diaspora.* New York: Crossroad, 1983.

Cotter, Wendy. "The Markan Sea Miracles in the Literary Context of Greco-Roman Antiquity." Ph.D. dissertation. University of St. Michael's College, Toronto. 1991.

Deissmann, Adolf. *Light from the Ancient East.* Trans. L. R. M. Strachan. London: Hodder & Stoughton, 1927.

Dibelius, Martin. *From Tradition to Gospel.* Trans. Bertram Lee Wolf. 2nd ed. New York: Charles Scribner's Sons, 1935.

Farnell, L. R. *Greek Hero Cults and Ideas of Immortality.* Oxford: Clarendon Press, 1921.

Ferguson, Everett. *Demonology of the Early Christian World.* Symposium Series 12; Lewiston and Queenston: Edwin Mellen Press, 1984.

Fiebig, Paul. *Jüdische Wundergeschichten des Neuentestamentlichen Zeitalters.* (Tübingen: J. C. B. Mohr, 1911.

—— *Rabbinische Wundergeschichten.* Berlin: Walter de Gruyter, 1933.

Flintermann, Jaap-Jan. *Power, Paideia and Pythagoreanism: Greek Identity, Conceptions of the Relationship between Philosophers and Monarchs and Political Ideas in Philostratus' Life of Apollonius.* Amsterdam: J. C. Gieben, 1995.

Frank, Tenney. *An Economic Survey of Ancient Rome.* 4 vols. Baltimore: Johns Hopkins Press, 1938.

Gundry, Robert H. *Mark: A Commentary on his Apology for the Cross.* Grand Rapids, MI: Eerdmans, 1993.

Hack, Roy Kenneth. *God in Greek Philosophy to the Time of Socrates.* Princeton: Princeton University Press, 1931.

Hardie, Philip. *Virgil's Aeneid: Cosmos and Imperium.* Oxford: Clarendon Press, 1986.

Heil, John Paul. *Jesus Walking on the Sea.* Analecta Biblica 87. Rome: Pontifical Biblical Institute, 1981.

Hock, Ronald F. and Edward N. O'Neil. *The Chreia in Ancient Rhetoric, Volume I: The Progymnasmata.* Society of Biblical Literature Texts and Translations 27, Atlanta: Scolars Press, 1986.

Horsley, Richard A. *Sociology and the Jesus Movement.* 2nd ed. New York: Continuum, 1994.

Jones, C. P. *Culture and Society in Lucian.* Cambridge, MA: Harvard University Press, 1986.

Jones, Rodney. *Apocalyptic Narrative and Other Poems.* Boston: Houghton Mifflin, 1993.

Kallas, J. *Jesus and the Power of Satan.* Philadelphia: Fortress Press, 1968.

Kee, Howard Clark. *Medicine, Miracle and Magic in New Testament Times.* Cambridge: Cambridge University Press, 1986.

—— *Miracle in the Early Christian World: A Study in Socio-historical Method.* New Haven and London: Yale University Press, 1983.

Kümmel, Werner Georg. *The New Testament: The History of the Investigation of its Problems.* Trans. S. Mclean Gilmour and Howard C. Kee. Nashville and New York: Abingdon, 1972.

Ling, Trevor. *The Significance of Satan.* London: SPCK, 1961.

Long, A. A. *Hellenistic Philosophy: Stoics, Epicureans, Sceptics.* London: Duckworth, 1986.

Mack, Burton L. and Vernon K. Robbins, eds. *Patterns of Persuasion*. Sonoma, CA: Polebridge Press, 1989.

Malherbe, Abraham J. *Social Aspects of Early Christianity*. Baton Rouge and London: Louisiana State University Press, 1977.

Meeks, Wayne A. *The First Urban Christians: The Social World of the Apostle Paul*. New Haven: Yale University Press, 1983.

Munitz, Milton K. *Theories of the Universe*. New York: Free Press of Glencoe. 1957.

Neusner, J. *Judaism: The Evidence of the Mishnah*. Chicago: University of Chicago Press, 1981

Pearson, L. *The Lost Histories of Alexander*. London: Blackwell, 1960.

Reitzenstein, Richard. *Hellenistische Wundererzählungen*. 1st ed. 1906; repr. Damstadt: Wissenschaftliche Buchgesellschaft, 1963.

Remus, Harold. *Pagan–Christian Conflict over Miracle in the Second Century*. Patristic Monograph Series 10. Cambridge, MA: The Philadelphia Patristic Foundation, 1983.

Ronan, Colin A. *Changing Views of the Universe*. London: Eyre & Spottiswoode, 1961.

Sanders, E. P. *Jewish Law from Jesus to the Mishnah*. London: SCM; Philadelphia: Trinity, 1990.

Smith, Morton. *Jesus the Magician*. San Francisco: Harper & Row, 1978.

Staden, Heinrich von. *Herophilus: The Art of Medicine in Early Alexandria*. Cambridge: Cambridge University Press, 1989.

Tagawa, K. *Miracles et Evangile. Etudes d'histoire et de philosophie religieuses* 62. Paris: Presses Universitaires de France, 1966.

Theissen, Gerd. *The Miracle Stories of the Early Christian Tradition*. Trans. Francis McDonagh. Philadelphia: Fortress Press, 1983.

Tran Tam Tinh, Vincent. *Le Culte d'Isis à Pompei*. Paris: Editions E. de Boccard, 1964.

Twelftree, Graham H. *Jesus the Exorcist: A Contribution to the Study of the Historical Jesus*. WUNT 54. Tübingen: J. C. B. Mohr (Paul Siebeck), 1993.

Weinstock, Stefan. *Divus Iulius*. Oxford: Clarendon Press, 1971.

Weiss, Johannes. *Die Predigt Jesu vom Reiche Gottes*. 3rd ed. Göttingen: Vandenhoeck & Ruprecht, 1964.

——— *Earliest Christianity: A History of the Period A.D. 30–150*. Trans. Frederick L. Grant. 2 vols. New York: Harper, 1959.

Witt, R. E. *Isis in the Greco-Roman World*. London: Thames & Hudson, 1971.

Wright, M. R. *Cosmology in Antiquity*. London and New York: Routledge, 1995.

Articles and chapters in books

Achtemeier, Paul J. "Gospel Traditions and the Divine Man," *Int* 26 (1972) 174–197.

—— "The Origin and Function of the Pre-Marcan Miracle Catenae," *JBL* 91 (1970) 198–221.

—— "Person and Deed: Jesus and the Storm-Tossed Sea," *Int* 16 (1962) 169–176.

—— "Toward the Isolation of Pre-Markan Miracle Catenae," *JBL* 89 (1970) 265–291.

Aune, David E. "Magic in Early Christianity," *ANRW* II 23/2 (1980) 1507–1557.

—— "Septem Sapientium Convivum (Moralia 146B–164D)," in *Plutarch's Ethical Writings and Early Christian Literature*, ed. Hans Dieter Betz. Leiden: Brill, 1978. 64–65.

Birley, Eric. "The Origins of Legionary Centurions," in *The Roman Army: Papers 1929–1986*. Mavors Roman Army Researches, ed. M. P. Speidel. Amsterdam: J. C. Gieben, 1988. Vol. 4. 189–205.

Bonner, Campbell, "The Technique of Exorcism." *HTR* 36 (1943) 39–40.

Brenk, Frederick E. "In the Light of the Moon: Demonology in the Early Imperial Period," *ANRW* 16.3 (1986) 2068–2145.

Brown, P. "The Rise and Function of the Holy Man in Late Antiquity," *Journal of Roman Studies* 61 (1971) 80–101.

Cotter, Wendy. "Cosmology and the Jesus Miracles," in *Whose Historical Jesus? Studies in Christianity and Judaism* 7, ed. William E. Arnal and Michel Desjardins. Waterloo, Ontario: Canadian Corporation for Studies in Religion by Wilfrid Laurier Press, 1997. 118–137.

Heichelheim, F. M. "Roman Syria," in *Economic Survey of Ancient Rome*, Ed. Tenney Frank. Baltimore: Johns Hopkins Press, 1938.

Kajanto, Iiro, "Fortuna," *ANRW* 17.1 (1981) 502–558.

Kolenkow, A. B. "Relationships between Miracle and Prophecy in the Greco-Roman World and Early Christianity," *ANRW* II.23/2 (1980).

Pépin, "Cosmic Piety," in *Classical Mediterranean Spirituality*, ed. A. H. Armstrong. New York: Crossroads, 1986.

Phillips, Charles Robert. "The Sociology of Religious Knowledge in the Roman Empire to A.D. 284," *ANRW* II 16.3 (1986) 2677–2773.

Sandmel, Samuel. "*Parallelomania*," *JBL* (1962) 1–13.

Smith, Jonathan Z. "Towards Interpreting Demonic Powers in Hellenistic and Roman Antiquity," *ANRW* II 17/1 (1978) 425–439.

INDEX OF TEXTS

Text numbers in bold present the part number, followed by the number of the text entry in that part.

Ancient sources

Ancient Authors

Inscriptions.

INDEX OF TEXTS OF THE
JESUS MIRACLES

The Jesus miracle stories are listed below according to their order in the canon. Numbers represent the part of the book, and the number of the entry in that part. The letters A and B refer to the two appendixes.

Mark 7:24–30 (Matt. 15:21–28): Jesus exorcizes the daughter of the Syrophoenician woman 2.35; **B.30**

Mark 7:31–37: (Matt. 15:29–31): Jesus heals a man who is deaf and has a speech impediment, 1.74; **B.41**

Mark 8:22–26: Jesus heals the blind man of Bethsaida, 1.75

Mark 9:14–29 (Matt. 17:14–21 //Luke 9:37–43): Jesus exorcizes and heals a man's possessed son, 2.36

Mark 10:46–52 (//Matt. 20:29–34//Luke 18:35–43): Jesus heals the blind man Bartimaeus, 1.76

Mark 11:12–14, 20–24 (Matt. 21:18–22): Jesus curses the fig tree, 3.62

The gospel of Luke

Luke 4:16–30: Jesus' miracles fulfill the prophet Isaiah 1.78

Luke 5:1–11: Jesus causes a miraculous catch of fish, 3.60

Luke 7:11–17: Jesus raises the only son of a widow from the dead, 1.80; **B.16**

Luke 11:14–26: Jesus exorcizes a demon causing a man to be mute, 2.38

Luke 13:10–17: Jesus heals a woman from her eighteen-year infirmity on the sabbath, 1.71; 2.37

Luke 14:1–6: Jesus heals a man with dropsy on the sabbath, 1.72

Luke 17: 11–19: Jesus heals ten lepers, **B.2**

The gospel of John

John 2:1–11: Jesus changes water into wine at the wedding feast of Cana, 3.54

John 4:46–54 Jesus heals the sick child of a royal official, 1.68

John 5:1–18: Jesus heals the man by the pool called Bethzatha, 1.69

John 9:1–41: Jesus heals a man born blind, 1.77

John 11:1–46: Jesus raises his friend Lazarus from the dead, 1.81

John 21:1–14: Jesus causes a miraculous catch of fish, 3.61

Acts

While the miracles in the Acts of the Apostles are not Jesus miracles *per se*, the writer of Luke–Acts clearly intends that the miracles be due to the power of the hero Jesus.

Acts 3:1–16: Peter heals a crippled beggar in Jesus' name, 1.82

Acts 9:1–19: Paul is given his sight by Ananias in Jesus' name, 1.85.1–2

Acts 9:32–35: Peter heals the paralyzed Aeneas in Jesus' name, 1.83

Acts 9:36–42: Peter raises Tabitha from the dead in Jesus' name, 1.84

Acts 14: 8–18: Paul cures a lame man, 1.86

Acts 16: 16–18: Paul exorcizes a spirit of divination in Jesus' name, 2.40

GENERAL INDEX

Aaron 167
Abana river 50
Abaris the Hyperborean 132, 145, 151, 190
Abba Saul, Rabbi 247
Abraham, Abram 98, 99, 100–3, 195, 242
Adam 115, 154
Admetus 13–14
Aegina 24
Aelian 16
Aelius Aristides 12, 13, 137
Aeneas 69
Aeolus, King 134
Africa 15, 183
Ajax 145
Akiba, Rabbi 98, 247
Alcestis 13–14
Alcetas of Halieis 18
Alcinous the Phaeacian 85
Alexander the Great 132, 153, 156–7
Alexandria 40, 41
Amastras 108
Ambrosia of Athens 17
Amoraic period 138, 142
Amorites 154
Amphiaraus 15
Ananias 70
Andrew 54
Andros 165
angels 93, 95; and begetting of children 108, 113; punishment

of 109, 110, 113; as teachers 108
Antigonus, King 209
Antonine period 177
Antoninus Pius 203n
Antony, Mark 147
Apellas, M. Julius 23, 24
Aphrodite/Venus 31, 88, 131, 132–3
Apion 239
apocalyptic texts 90, 106; 1 Enoch 106–12, 116, 118, 120; Jubilees 112–17, 118
Apollo 12, 13, 16, 29, 33, 151, 190
Apollodorus 13, 26, 189
Apollonius Rhodius 143
Apollonius of Tyana 36, 43–5, 83–9, 131–2, 145–6
apothegms 1, 2–3
Appian Way 158
Apuleius Lucius of Madaura 15, 46–7, 80, 136, 137, 177, 190, 212–13, 220–1
Arabah, sea of 154
Aram, Arameans 50
Arata of Lacedaemon 18–19
Arcadians 29
Aresthanas 30
Argo 143
Argonauts 16, 142–3
Aricians 30
Aristippus of Cyrene 38